Behind the Veil

SERIES ON INTERNATIONAL, POLITICAL, AND ECONOMIC HISTORY

Behind the Veil

An American Woman's Memoir
of the 1979 Iran Hostage Crisis

Debra Johanyak

The University of Akron Press
Akron, Ohio

All inquiries and permission requests should be addressed to the Publisher,
The University of Akron Press, Akron, Ohio 44325-1703.

Library of Congress Cataloging-in-Publication Data
Johanyak, Debra, 1953-
  Behind the veil : an American woman's memoir of the 1979 Iran Hostage
Crisis / Debra Johanyak. — 1st ed.
      p. cm. — (Series on international, political, and economic history)
  Includes bibliographical references and index.
  ISBN-13: 978-1-931968-38-6 (cloth : alk. paper)
  ISBN-10: 1-931968-38-1 (cloth : alk. paper)
  ISBN-13: 978-1-931968-40-9 (paper : alk. paper)
  ISBN-10: 1-931968-40-3 (paper : alk. paper)
  1. Iran Hostage Crisis, 1979-1981—Personal narratives. 2. Johanyak,
Debra, 1953- 3. Americans—Iran—Shiraz—Biography. 4. Women—Iran—
Shiraz—Biography. 5. Shiraz (Iran)—Biography. 6. Danishgah-i Shiraz—
Biography. 7. Dual nationality—Case studies. 8. Intercountry marriage—
Case studies. 9. Iran—Politics and government—1941-1979. 10.
Iran—Social conditions—20th century. I. Title.
  E183.8.I55J64 2006
  955.05'4092—dc22
  [B]
                                    2006030909

The paper used in this publication meets the minimum requirements of
American National Standard for Information Sciences—Permanence of
Paper for Printed Library Materials, ANSI z39.48(EN)1984. ∞

Cover photo by Jamie Newhall.

This book is dedicated to

El Shaddai,
Almighty God,

and

Jason and Mathew Kamalie

Contents

Preface

This book is a testament to the Iranian people who supported me during important phases of my personal development. It also tells the story of two nations in conflict over a series of political events involving rulers like Shah Reza Pahlavi and the Ayatollah Khomeini as well as the nameless masses that included me, a woman with dual citizenship, suspended between two feuding governments. Like divorced parents with shared custody, the United States and Iran nurtured our family in differing yet complementary ways. It is unfortunate that they remain estranged more than a quarter century after the 1979 diplomatic break.

Both nations boast illustrious histories, and both wield global influence. The United States has long been recognized for helping economically-disadvantaged countries and promoting peacekeeping efforts in war-torn regions. Iran offers an exotic culture and boundless hospitality. My birth links me to the first country, and marriage, to the second. While I enjoyed a comfortable upbringing in the United States, I experienced personal and professional growth in Iran.

No government is perfect. Many criticize several U.S. presidents for overstepping sensitive boundaries to defend weaker nations, leaving an imperialist legacy that discourages trust. Iran's Islamic Republic has been denounced for imposing fundamentalist Muslim rule on its people. Both governments appear to want what is best for their respective nations, and yet, complex problems defy simple solutions.

Grateful for freedoms enjoyed by U.S. citizens, I question some of our foreign policies. Appreciative of Iran's tolerance of an "in-law" by marriage, I felt pressured to conform to rules I did not endorse.

In this book, I have tried to recreate memories, conversations, and anecdotes from that intense time. Sometimes I have guessed at phrasing or details when I could not be sure of dialogue. Letters, periodicals, and my personal journal were sources for many statements. In certain cases, names and descriptions have been altered to protect privacy, while some figures represent multidimensional composites. Key players are drawn from life. Any errors are unintentional, as truth remains an important means of healing the past and building the future.

Much remains to be done toward renewing relations between the United States and Iran. Both governments must set aside the veil of pretense to face past indiscretions and embrace future goals. I hope this book contributes toward those efforts.

Acknowledgments

Steeped in classical legends and Islamic mysticism, Iran became a modern enigma following the militants' capture of sixty-six hostages at the American Embassy in Tehran on November 4, 1979. Many Americans, Iranians, and other nationalities played the roles that produced the hostage drama and corresponding events that unfolded in my life. This book is an attempt both to present a personal account of the international crisis from the perspective of a dual American-Iranian identity, and to recount the repercussions I experienced as an American living in Iran during that period. The clash of cultures that shook the world echoed through the lives of many individuals, including those of my family. It was a fateful time to be an American in a country that had in effect declared war against my homeland.

While I am not a historical scholar, and this book cannot be considered a pristine record, I have attempted to describe meaningful experiences as an American woman married to an Iranian national to share with readers interested in the 1979 hostage crisis. I would like to thank those who found the story worthy of print and donated valuable time to reading it and offering helpful feedback, including Elton Glaser, interim director of the University of Akron Press, and the thoughtful reviewers of my manuscript. Amy Freels, production coordinator, Jena Lohrbach, graduate assistant, and Julie Gammon, marketing manager, contributed valuable expertise as well. Dr. Ali Akbar Mahdi of Ohio Wesleyan University provided insightful feedback and assistance. There is not enough space to thank everyone whose comments and questions helped shape the book's development. Some may recognize themselves in these pages.

Special appreciation is given to my former sister-in-law, Parvin "Pari" Kamalie and her sisters, especially Esmat and Tooran (with daughter Mithra), whose friendship and generosity are beyond compare. Abdolah and Mina shared their home and their hearts with us.

I want to thank Nas for introducing me to Iran. Mamanbozorg and Bababozorg, having departed this earth, are remembered with affection. I appreciate the opportunity of teaching and studying at Shiraz University, where I received a graduate assistantship, and the many students and colleagues who made that experience meaningful.

I am grateful to my sister Becky for letters and phone calls during that trying time. My mother, father, and Annie are now gone, but their letters witness our closeness during those days. My brothers, John and Scott, supported my departure for Iran, and cheered our return.

The fifty-three hostages who spent 444 days in captivity deserve recognition for their service to the United States, which in turn should be commended for a general if not universal show of restraint during the hostage crisis. I thank the government of Iran for allowing me to remain in that country following the break in diplomatic relations with the United States. I am especially thankful to the Iranian people for their unparalleled kindness and acceptance.

I thank God for protecting the hostages, my children, and me. I cannot imagine He is pleased when His children hate and hurt each other. We should rather rise above the past to share our strengths and overcome weaknesses.

Of Kings and Conflicts

I RAN'S MIDDLE EASTERN HISTORY, ISLAMIC GOVERNMENT, AND rich oil supply claim a place of note in contemporary news media as well as in political, social, and religious studies. Of ongoing concern to Americans is the fact that for twenty-seven years Iran and the United States have remained diplomatically estranged as a result of the 1979 hostage crisis. While mutual distrust continues over oil supplies and nuclear capabilities, it is time to put hostilities aside and begin building a new relationship based on mutual respect.

Diplomatic relations between Iran and the United States, which had been growing unstable for some time, shattered on November 4, 1979, when Iranian militants broke into the U.S. Embassy in the capital city of Tehran and captured dozens of staff secretaries, administrators, and marines. Supported in principle by Supreme Ruler Ayatollah Khomeini, militants demanded concessions from the American government in exchange for the hostages' release, including the return of cancer-stricken former monarch Mohammad Reza Pahlavi for trial, and a formal apology from the United States for interfering with Iranian affairs. The United States refused all demands, and despite worldwide negotiations and a failed rescue attempt, fifty-three hostages remained captive for 444 days. They were released on the day that President Ronald Reagan, Jimmy Carter's successor, was sworn into office, but diplomatic ties between the two countries remain severed as of this writing.

In recent years, hints have surfaced that both countries might be willing to rebuild a productive relationship. But neither government has found a way to initiate negotiations. Despite President George W. Bush's labeling of Iran, along with Iraq and North Korea, as an "axis of evil" in January 2004, U.S. government representatives made overtures to send a diplomatic team that would include Senator Elizabeth Dole, former president of the American Red Cross, to discuss Iran's nuclear program, human rights, and terrorist role in the global arena. Iran's foreign minister Kamal Kharrazi responded by saying the proposal appeared "lopsided," lacking serious intent to resolve long-standing differences,[1] and Iran rejected the visitation bid. Both governments remain wary.

There is still much that we do not understand about this Middle Eastern country, with its variegated culture and diverse people. Although Jews and Christians seem to expect others to know and respect the Ten Commandments, how many westerners understand the five pillars of Islam? Why are we hard pressed to explore differing definitions of values, like honor and modesty? Why can a European nation like France strip schoolgirls of their traditional headgear and yet Iran be criticized for insisting that women cover themselves? If East and West can set aside disagreements to focus on shared goals, a strategic partnership might form to create a united front against destructive forces like terrorism and prejudice.

As a citizen of both countries in 1979, I witnessed Iranian and American responses to the hostage crisis and found myself at times caught within intercultural hostilities. Though I had avoided political involvement and religious commitment while coming of age in the United States, critical issues stemming from these belief systems in Iran demanded a public response or personal compliance. My first national voting experience occurred in Iran's 1980 presidential election. The hope of making a positive impact on government leadership during a critical time of national unrest and international crisis stoked my involvement in political events and influenced me to become a registered voter after my return to the United States. In parallel fashion, though I had attended church sporadically before moving to Iran, it was in that Islamic nation that I confronted and confirmed my Christian beliefs while reflecting on Muslim doctrines.

This book highlights my observations as an American married to an Iranian in the 1970s while students at a midwestern university. We later lived in Iran under two regimes. In 1977, after earning bachelor's degrees, my husband Nasrolah and I, with two young sons, moved to Iran to build our future. At that time, the country was under the reign of Shah Mohammad Reza Pahlavi, who would be Iran's last monarch. After several months, a medical emergency requiring surgery and convalescence led to my departure. I left Iran with mixed feelings, sad to leave the friends I had made, yet relieved to return to familiar surroundings. My husband later followed us to the States, and for a time we worked at establishing a life in this country.

But, in 1979, we decided to return to Iran after the Ayatollah Khomeini had come to power. Neither my husband nor I was much interested in politics. We assumed Iran's governmental transition would be smooth, and we expected to live life largely on our terms without government interference. But in the fall of 1979, the political situation whirled out of control when anti-American fervor swept the country and climaxed in the embassy takeover. Our family remained in Iran through the spring of 1980, determined to give our relocation every chance, and hoping to ride out the storm. But tremors far more violent and far-reaching than any earthquake forced our eventual evacuation.

My husband's family was affectionate and considerate; I am still very fond of them. The university students were among the best I have taught, having instructed students from around the globe in English as a Second Language. Iran's mountains, rivers, and waterfalls were as welcoming as its tribal, intellectual, and rural people. Iranian hospitality is matched only by Islamic faith. Both of these strong, pervasive forces embrace strangers in all-encompassing terms.

"Stay and dine with us," a housewife pleads, following centuries of tradition.

"Conform or die!" extremists warn, echoing terrorists of contemporary times.

Most Iranians revealed themselves as loving, gracious, loyal people who desire to live peacefully with each other and in harmony with global neighbors. Like all of us, they want to be treated with the same kindness and respect they extend to others. Yet, every country, race, and belief system has its share of fanatics. I came face to face, literally, with those who were determined to rid Iran of Western influence—including me. Fortunately, those encounters were rare. I later learned that Iranians studying, working, or living in the United States experienced similar confrontations.

Coming of age with a feminist perspective and marrying a man from the Middle East set the stage for inherent conflicts. But the tensions that soon beset me were very different from those I might have expected. While the story of a Christian married to a Muslim against the backdrop of their feuding nations suggests a modern Romeo and Juliet theme, the drama we enacted climaxed in a cataclysmic collision of culture and politics with far-reaching implications.

This book offers a brief overview of Iran's history. Included is the background of its two most recent governments, the Pahlavi monarchy and the Islamic Republic, and their clash that shook the world. My narrative weaves together three themes that intersect at the historic 1979 crossroads—the role of the U.S. government in Iran, Islamic leaders in conflict with the United States and each other, and representative people of both nations. Chapters describe my marriage and family life; the moves to Iran in 1977 and 1979 that include personal struggles such as a sandstorm, house rats, and verbal assault; and a campus takeover that threatened our freedom and perhaps my life. Overarching these events was the day-to-day breaking news of the hostage crisis. It was a time I will never forget.

The chief symbol of my private and political dilemma was the veil, or chador. Resisting urgings and threats to cover myself in public during that chaotic epoch of 1979–80 grew out of a resolve to maintain my personal identity. After November 4, 1979, the veil came to embody increasing pressure to conform to Islamic principles. I felt that wearing the chador would be to capitulate to government control. Not wearing it, on the other hand, exposed me to criticism and danger. I was destined to confront new meanings to being American, female, and Christian that were very different from those I had grown up with in the Midwest.

Some of my interpersonal conflict grew out of youthful naiveté. At twenty-four, fresh from college, I expected the world to accept me "as is." What I had learned in college about democracy and feminism I assumed would be embraced everywhere. Though I did not expect Iranian women to hold feminist views, I somewhat smugly assumed that all who knew of my American heritage would respect it and allow me to follow my beliefs. If they did not know I was American, surely my public appearance without a veil would be telling—and it was, but not in the way I expected.

What I failed to understand was that presuming upon the right to follow my own path might distract those who walked a different road. While I meant no harm in avoiding the veil in my quest for physical, spiritual, and political freedom, my refusal to adopt protective covering could be interpreted as spitting in the eye of my host country. Generally familiar with Islamic teachings, I did not grasp the full symbolic and practical meanings of the chador. Thus, appearing in public "exposed" to the new Islamic regime, I might as well have thumbed my nose at any passing ayatollah. Simplicity could be readily construed as arrogance, especially since my dark features suggested a possible Iranian lineage that would make me beholden to Islamic mandates. I should have better respected the spiritual views of the people I lived with instead of expecting them to accept me on Western terms.

Like the captives, the world was taken by surprise when dozens of American Embassy staff were captured in Tehran on November 4, 1979. Yet the takeover should not have been unexpected. In fact, there had been ample warnings of anti-American violence for some time. Long-term conditions leading to the crisis can be traced through the first three-quarters of the twentieth century. But to understand the background of Iran's modern conflicts, it is helpful to look at earlier history.

Despite living in Iran for several months before the embassy takeover, I knew little about the country's political background, and had no hint of impending events that would drastically affect our lives. Oh, there had been rumors and rumblings, but we had grown accustomed to the fundamentalist lifestyle that was implemented when Ayatollah Khomeini returned to Iran. We heard the random news stories about anti-Western demonstrations on the television. My mother, aunt, and sister wrote letters expressing concern and begging me to come home.

But having known many Iranians in the States, and living among such welcoming folk in the Persia I was learning to love, there seemed to be no real reason for alarm. Nas and I were complacent; his family members were reassuring. Only later would I discover how far many people go to convince others and themselves to believe that all would be well, a survival strategy they had practiced for centuries when faced with imminent danger.

On the night before the embassy assault, alone in my bed in the flat above the one shared by Mina and Abdolah, I slept dreamlessly, little suspecting the shocking news that would greet me in the morning. Before that, however, many cumulative events would fall into place and bring me to the historic 1979 crossroads.

CHAPTER ONE

Meeting in America

THE IRANIAN PEOPLE EXPERIENCED SIGNIFICANT REGIONAL
and national turmoil throughout the twentieth century.
The 1979 hostage crisis was a continuation, in some re-
spects, of earlier tensions. Or maybe it was a climax to these events. My
life, by contrast, was ordinary. Nothing in my American upbringing
prepared me for the critical juncture I would reach in 1970s Iran.

Growing up in Akron, Ohio, a city with a population of about
230,000, I had a fairly normal childhood. My father, an immigrant's
son, worked as a construction foreman, supervising the building of universities, hospitals, and factories. His father (my grandfather) had left
Eastern Europe when his widowed mother married a man who insisted
his son share my grandfather's inheritance. Abandoning lands and
family, my grandfather sailed to New York in the early 1900s and came
to the Midwest as a coal miner. Before leaving his country, which according to the borders in those days was probably Russia, he made
an arranged marriage. Family legend has it that Grandfather Luke
Holodnak (or "Holodnyak") purchased his bride before coming to
New York. Maria Halus, my grandmother, probably had little say in

the matter. Her parents wanted a better life for their daughter in the land of the free. Her father sailed with Maria to the New World in 1912, when she was fifteen, and delivered her safely to Luke, who had been renamed "Louis" at Ellis Island. The young couple joined a community of Eastern European immigrants who moved from coal mines to cities in search of factory work generated by two world wars. The community stayed connected through the Eastern Orthodox Church, which provided social organization as well as spiritual guidance. Over several decades, Louis and Maria raised three sons and four daughters in a blend of Old World and New World traditions. Together, they pioneered a new life in a land where neither initially spoke the language or had family to help them.

My mother was born into a farming family, the youngest of seven children. Her parents' families had known each other for generations, with towns named for progenitors who had founded them. My mother was proud of the doctors and pastors who gentled her matriarchal heritage, although her father was a farmer and a blacksmith, with rumors of an intersecting Native American bloodline. Graduating high school with top grades, during the World War II industrial boom, my mother came to Akron in search of employment, and got a secretarial position in a textile company. Her parents had offered to put her through college, but she felt they already had done enough, and her father was dying of tuberculosis. At the company where she was employed, she met my father. While their "mixed" marriage seems odd—a Baptist marrying someone of Russian Orthodox background—it may have emboldened me to make the union I did a generation later with an Iranian Muslim.

As the oldest of their four children, I handled many household duties. My mother continued working after marriage, while my father was occasionally unemployed during the cold winter months when construction was slow. I accompanied my sister, Becky, and brothers, John and Scott, to and from school, and helped cook meals, do laundry, and clean house. When I was thirteen, our mother contracted tuberculosis and was sent to a sanitarium for a year. My sister and I assisted our mother's sister, Aunt Anna (or "Annie"), in caring for us, so that she was able to keep her nursing job. My father worked out of town then. When he came home, he stayed with his parents in their modest eastside home in deference to my aunt's presence in ours. Eventually, my mother was released and pronounced healed, but she continued to experience health problems the rest of her life.

During adolescence, I longed to escape the responsibilities and dreariness associated with my mother's poor health and my father's long absences. Intrigued by Hispanic neighbors whose language I could not understand, I grew eager to share their "difference." In fifth grade, I jumped at the chance to study Spanish, and continued its study through high school. I tried out for and was selected as a middle school cheerleader, which was my effort to celebrate life rather than remain a sidelines spectator.

Following my mother's tuberculosis diagnosis, my siblings and I were tested for the disease, and I was found to have lung scars that forced me to quit cheerleading and take twenty-one pills daily to keep from getting the deadly disease that had killed my grandfather and hospitalized my mother and an uncle. Reluctantly, I assumed a leisurely schedule, turning to the books I had loved since childhood. Instead of *Little Women* and *Sir Pagan,* though, I now delved into *War and Peace, A Tree Grows in Brooklyn,* and anything else the school librarians recommended.

My siblings and I spent our formative years on a quiet street in the heart of town. Our family was neither religious nor politically active, though our mother sometimes took us to church at the top of the hill. My father rarely attended Mass, although he went occasionally, as he grew older. He watched the evening news after work, complaining about each president and national budget.

"Are we Democrats or Republicans, Dad?" I asked one evening as the television news ended about 7:00 P.M. I assumed that political status and religion were inherited.

"Democrats," he grunted.

"Why?"

"Democrats fight for the underdog."

Unsure of his meaning, I held on to my father's words. But I did not register to vote when I reached legal age, nor did I follow political candidates or issues. Despite occasional church attendance, I was not particularly religious. As a teenager, I explored life without politics, spirituality, and social issues. Little did I expect to encounter all three ten years later, halfway around the world.

I loved talking to my father about things like this, for he seemed to value my opinions. Having dropped out of high school to join the army during World War II, he had visited India, the South Seas, and Europe, all of which left vivid impressions that he shared with me. After the war, he obtained a GED (or its equivalent at that time) and enrolled at Kent State University for a term or two, mainly "to play football." Though he did not graduate with a degree, he understood the value of education in a world that was rapidly evolving from the one in which he had grown up.

"Knowledge is golden," he said more than once as I poured coffee, adding a teaspoon of sugar and a splash of milk. He would take a hearty swallow, set his cup on the coffee table, and swing his legs onto the sofa to recline comfortably after dinner. He continued talking as I stood patiently listening or settled on the floor beside him. He reflected on the nature of the universe and physical matter, about spiritual ideas and government reform. As my siblings and I were raised in the Old World tradition, the services rendered our father evidenced respect. I learned to honor rather than question him, and grew up with an obedient attitude that reflected love, not repression. I would encounter a similar family attitude in Iran.

"People can take your name, your money, and anything else you have, but they can't take what you know. Go to college—get an education," my father instructed me.

He began writing a book when I was ten. Printing in capital letters, Dad wrote "Immortality" at the top of the first sheet of lined notebook paper that he had requested from my schoolbag. Sitting in his living room easy chair, he wrote page after page each night after dinner one winter when there were no construction jobs. Sitting at his feet or standing at his shoulder, I glanced at the words while he wrote, trying to comprehend his philosophical thoughts. I realized later that my father was an intellectual, and although he eventually gave up on the book, his mode of deep thinking left a strong impression on me.

Inspired by his confidence in my ability to succeed, I followed my father's advice. After high school graduation, I got a job as a secretary to pay for college. Curious about new things and people, I began dating a Jewish boy who had been introduced by a mutual friend. Different from the boys I had grown up with because of his European ancestry and curly dark hair, Ben revealed glimpses of an outside world I had never seen. His grandparents had been imprisoned at Auschwitz during World War II, and his wary parents did not approve of dating outside the Jewish faith. So we kept our relationship a secret. Developing an interest in Jewish culture, I learned the Hebrew Shabbat prayers and how to keep kosher. I admired the strong family ties that united Ben's extended family in weekly visits and overseas trips. Yet, aware that his parents would not approve of our dating, he and I separated ourselves from the harsh realities that threatened to destroy our intimacy. After six months of dating, we became engaged when he placed a quarter-carat diamond on my left ring finger—unknown to his parents. I was thrilled by the prospect of uniting with his millennia-old bloodline and joining the secure network of extended family—if only they would accept me! We were young and idealistic, and we loved each other, I thought.

But we never found an occasion to tell his parents about our engagement. I became pregnant the following year, and my fiancé decided he did not want to get married, after all. A few months later, he told his family about the impending birth, and they sent him away to college to keep us apart. My parents, disappointed by the broken relationship, welcomed my son Jason the following summer.

My college secretary position allowed me to take a tuition-free class each semester at the University of Akron, and I became determined to build a future for Jason, who was now the focus of my life. I found a competent retired woman whom we called "Nanny" to look after my son when I returned to work a few weeks after his birth. My wounded emotions slowly healed. In fact, I chose Jason's name, which means "healer" in Greek, to help me get past my broken engagement. I decided not to date anymore, following the unsatisfactory outcome of two-and-a-half years with my fiancé. I spent evenings at home with my child, and resumed reading classical and popular literature.

Several months later at my campus job, I was promoted to the position of assistant to the international student adviser. My work included preparing visa applications and assisting international students with enrollment documentation. Friendship with foreign students filled the void of diminished family contact, since my father and brothers worked out of town, my sister was married, and my mother had her own circle of friends. I cooked dinner for Aruna from India and Tranh from Vietnam, and they hosted Jason and me in return. I went to the opera with Turkish and Colombian acquaintances. These friendships nurtured my appreciation for ethnic cuisine and cultures. I could once more savor adventure vicariously via food, friends, and fun.

Choosing a college major of English, I read for my courses literature by authors like Saul Bellow, Jane Austen, Nathaniel Hawthorne, the Brontes, Shakespeare, Chaucer, Montaigne, and others whose work encapsulated worldviews I had never imagined. Hungry for ideas, I also desired to help others. I told myself if a conventional marriage and family were out of the question, perhaps Jason and I would join the Peace Corps or volunteer for short-term VISTA assignments, until I soberly realized Jason could not go with me. I daydreamed of university study in another country, like England. But without funding, I found my goal blocked by prohibitive fees. Youthful and energetic, I explored one exciting option after another. I relished my independence, but pined for a focus. Meanwhile, I took my son to the park and the zoo, and in quiet moments we shared storybooks. I held him in my arms as we laughingly danced to the beat of pop music in our small living room. Then I would return to the kitchen table of our two-bedroom apartment and resume studying, my dreams on hold.

One September morning as I folded letters for mailing at my office desk, I looked up to find an attractive woman with a baby on her hip standing before me. I had seen her before and knew that her husband had just graduated with a master's degree in economics. Receiving a job offer from an international bank in the Middle East, he already had left the country. His wife had one more semester to complete for her bachelor's degree in psychology. This I had learned from processing the paperwork for this young Iranian couple. Our university, famed for engineering and polymer science programs, attracted many international students, including a fair number of Iranians.

"Good morning, Miss," she said with a smile as the baby cooed. "May I post this on the board?"

She showed me a handwritten sign that said "Roommate Wanted" with details in smaller print. I gestured to the bulletin board opposite my desk.

"Certainly—there's a tack."

I got up to take the baby while she hung her sign. He was a solid infant, not quite six months old.

"Thank you," she replied, taking the baby again.

"What's his name?" I smiled.

"Peymon."

"He's cute. Where are you staying?"

"We are with my husband's brother. But he has a roommate."

I would not want to share cramped quarters with two men either, especially if neither was a blood relative.

"Do you know anyone who is looking for a roommate?" she asked anxiously. Her English was accurate and clear, with a slight foreign inflection.

"To be honest," I replied, "most students already have found room-mates this term. I can't think of any women who are looking."

She appeared disappointed as an odd thought sprang to my mind.

"Maybe—," I began.

"Yes?" Her face grew animated.

"Maybe you could stay with me this semester."

Why had I said that? In our rather small apartment, I would have to move Jason into my room to let Nika and her child have his. I did not need the burden of looking out for another person. Besides, I enjoyed quiet and privacy.

"That would be wonderful!" Excitement danced in her brown eyes.

Immediately, I sensed the trade-off would be worth it. If I could not travel abroad to visit other cultures, perhaps they could come to me via Nika. Then I realized she might not know about Jason.

"I have a young son. Will it bother you to have another child in the apartment?"

My question really asked if she wanted to room with a single mother.

Nika's eyes looked blank as she registered this information, then she quickly smiled and extended her free hand.

"I am very happy to share the apartment with you and your child. What is his name?"

"Jason."

We exchanged telephone numbers after I explained her share of the rent. She wrote a check and asked to move her things to the apartment on Saturday. That evening after work, with only a few misgivings, I cleared Jason's room of his larger toys and pulled out the rollaway bed from his closet. Even if things became tense, it would only be until Nika's graduation in December. Then my life could return to normal.

On Saturday, the door buzzer rang as I washed a few breakfast dishes while Jason watched television cartoons.

"Yes?" I called into the door speaker panel.

"It's Nika."

Pressing the "open door" button, I soon heard a quick foot on the six steps leading from the first-floor entrance, and I opened the door to welcome my new roommate. Instead, I found myself face to face with a man whose hazel eyes caught me off guard.

"Yes?" I asked.

He held out his hand politely.

"I'm Nas, the brother of Nika's husband. Can I bring in some boxes?"

"Come in."

Jason looked up as the tall stranger with dark, wavy hair and a trim beard strode through the living room.

"Hi!" he smiled at Jason, who grinned shyly.

"In there," I pointed to the bedroom at the end of the short hall.

Nika appeared in the doorway. I took the baby from her as she struggled with a large paper bag of groceries.

"There's one more in the car, and we'll be done."

"I'll make tea."

"That sounds good." Her brother-in-law threw a smile over his shoulder as he left.

I knew enough about Middle Eastern culture from my job and friendships to realize that hot tea is a cultural staple. Within the hour, Peymon lay sleeping in the playpen, and Jason ran a toy truck over the living room carpet as four adults drank tea and munched cookies in the small dining area between the kitchen and living room. I was impressed by Nas's aid to his sister-in-law, first by moving her, then by offering to take her to the bank and a doctor's check-up the following week, since she did not have a car. His roommate Bill, who had helped with the moving, was personable, and said he was working on a business degree. Nas was studying industrial management.

"Bye!" He leaned around Nika at the door to add a statement for me. "Thanks for the tea and cookies."

"You're welcome."

He and Nika exchanged a few words in Persian before she closed the door and began helping me clear the table.

"Nas says you are like a Iranian girl."

"Why?"

"Because you are nice, and you made tea for us."

"It's the polite thing to do. I'm sure you would do the same."

"Yes," Nika said, rinsing a cup. "In Iran, everyone offers tea or fruit to guests. But it is not like that in America."

"We're always in a hurry here. People don't take time to visit."

She nodded. "Visits are very important in my country. Everyone goes to somebody's house for tea or dinner. They make you feel welcome."

So went my first lesson in Persian culture. I was intrigued by customs that seemed so hospitable compared to the contrasting coldness in American society. It was true that in the South, among my mother's people, guests were readily welcomed and offered full-table spreads and afternoon chatter. And my father's relatives had hosted our family for many Sunday dinners and holiday meals. But in Persian culture, hospitality appeared to be a daylong, year-round event.

The fall term passed quickly. Soon we were pelted with snowflakes and whipped by chilling winds. Nika and I traded babysitting while each of us went to class on alternate evenings. We ate supper together when our schedules overlapped, and shared morning tea and toast before heading our separate ways. Sampling my roommate's eggplant stew or saffron rice was delicious, and I practiced her recipes when time permitted. Nika cooked with plenty of vegetables and a little meat, which seemed far healthier than greasy fried chicken or burgers, often the norm for busy students. I watched Nika serve tea and fresh fruit on small plates with delicate forks to Iranian students from campus or occasional out-of-town guests. Sometimes I kept out of the way by visiting my mom and sister or taking Jason for a stroller ride. My roommate treated her visitors like family. No one was a casual guest. That warm camaraderie beckoned my lonely soul.

While the auburn-haired girl and I did not argue, occasionally we got on each other's nerves, as when she spoke Farsi with her guests or I went out with friends, leaving her at home. Neither of us relished being excluded from the other's social life, but we respected one another's boundaries. Each month her husband called from Lebanon, and once she spoke to her parents in Tehran. She also received letters addressed both in English and in the mysterious Farsi script. I almost was jealous of the closeness her family members shared, since I did not see that much of my relatives who lived in the same town. I later heard an Iranian woman living in this country say that she could not imagine going more than a week without a telephone call from her brother, who lived in another state. I found this family closeness to be pervasive in Iranian culture.

Nas came around or called frequently to see if Nika needed anything, or to play with Peymon. He liked children, and he invited Jason to join their games. After he left, Nika revealed some of his comments about me:

"She's so quiet."

"Isn't she nice?"

"She looks Persian."

With waist-length hair and a dark complexion, I resembled someone of Middle Eastern descent. Maybe I reminded Nasrolah of a girl from home. Nika told me he had been semi-engaged to a girl there, but had broken it off before coming to the States. I wasn't completely surprised when he invited me to dinner to thank me for helping Nika and Peymon. Yet I was unsure about whether to accept. I pulled my hair into a knot and wore a touch of makeup, preferring my usual natural look to a glamorous image. Nas's eyes brightened when I met him at the door. He wore a sport shirt and jeans with a corduroy jacket.

I was pleasantly surprised by his gentlemanly behavior. During the 1960s and 1970s, many men took advantage of women's liberation to let us pay for dates or to treat us as "pals" by not opening doors or letting us go first. My mother had raised us to practice and expect good manners, feminism notwithstanding. There also was the so-called free love movement that often resulted in serious consequences to women who had casual relationships. I wondered how Iranian men would be. Demanding? Controlling? Stereotypes floated like rumors around all the nationalities I met at the International Student Office. I was determined to maintain good boundaries. My broken engagement had taught me a difficult lesson, and I would hold myself in reserve for the right man, if one ever came along. With Nas, I was casual and friendly. I had not dated since Ben, and I did not really know why I had come this time. Perhaps I was ready for adventure again. While I did not expect to find it with this shy student, our date was a start.

Over a steak dinner at a family-style restaurant, we discussed college goals. Nas planned to return to Iran for two years to repay the government's financial aid that was funding his education.

"What are your plans?" he asked over salad.

"Something to do with English, I hope," was my tentative reply, hoping there were no shards of lettuce stuck in my teeth. While I didn't need to make a romantic impact, neither did I want to give the impression of a T-rex.

He must have understood the reflective glint in my eyes.

"Many students don't know where they will work after graduation."

"True, but I should be getting some idea. I don't want to be a secretary forever."

"Is your job hard?" he asked politely.

"No, but it's not exciting, either."

Nasrolah nodded. He had good table manners.

The rest of the evening was comfortable, without pretense, and we returned to the apartment by ten. My roommate looked up from the sofa where she was poring over an industrial psychology text; the kids were asleep in their beds.

"Thank you," I told her brother-in-law at the door.

"I must thank you. You have been kind to my family. We will not forget."

With a few words to Nika, he was gone, and I was grateful he had not tried to kiss me or plan another date.

"He likes you," she said as I turned after bolting the door.

"How do you know?"

"I know him. He loves children, too."

"I can see that."

While it was nice to feel valued, I wondered at this turn of events. Did I really want to date a foreign student? Maybe the whole thing would dissolve, and I would have no decisions to make. I admired Nas because he lived life on his terms. There was a certain fearless quality in his nature that made me feel safe around him. I just was not sure if I was ready for the responsibilities of a permanent commitment. Shaking my head at these whimsical musings, I realized I had jumped too far ahead. Who had said anything about marriage?

A week later, Nas asked me to his apartment to watch *The Godfather* on television. It would be a casual date, one I could view from the perspective of friend. But I felt Nas was not the kind of person to spend time lightly with someone he was uninterested in. Our lives were too busy to play games. His quiet strength fostered a responsive dependency that surprised me, since I was used to taking care of myself.

"I'm not getting involved," I muttered after dismissing all the reasons why I should not go. But I found Nasrolah attractive, with his dark, curly hair, tall form, and hazel eyes. And I liked the manly way he looked out for his sister-in-law and was enrolled in college in a country where he had had to learn the language first. Nas was a man of purpose who appeared to be on the road to success. I, on the other hand, was on a byway. How could our paths converge?

Nika smiled knowingly as we left about 7:30 P.M., with Jason tucked into bed as she wrote a research paper. We walked a few blocks to Nas's apartment. He unlocked the door and led the way to a familiar layout, one that I had seen in other apartments designed for students. The place was clean and neat, not what I had expected from a couple of guys. Bill was out for the evening, so we had the place to ourselves. Two hours later, the movie was over, and my virtue, if not my ego, was intact. Nas walked me home; it was a crisp autumn evening, and the moon shone brightly above the nearly bare treetops over our heads. At my apartment, he nodded a "thank you" before leaving. I closed the door behind him thoughtfully, feeling Nika's curious glance at my back. Saying nothing except "good night," I went to bed.

The next day, he came for tea. Nas and I talked about our formative years. He enjoyed hunting and fishing, as my father did. Nas seemed to enjoy asking questions and listening to my answers. I had never been with someone who had shown interest in my relatives. Later, I asked Nika about it.

"Is he curious, or does he suspect something bad about me?"

She laughed. "All Persian people ask about family. That means they like you very much."

That really caught me by surprise. In high school, before I began dating Ben, many guys got to "know" girls by dating them casually. This typically led to short- or long-term romances. Some wanted a date to meet the status quo. Others were looking for a companion to special events. Then there were those in search of a "good time," whatever that meant individually, but always linked to personal gratification. Nas was different. Cautious, reserved, and slow by American dating terms, he spent time talking about career goals, family interests, and contemporary events. I felt respected. He admired my academic progress and my perseverance in raising a child alone. Some women, he told me later, would have given the baby to their parents, let someone adopt it, or had an abortion. He liked the fact that I had accepted the responsibility of single parenthood, and that I gave my child good care.

The next weekend, I invited Nika, Peymon, and Nas to my mother's house for dinner. My sister Becky stopped by after her anatomy class, since she had just begun nursing school. Mom made an American meal of hamburgers, french fries, and apple pie. Our guests ate seconds and seemed to enjoy it all. My petite mother, usually shy around strangers, opened up to ask about life in Iran as she took Peymon on her lap.

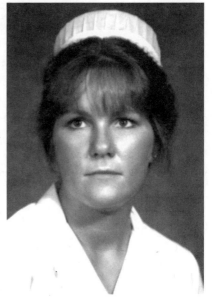

"Are the roads like the ones we have here?" she asked.

"Many of them are," Nika answered. "When Nas gets his degree, he wants to build more highways in Iran."

My sister Becky

"That'll be nice," my mother replied with a smile. Nas asked about photographs on our fireplace mantel. I pointed out various family members, as Nika complimented my mother's afghan sofa cover.

"Your home is very comfortable."

"Thank you," Mom said, brightening. Good manners transcend all cultures.

Soon it was time to go.

"Thank you for inviting us." Nika embraced my surprised mother, who was not a demonstrative woman. Persian women, on the other hand, typically kiss other females on one or both cheeks in greeting or departure.

"Come back," my reserved parent said in her low voice.

A week or so later, I came home from work to find my roommate entertaining two Iranian brothers. Visiting the United States for a few weeks, they wanted to stop by and see Nika and Peymon, having known Nika and her husband in Iran previously. After the introductions, one of the brothers sent covert glances my way. I assumed he had not met many American women. Heavyset, scholarly looking, and shy, his thoughts were hidden. After they left, Nika told me the shy one wanted to know if I would consider marriage.

Shocked, I answered, "Why would he ask that?"

Laughing, she explained, "He sees you are a single parent and a student, and thinks you may be looking for a husband. He also thinks you are pretty and smart. Their family has money, so you don't need a dowry. If you are willing to consider him, he will begin the negotiations."

I laughed, too. "I'm not in the market for a husband. Tell him thanks, anyway."

Here was something new—arranged marriages. Well, it was new for my generation, although my grandmother had had an arranged marriage. Tentative inquiries are made about a prospective spouse who is known generally by one or more family members. If inquiries pan out, negotiations proceed to the point of checking family backgrounds and discussing financial details. Evidently, I had passed the first round with our visitor. I guess the brother's query posed an example of marriage by recruitment, since I had not sought this particular honor.

Nasrolah must have been told of potential competition, a wealthy suitor at that, for he proposed marriage a month later. Again he invited me to dinner.

"We have known each other a few months," he began as the server set down our plates of broiled seafood.

"Our family is grateful for all you have done for Nika and Peymon." He paused before continuing as I looked at my plate, hardly daring to glance at his earnest face.

"I want to marry you."

Gazing solemnly at this twenty-four-year-old man, I realized there was little I knew of him, except his name, his nationality, and something of his family. Yet what did I have to look forward to? My married sister was in nursing school. My best friend, Karen, had just gotten engaged and was busy making wedding plans. Jason needed a father, and Nas had proven himself interested in Jason's well-being. My suitor had accepted my unmarried situation by saying Jason's father had surrendered a priceless gift, and he had expressed a desire to legally adopt Jason. I knew that marriage to me would make Nas eligible for permanent residence—a green card. This would facilitate travel between our two countries. Was that his primary motive? At the moment, I did not care. He was offering the marital legitimacy that my former fiancé had denied me. Nas seemed sincerely concerned for his sister-in-law and genuinely affectionate toward Peymon and Jason. He had been attentive to and respectful of me since the day I had met him, and he was good-looking as well as hardworking. I had grown fond of Nas, and would miss him if he were to leave my life.

"Yes," I smiled, squeezing his hand. "I will marry you."

He handed me a large envelope. Inside was a glittery romantic card. Opening it, I saw Nas had scrawled, "Friday is coming, and you are going to get a ring." Friday was his payday. "I don't need a diamond," I told him. "Just get me a band, and I will buy a matching one for you."

Our announcement a few days later amazed my family. My mother might have been a little dismayed, but she was not shocked. Becky showed pleasure, while my brothers congratulated me by telephone. My father said little when he got back in town, though I caught

My wedding day

a gleam of uncertainty in his eyes as he gripped Nas's hand. Having gone against his parents' advice in marrying my mother out of the faith, my dad could say little to me.

Nas and I were married on December 6, 1974, at the Summit County Courthouse, with Nika as our witness. A heavy snowfall forced us to climb over icy banks in the downtown parking lot. Nas moved his

Nas soon after our wedding

things to our apartment that weekend while we studied for final exams. His Eastern-style divan, Oriental wall hangings, and silk table covers gave our place an exotic air. The 1970s influenced us, too, when Nas hung up a large color poster of Che Guevara, Cuban revolutionary. Though I knew little about the cigar-smoking rebel, the poster suggested a rebellious streak that was reflected in our mixed marriage.

Nika planned to leave the United States by mid-December upon receiving her bachelor's degree, and we would drive her to New York as our honeymoon getaway. We helped her buy a Camaro and arrange shipping for it. Then we accompanied her to JFK Airport and watched her and Peymon board the plane that would reunite them with Nas's brother in Lebanon. All of us had tears in our eyes at this sad parting. Afterward, it was just Nas and me, alone but for Jason, who was waiting for us with my mother in Ohio. We spent the seven-hour drive home partly in shy silence, and partly in discussing class schedules for the coming term. The transition from single to married status came readily, perhaps because we led such busy lives that marriage did not seem to make much difference. I had exchanged one Persian roommate for another, albeit one I was committed to in affection and respect with a marital bond.

Within a few months, Nas began the adoption proceedings for Jason, and after Ben, the biological father, did not respond to written notices, the court allowed Jason to take my husband's surname and become his legal heir. It seemed unusual that a Muslim father would raise a Jewish boy, but I was gratified that Nasrolah could look beyond racial boundaries to adopt my son—our son.

College classes dominated our schedule. When the new term began, we rushed from one to the next, barely with time enough to sit back and enjoy our family relationship. On weekends we hiked in local parks or barbecued on the apartment terrace. Sometimes we visited Iranians in mixed marriages like ours, and we would go swimming at a community pool or host guests for dinner. Those early years sped by in a blur.

I became pregnant the following November, but miscarried in January. Nas comforted me after we returned from the hospital.

"We'll have a baby later," he said softly, holding me.

"It won't be the same," I wept.

In time, I put the loss into perspective. We had other considerations to focus on, including Jason's enrollment in preschool and completing our bachelor degrees. Nas and I got along as well as other newlyweds. Disagreements usually centered on money, since finances were tight with both of us in school. Our biggest argument was about Jason, ironically, when Nas became angry for my disciplining the toddler when he threw food on the floor. My spouse and I did not speak for three days,

Mom, Nas, and Jason at Christmastime in the United States.

until common sense got the best of us. Many Persian people have a soft spot for children, but rather than becoming spoiled, the young Iranians I met were respectful and well mannered.

I cooked Persian food, with rice a daily staple. Nas liked to bake roasts or grill chicken, and we entertained his friends or my family for dinners that included steamed rice with baked or grilled beef or chicken, and sometimes fish. He enjoyed being a father and taught Jason how to ride a tricycle and shoot a popgun. There were no cultural bridges to cross—not then. We joined the thriving Persian community at our campus, celebrating Iranian holidays like Now Rooz, or the New Year, with the group of people that became our friends. At last I was immersed in a supportive community of those in similar lifestyles. I took a Persian language class in which I learned basic principles, like the Farsi alphabet and simple sentences:

Ob me kham. (I want water, or I'm thirsty.)

Koja meeri? (Where are you going?)

The Immigration and Naturalization Service eventually approved Nas's application for a green card, after several highly personal interviews that were conducted first jointly, and then separately. Though investigators' questions were intimate and pressing, we could honestly assure them that ours was a marriage of commitment, not convenience.

During our last year of college, I became pregnant again. Nas was concerned a baby would disrupt graduation and relocation plans, but I was confident the time was right, and that things would go well for us. Though I developed toxemia in the final trimester, which forced me to go on bed rest for the remainder of the pregnancy, everything turned out fine, and our son, Mathew Borzu Kamalie, was born safely two weeks after I completed my final class.

We graduated in 1977, and Nas went to Iran a few weeks later to arrange our relocation. He returned from Iran just one day before black-haired, blue-eyed Mathew was born on July 16, 1977. Though I attempted a natural delivery, a C-section became necessary, requiring a longer recovery over the next four weeks. Jason loved having a baby brother, and Nas enjoyed rocking and bottle-feeding the baby when my milk did not come in, as hoped. Watching the three of them nestle on the sofa, my heart was full.

We packed up the apartment and booked tickets on an Iran Air overnight flight to Tehran in August 1977. But we ran into a hitch selling Nas's black Impala and switching utilities into the apartment manager's name. Reluctant to cancel our reservations, I agreed to fly without Nas, taking the kids with me. He would join us a week later after finalizing last-minute matters. My parents were not happy about my traveling without him, but it was my decision. I was ready to embrace my new adventure.

CHAPTER TWO

The First Journey

I DID NOT ANTICIPATE PROBLEMS IN MOVING WITH NASROLAH and the children to Iran. But in fact, Nas did not prepare me for the confrontation of cultural challenges after we relocated. Like many men, my husband said little about his childhood, and he assumed the move would not seriously affect me. Things like bathroom hygiene and flies, irrelevant to him, shocked me, requiring a prompt attitude adjustment.

Elvis Presley died the day we left the United States. The startling loss seemed to underscore the sobering notion that I was leaving behind Western culture, with all its celebrity glitz and youthful idealism that performers like Elvis embodied. It was clear even to my uninformed mind that there would be nothing similar to him in Iran, although Iranian youth admired pop music. Hearing the news of Elvis's death two days later, coupled with the announcer's pronouncement that a cultural era had died with the King, I sensed that I had left my coming-of-age milieu and had entered a phase that would be extraordinarily challenging, requiring adaptation and open-mindedness. I was growing up.

Settling into the seat of the jumbo jet for the transatlantic flight, I cuddled Jason at my side while Mathew slept at our feet in a bassinet provided by the airliner. Our nonstop ten-and-a-half-hour flight was uneventful. Flying over the Asian steppes, I felt as though we had entered a time tunnel, expecting any moment to see a colorful caravan traversing the hills below.

As our plane touched down, I gathered the kids' toys and my book, bundling the boys into seat and carrier. Excitement welled up: What would our new life be like? Would people like us? Would everyday schedules be very different?

Abdolah, Nas's older brother who was one of the shah's motorcade escorts, met us at Mehrabad Airport with tears for our arrival and kisses for the kids. His emotion was heartwarming and his manner reassuring as he whisked us through customs. Stepping out of the terminal, I encountered the bluest sky I had ever seen—and the warmest sun. In the parking lot, a cluster of relatives met us with cries of pleasure, as the women, most about my age, kissed my cheeks and embraced us warmly, taking the baby and fussing over Jason. Abdolah's wife Mina, a year younger than I, looked us over with frank brown eyes. She stepped forward with a bouquet of fresh flowers, kissed both my cheeks, and smiled haltingly as she tried out her few words of English:

"Welcome—Iran."

"Thank you! We're glad to be here."

The younger girls pecked my cheeks as I caught comments like, "She's young" and "Pretty!" Following social protocol, the men did not stare or get close. Relieved by the welcome, and travel weary, we settled into the back seat of Abdolah's tan Pekan and soon joined the streaming traffic that fed into Tehran's main thoroughfares. Passing through the business district, I saw large department stores and fashionable shops, as well as commemorative fountains accenting circular drives. Amused, I watched an elderly man in shabby coat and cap drive a donkey-pulled cart past a parked Chevrolet Blazer. Raw carcasses stripped of their hides hung before butcher shops, and skyscrapers graced a skyline darkened by lead toxins.

Within thirty minutes, we reached a narrow "kuche," or street, where Mina and Abdolah rented a small, first-floor apartment. They settled us into their bedroom, taking the dining room floor for themselves. A

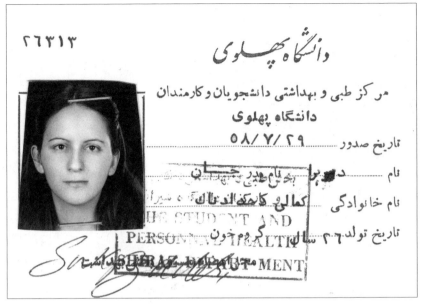

My Iranian identification card

dozen relatives living in Tehran and visiting from Shiraz celebrated our arrival by stopping in to share fresh watermelon and cantaloupe, along with the most luscious grapes I had ever tasted. Hot, strong tea was served in small glass cups called "estekans." A handful of teenage boys practiced schoolbook English with Jason:

"How are you?"

"We happy you come Iran."

"You speak Persian?"

Catching their efforts with pleasure, I tried out the Farsi I had learned in the Persian class:

"Ma khoobeem." (We are good.)

"Ma doost dareem eeran." (We like Iran.)

"Man Farsee hanooz yad nagereftam." (I have not yet learned Farsi.)

The young women fingered my denim skirt and cast admiring glances at the leather clogs I had removed upon entering the apartment. Everyone wore "house shoes," the rubber kind widely used throughout the Orient. Abdolah's wife had thoughtfully provided new pairs for the children and me, as this was one of those household adjustments Nas had not thought to prepare us for.

Assisted by two teen sisters from Shiraz, Mina prepared chelou kebab, the national dish, for dinner. My offer of help was kindly rejected, and I was told to rest following the long trip. The girls shook out a flowered vinyl tablecloth and placed it on the living room floor, then added melamine plates and silverware for the twelve of us who would be dining. When everything was ready, we assembled around the "sofreh" and passed around platters heaped with steamed rice, plates of ground beef chunks skewered with grilled tomatoes, onions, and seasonings, and a salad of fresh tomatoes and cucumbers with a vinegar dressing. Coca-Cola and two-foot sheets of warm, flat bread fetched from the neighborhood baker completed the meal. Desserts were uncommon, although we did enjoy occasional sweets from guests or while shopping.

Afterward, I tried to help the women clear dishes, but again I was urged to sit, while a laughing fifteen-year-old gently pushed me down. All the while, Jason sat jabbering with two cousins who appeared to be ten or twelve, and they took him to the patio to play with a slingshot as I reminded him to be careful. With the time difference that made Iran's clock about eight and a half hours ahead of American time, Mathew fell asleep for nearly two hours, waking briefly to be passed from one set of arms to another before dozing off once more. Hot tea again was served—stronger than I was accustomed to, but welcome after the long day.

Abdolah periodically offered to help us acclimate. After tea, as I pulled a few clothing items from a carry-on bag, he paused by the open bedroom door.

"What do you need?"

"Nothing right now, thanks." I helped Jason pull on a pajama top, but turned with a quick smile of thanks for our host.

"Please say what you want, and Mina or I will get it for you."

"I will let you know. Thanks very much." I watched Jason dash off to wrestle with Abdolah in the living room, and I went to talk to Mina and the girls while they cleaned up the sofreh. Abdolah had visited us in the States a few months before Mathew's birth, and later telephoned to say he dreamed we had a baby boy. The second-oldest son of his family, Abdolah was the one who looked after his aging parents and two unmarried sisters who were still at home, Parvin (whom we called "Pari") and Esmat.

Esmat with her first son

Everyone made us feel comfortable with smiles and words of welcome, and I did not feel like an outsider at all. Neither did Jason. Despite potential language barriers, we knew enough Farsi, and the relatives knew enough English—bolstered by Abdolah's interpretations—to bridge customary needs, such as finding the bathroom, getting something to drink, and making baby formula. Abdolah and Mina had no children yet, and he seemed especially fond of Jason and Matt.

An hour or so after our second round of tea, the company began to disperse. Two of the girls went by taxi to their aunt's house in another part of the city, while the other two girls made beds on the living room floor. Their brothers and cousins camped on the patio. Surrounded by walls, the patio faced nearby apartment buildings. While not particularly scenic, the concrete slab was adorned by a pool of water that was customary in all the patios I visited. Surrounding the pool were

Parvin Kamalie (Pari)

potted shrubs and flowering roses, suggesting a garden respite in the city's midst.

I appreciated the bedroom's privacy and, closing the door, got undressed before settling the sleeping baby beside me. Nursing a bottle of formula made with purified water, Mathew was ready to sleep once more, no doubt tired by our travel and the many relatives' kisses. I placed the can of formula on the bedside table, pulled the sheet over us, and turned off the table lamp. I could see under the door that lights were being turned down in the other room, as Abdolah's voice, echoed by Mina's, softly called in English,

"Good night."

"Good night," I replied, "and thanks."

At first, I could not sleep. Though after ten o'clock in Iran, by American time it was midafternoon. Turning gently so as not to waken the sleeping boys, I forced my eyes to close, and after several minutes, I drifted off. Mathew's soft cry woke me hours later. Straining to read the digital clock on the bedside stand, I saw that it said "2:30." I reached for the lamp and turned it on so I could prepare the baby's bottle from purified water in the thermos that kept it warm for this purpose. Just as my hand touched the formula, I felt something move. Snatching my fingers away, I saw the hugest insect imaginable—the size of a mouse—clinging to the side of the formula can. I wanted to scream. Instead, I stared at it, paralyzed with fear. In a moment, Mina's soft voice asked in Persian,

"What is it?"

"Nothing," I whispered loudly. "I just want to make a bottle."

She opened the bedroom door slightly.

"Do you need help?"

Relieved, I pointed to the bug.

She took off a slipper and whacked it. Picking up her victim by an antenna, she carried it out of the room. I heard her go out on the patio where she disposed of the remains. I got out of bed, looking around for the giant bug's kin. Finding none, I cautiously mixed the formula and made sure to replace the lid tightly on the can.

Peeking in the door and seeing that I was settled again, Mina asked why I did not nurse Matt, which was more universally practiced in Iran than in the States. I explained that my milk had not come in, and she nodded, while closing the door. After drinking several ounces from his bottle, Matt burped, and I turned off the light. This time I lay awake for a long time, wondering about other surprises in the dark.

The next few days passed quickly, bringing new discoveries. Nas was to arrive at the end of the week, but in the meantime Mina took us shopping by day while Abdolah showed us the city at night when he came home from his policeman's job. Mina's pink-cheeked sisters accompanied us, their youthful enthusiasm a fun addition to our sightseeing expeditions. Interested in American culture, they wore jeans and trendy tops, and some wore headscarves when we went out in public. The brothers and cousins went with Abdolah or watched television in the apartment. This was their summer break from school, which would start in another two weeks. Mina helped me wash baby bottles and diapers; the disposables in Tehran were prohibitively expensive. Nas had arranged for Abdolah to handle our expenses until he arrived, so I had no Persian money in hand until Abdolah exchanged my American bills for Iranian currency. I did not have to ask for anything because all our needs were met. But, by the end of the week, I was ready to have Nas around, so I could ask for things that might be needed, without embarrassment.

The most difficult challenge of those days was the alarming revelation of the Eastern toilets—ceramic bowls set into the floor instead of perched on pedestals. Nas had not mentioned them. At first, I found these awkward, especially when we later visited families whose "toilets" were built into patio cubicles rather than indoors. To compound the culture shock, many Easterners substitute their left hand (sometimes called the "hygiene hand") and a spray hose for toilet tissue. Others used a plastic pitcher with a long nozzle. I quickly learned to carry a supply of tissue wherever we went.

The prolific "soosk," or palmetto bugs, scampered up walls or ran across the floor, much to my dismay. Sometimes I saw them on sidewalks or in restaurants. One night when we got home from a sightseeing trip that had included a lovely green park and a drive past the royal palace, Abdolah turned on the bathroom light, and literally hundreds of bugs darted out of the toilet! Abdolah and the boys grabbed some spray and a broom and destroyed as many as they could. I had no idea where they had come from or why they were invading us, but fortunately, that experience was not repeated. I tried not to think about the ones that got away.

Another adjustment came with the afternoon siesta, which at first I found a nuisance. Used to nonstop activity in an eight-hour job five days a week as well as back-to-back college classes, taking a two-hour nap after a midday meal seemed unnatural and wasteful. Urging Jason to color quietly with crayons and paper, I coaxed Mathew to take a nap, and laid him on Mina and Abdolah's bed. Soon I felt my eyes grow heavy in the afternoon quiet, especially following a busy morning shopping with Mina or preparing lunch for a dozen guests. Before long I was taking advantage of the afternoon break. Sometimes I read history or romance novels. Later, I wrote letters home. Then I welcomed the reprieve from daily chores, especially when Jason likewise slept, and I could cast off the day's cares, at times falling asleep myself.

The custom of expectant gifting nearly got the best of me. Shortly after our arrival, I distributed cologne, jewelry, and jeans to Mina and her sisters, following the custom of presenting gifts to a host, a system that I had learned early in our marriage. In fact, Abdolah had sent boxes of gifts that included gold jewelry, pistachios, and traditional garb following our marriage. But now I was to encounter an unexpected variation. When someone strongly admires something of yours, it is a supreme (and expected) act of kindness to bestow that item on the admirer. It took nearly an hour of Mina's constant praise of my denim skirt before I realized that she wanted me to give it to her. Being about the same size, I knew it would fit her. But I was reluctant to part with the skirt, as it was new, and I had planned to wear it after losing my pregnancy weight in another month or so. In the end I gave it up, feeling noble if not pleased, and she wore her prize the next day with many expressions of gratitude. Seeing her joy, I felt guilty about my initial reluctance. Later, I would learn how it felt to be on the receiving end of the custom.

Shopping in Tehran's downtown area, I was amazed by terrible traffic snarls and surprised to find American products like Rubbermaid containers and Wishbone salad dressings—at $6 a bottle. Fortunately, the kids and I enjoyed Persian food, so imports were not a priority. We visited Mina's uncle and his wife, who took to us immediately. The wife rocked Mathew in her lap as we talked, for they spoke good English and were well traveled. One time we visited an indoor mini-mall, with trendy shops boasting the latest Italian and French fashions. Of course, everything was pricey, but it was fun to look. I began to notice that Iranian women like to look their best when they visit or go out in public. Accustomed to the casual look of the '70s in the States, I soon began to dress up a little more before leaving the house.

With Mina's sisters, we explored the underground bazaar where pungent spices and colorful fabrics competed with the latest Eagles' eight-track tapes and designer auto accessories. We rambled from one stall to the next, comparing prices on imported and native clothing and admiring the famous carpets and tapestries. Jason quickly learned Persian expressions and became more fluent than I in those first weeks.

The cousins treated him like a brother, and he soon adapted to their games and play.

Later, we visited city parks with beautiful rose gardens and rolling lawns and dined at swank restaurants, with a choice of Western or Persian food. Once we took a monorail ten thousand feet into the Alborz Mountains for a picnic of sandwiches and tea on a ledge overlooking a magnificent valley laced with lingering shadows. Staring into the abyss brought a shudder as I realized the potential danger below, if I should lose my foothold. But all around us, steep, rocky crags promised protection from the buffeting wind as wispy clouds sailed overhead, almost within reach. The precariousness of our small pocket of protection within the mountains came home with sharp reality. I must watch every step, above and below.

We drove by the regal residence of the country's ruler, the shah of Iran. Mohammad Reza Pahlavi (1919–80) was the oldest son of Reza Khan, the military leader who had seized government control in the early twentieth century. Completing studies in Switzerland and an Iranian military school, in 1939 Pahlavi had married the sister of Egypt's King Faroq I. Their marriage produced a daughter, Princess Shahnaz, but ended in divorce ten years later. In 1951, the shah married Soraya Esfandiary Bakhtiari, who was titled queen, or empress, of Iran. Her father was the ambassador to Germany. When Soraya did not bear a child, Shah Pahlavi divorced her in 1958, and she left for Paris, where she lived until her death in October 2001. In 1959, the shah wed Farah Diba, daughter of the captain of the Imperial Iranian Army. Their union produced four children: Crown Prince Reza Cyrus (October 31, 1960), Princess Farahaz (March 12, 1963), Prince Ali Reza (April 28, 1968), and Princess Leila (March 27, 1970). The younger daughter died in London on June 10, 2001.

In the metropolis of Tehran were tiny alleys and multilane highways. Complacent donkeys trotted in the wake of roaring Camaros. Photos of the shah adorned windows and doorways of many shops and stores, but Western influences were everywhere, as well. Neon signs invited hungry shoppers to dine on pizza and burgers, while traditional eateries offered the famous chelou kebab or the popular khorosht sabsi, a stew made with greens like spinach and dill to which beans and chunks of meat are added. Jujee kebab, roasted young chicken, or chelou mahee, fish and steamed rice, are among other tasty dishes we sampled.

Iran was a land of contrasts. Discos and nightclubs operated discreetly, but I saw no all-night bars or the common drug use that was prevalent in the States. Women typically did not go out alone; rather, families escorted them, or they ventured out in pairs or groups. To appear in public without a companion might betoken a woman of loose morals, as I would later learn, to my chagrin. Western women used to freedom sometimes shopped alone, but I did not hear of any dangerous incidents then. "Foreigners" were common in Iran at that time, and during our shopping trips I saw blonde, brown, or mahogany heads in the downtown streets. Shopkeepers were friendly and helpful, and many knew a little English.

Evidence of progress was everywhere. Many buildings were new, highways were in good condition, and stores offered goods from all over the world. British Land Rovers and Japanese trucks jostled European and Iran-made automobiles. Many Iranian women went unveiled, revealing hairstyles I had admired in fashion magazines. Wearing the latest makeup, gold jewelry, and stylish outfits, they resembled women I had seen in New York. Yet, there were street beggars, too, the real-life kind missing their sanity or a body part for which they petitioned our donations. Iran did not yet offer the kind of welfare support that is widely available in the United States and other industrialized nations. Life in Tehran was multifaceted, and it moved at a fast clip. Shiraz would be a welcome change for me, since it was smaller and less commercial, I hoped.

Nas did not arrive until August 30, delayed by a stop in France to visit cousins who were studying at a university there. Abdolah met him at the airport, as his plane landed after dark, and family convened once more when he arrived at the apartment. Everyone was thrilled to see my husband after six years of his being away; the boys hugged him, and the girls wept. You would think he had come back from the dead. Perhaps in their eyes he had, since when Iranians left their native land for jobs or education, they did not always return. This was the era of the Asian "brain drain," when fertile minds traveled Europe and North America in search of opportunities that were unavailable in their homelands. There were, however, many Iranians who had graduated from Western universities and returned to Iran to lend expertise to enriching their country.

We did more sightseeing with other family members who had come to rejoice over the return of the lost sheep, and then turned our attention to plans for driving south. Nas was just as eager as I was to get to Shiraz, so we borrowed a car and packed up to leave a few days after his arrival. Shiraz, the city of nightingales and roses, the final resting place of beloved poets Hafiz and Saa'di, was home for Nas, and beckoned the boys and me.

Our trip began at 6 A.M. on Friday morning, September 2. I was thrilled to travel the semi-arid terrain and hilly mountain passes, past oil refineries and sleepy villages. As I watched pillars of smoke belch into the sky, I realized that the simple substance called "oil" was a major cause of violent international conflicts. Iran commanded respect in multinational energy negotiations over this valuable commodity.

During the long trip, while the boys were quiet and Nas concentrated on the road in his own reverie, my thoughts turned inward. Would Nas's parents like me? Since learning of our marriage, they had sent gifts of gold jewelry and Persian music cassettes. His father, who had corresponded faithfully during Nas's sojourn in the United States, had added postscripts for me in his letters. I later learned that in Iran, his father's title was "Borzu khan." The title "khan" dates to thirteenth-century Mongol figures like Genghis Khan and Kublai Khan, and indicates a tribal chief or ruler. Through bits of information gleaned from Nas and Abdolah, I learned that Borzu and two brothers had been chiefs of three villages. Their rule had weakened in the 1960s when the shah instituted land reform legislation, canceling feudal practices that had existed for hundreds of years. When his brothers died a few years later, Borzu gave up the village homestead to move the family of ten children to Shiraz for convenience, as he and his wife, whom we called "Mamanbozorg" ("Grandma"), were aging, and the children had matured; most had married. Taking a stately, two-story home on a tree-lined street near downtown, the parents continued to receive goods and reports from the village, though discontent among those who still worked the land bubbled over from time to time.

As the remaining children married and left, shrinking the family core further, moving to a smaller home in a modern housing development on the city's fringes seemed like a logical step for the parents. Their new house was our destination as the loaded vehicle made its way over hills and winding roads, through the heart of Esfahan with its architectural splendors manifested in famous mosques and tiles. This was the adventure I had always dreamed of, from the exotic artistry of the bazaar crafts to the gorgeous mosaics of Esfahan's buildings, viewed previously in textbooks.

Today, it was just Nas and the kids, as it had been in the States, travelling along the highway toward an unknown destination, one that I longed for and yet somehow feared. It was one thing to visit a strange city and be feted by people I might not see again. It was another to head toward a town and a family that might or might not welcome us into their midst. Maybe the letters had been a pretense. Maybe his parents were disappointed that their son was bringing home a foreign wife and children.

I turned inward, searching for memories of all I had learned about this nation and its people. A multicultural country, Iran is inhabited by diverse ethnic groups. The "Arien" or "Aryan" race emerged from the Indo-Europeans who originally settled on the Russian steppes. About 4,000 B.C., the Aryans began to migrate east to India, as described in the *Rig-Veda,* and south to the modern-day Iranian plateau, which then was called "Arya." Later, the region became known as "Iran." Archeology revealed a settlement of Indo-Aryans east of Kurdestan in the second millennium B.C. Later, King Darius of Persia (521–486 B.C.) proclaimed his Aryan roots in an extant inscription near the city of Shiraz: "I am Darius the great King. . . . A Persian, son of a Persian, an Aryan, having Aryan lineage."[1]

Because some families arranged clan marriages rather than intermarrying with other groups, their descendents today still reflect Aryan traits, such as blond hair and blue or green eyes. Nas's family displays these features. Originally, the Iranian empire included part of Pakistan, Afghanistan, Bahrain, Syria, Iraq, Kuwait, Jordan, Israel, Turkey, and Lebanon. Iran's kings, including the last, Mohammad Reza Pahlavi, emphasized Aryan roots as part of a distinctive royal lineage that helped legitimatize their rule. Thus, Iranian ("Aryan") people are different from Semitic peoples of the Middle East that include Jews and Arabs. However, over the centuries, intermarriage has produced mixed bloodlines in many Iranian families.

The terms "Iran" and later, "Persia," derived from the sixth century B.C. and sometimes were used interchangeably to refer to the geographic area stretching from India to the Mediterranean, north toward Russia, and south to Egypt. However, they actually mean different things. "Persia" comes from "Pars" or "Persis," with respect to the mountainous area northwest of the Persian Gulf where the city of Pars and the ancient site of the Achaemenid citadel Persepolis are located. Persian or Farsi is the official language; its modern form emerged in the ninth century A.D. The word for Iran is Aryan, and it refers to a more expansive geographical area. The term has been in use since the Achaemenid period (ca. 550–331 B.C.).

Historians believe the Persian Empire is one of the world's oldest monarchies, with the first ruler, Cyrus II, dating from the mid-sixth century B.C. Later Persian kings conquered Egyptian, Asian, and Middle Eastern lands, progressing as far west as Greece before Alexander the Great defeated Darius III in a series of battles between 490 and 479 B.C. During this era, the Persian Empire played a key role in global affairs and influenced Judeo-Christian spiritual matters, as recorded in the biblical Old Testament books of Ezra, Nehemiah, and Esther. King Cyrus issued a proclamation allowing Jews who had settled there following the Babylonian captivity to return to Israel and rebuild the temple:

> The LORD, the God of heaven, has given me all the kingdoms of the earth and he has appointed me to build a temple for him at Jerusalem in Judah. Anyone of his people among you—may his God be with him, and let him go up to Jerusalem in Judah and build the temple of the LORD, the God of Israel, the God who is in Jerusalem. And the people of any place where survivors may now be living are to provide him with silver and gold, with goods and livestock, and with free-will offerings for the temple of God in Jerusalem. (Ezra 1:2–4 NIV)

Far from Iran adopting the Jewish religion, between 559 B.C. and A.D. 651 the area's chief belief system was Zoroastrianism: "The Maz-daayasni faith was revealed by Ahura to the Aryans under King Jamshid, thousands of years before Zarathushtra, and was meant only for the Aryans of Iran. . . . As such, there was no "conversion," because the Aryans were already Mazdayasnis when Zarathushtra came."[2] Zoroastrianism was a monotheistic faith that embraced tenets familiar to Jews and Christians: the war between good and evil, a coming messiah, the resurrection of the dead to judgment, and a spiritual heaven and hell. This belief system was evident in Iran through most of the first millennium A.D.

During this time, a series of dynasties emerged, including the well-known Seleucid and Sassanian lines. In A.D. 226, Ardashir Papakan founded the second great Iranian empire, the Sassanid, which lasted four hundred years. But in A.D. 642, the Caliphate of the Muslim faith seized control of Iran and established Islam as the country's prevailing religion, with Arabic as the official language. Between A.D. 820 and 1200, Iran grew into a great center for art, literature, and science. Poets like Ferdowsi (A.D. 940–1020) created beautiful language forms that are still admired today. Ibn Sina (Avicenna, A.D. 980–1037) catalogued an extensive medical work that remained a standard in Western medical studies until the seventeenth century. Al-Ghazali (A.D. 1058–1111) blended mystic and logical interpretations of philosophy in Islamic civilization. Omar Khayyam (A.D. 1048–1122), renowned in math and astronomy, wrote the *Rubaiyat* with poems that remain widely admired.[3] Saa'di (A.D. 1213–92) wrote poetry in collected works, including *Gulistan* (Garden of Roses) that emphasize human interdependence beyond race, nationality, or religion. Captured by Crusaders, he was enslaved and went to Africa, Asia Minor, and India. Hafiz, a title for one who has memorized the Koran, was born Mohammad Shamseddin (A.D. 1320–89). Brought to Shiraz in southern Iran as a child, he remained there the rest of his life, except for a brief exile. Best known for his ghazal form, Hafiz is honored as a literary success in the East and the West:

> Would you think it odd if Hafiz said,
> "I am in love with every church

and mosque
and temple
and any kind of shrine

. . .

Because I know it is there
That people say the different names
Of the One God"[4]

Both latter poets are buried in Shiraz, where tourists still flock to visit their tombs as commemorations of Persia's golden age of letters. Cultural achievements like these colored Iran's political landscape with a dynamic blend of religious, literary, and philosophical shadings. Though the Seljuqs controlled Iran from A.D. 1040 through the twelfth century, Genghis Khan and his descendants later organized the fragmented tribal areas into an interconnected empire as part of the Ilkhanid state, and by 1450 Iran fell under Turkoman authority.

In 1501, the Safavids came to power and created a stable government; they are believed by many to be the founders of modern Iran. Shah Abbas I, one of the greatest Safavids, ruled from 1588 to 1629. Shah Abbas fostered a multicultural society that hosted foreign merchants and promoted religious tolerance. European ambassadors from countries such as Spain, Portugal, and England initiated a rich tradition of cultural exchange. By 1722, the empire had begun to decline when Afghans captured the capital of Isfahan and controlled Iran's central and southern regions for seven years. Nadir Khan Afshar ended Afghan rule but weakened governmental administration and financial security until his assassination in 1747.[5]

In the nineteenth century, Russia and Britain played the "Great Game" of vying for control of central Asia, during which Iran became a major pawn and internal strife dominated. Following fifty years of civil war between the Zand and Qajar tribes, the Qajars ruled Iran until a 1921 coup d'etat by Reza Khan, a military official, ushered in the Pahlavi dynasty with a promise of reforms and modernization.[6] His son, Mohammad Reza Pahlavi, was the current ruler in 1977.

As I mused on all I had learned of this timeless land with its endless procession of rulers and intellectuals, I realized how different Iran and its people were from my homeland and me. It was beautiful and rugged, haunted and haunting. Would I fit in?

Hour after hour, we pressed toward our goal nearly six hundred miles south of Tehran. It was a clear, warm day, and we stopped at several restaurants and stores to buy cold bottled drinks and feed Mathew formula made of boiled water from the thermos. Jason was curious about everything, and Nas patiently answered questions about grazing sheep or colorful herdsmen alongside wheat and barley fields. After a while, Jason dozed off in the back seat, while Mathew slept in my arms a good part of the way.

As the day began to wane, we approached Shiraz with growing anticipation. Soon we passed beneath the Koran Gate, the awe-inspiring arch that vaults over the highway as you enter the city. The Koran Gate is so called because of a Koran manuscript that resides in the structure's top level to bless travelers below. The 1,300-year-old city has survived deadly earthquakes, military invasions, and disease outbreaks. In the afterglow of the warm day, I liked it immediately. A twilit peace hung over the panoramic view as we descended the final hill into the urban area. Street vendors offered roasted corn and turnips to evening pedestrians out for a stroll. The call to prayer on loudspeakers atop tall poles substituted for church bells I was used to hearing at home. Sensing the tremendous cultural differences between my native land and this new country, I was both elated and uneasy. Surely, this would be a fresh start for Nas and me, and for our marriage.

The sun, a fiery orange globe, slowly sank in the sky as our vehicle made its way along the busy evening streets of Shiraz. My eyes darted from one thing to the next. Distant mountains were robed in majestic purple beneath a darkening azure sky. We crossed an ancient-looking bridge over a riverbed that was nearly dry. I felt lost in the odd sensation of timelessness.

Nas skillfully maneuvered the car through crowded streets and back onto the highway that carried us to the far side of the city. There he pulled onto a newer side road that was flanked by a butcher's shop, a bassani (ice cream shop), a dry cleaning store, and several smaller streets of new single- and dual-family dwellings made of brick. All opened onto the street or were fronted by gated patios to protect their privacy.

While greenery was not abundant, many patios sported shrubs or slender trees that shot above the gates. Everyone prized flowers and foliage here, since rainfall is scarce in southern Iran, except during the autumn rainy season. A moment later, we turned onto a side road. Passing four or five small, neat homes, he pulled in at the next gate that was ajar for us and honked loudly. Immediately, family swarmed us.

Our car doors were pulled open, and we were assaulted with dozens of kisses from the unmarried sisters, Esmat and Pari, as well as two of the older married girls who, with their children that were jumping up and down excitedly, met us with elation. Pari grabbed my neck with one arm and Mathew, whom I was holding, with the other. Tearfully, she kissed us numerous times, murmuring in Persian that I only partially understood, "I am so happy you came," "I have wanted to see you for so long," "I am glad to have another sister." Overcome by this display, my own tears flowed as Nas nonchalantly hugged his clustering nephews, and our entourage moved toward the front door en masse.

Mamanbozorg waited to greet us, in voluminous skirts and long-sleeved tunic, her head veiled in the traditional manner, yet revealing a salt-and-pepper braid hanging to her waist. Her lovely dark eyes were fringed with thick lashes that defied the faint creases of age in her cheeks. Her low, rhythmic phrases sounded like prayer, and she expertly grasped first Jason, then Mathew and me, as tears shone in her eyes. I had not expected such emotion.

Bababozorg's sitting room, one of two on either side of the front door facing the patio with floor-length windows, was just around the corner, and he ambled toward us with the help of a cane, the victim of arthritis or muscular degeneration. A tall man whose spare frame had weathered the storms of life, his proud features and regal bearing suggested someone who was used to giving orders and having them obeyed. Yet his expression showed curiosity and warmth when his eyes found us in the family's midst. Pausing before him, I saw my father-in-law nod and heard him murmur something with a gentle smile that I sensed was a welcome. Nas flung an arm around his father's neck, and Borzu embraced him fully, his face lit with joy upon having his prodigal home. Nas had left Iran against his father's wishes. Now the men, one young and strong, the other old and failing, stood face to face as their hearts met and mended.

Mamanbozorg in mourning

Bababozorg on a Dasht Arzhan rooftop for cool air

My husband and the nephews followed his father into the aged man's room, where, I learned, he stayed most of the time. His wife slept off the dining room in a bedroom shared with her two daughters. The large room on the other side of the front hall, parallel to Bababozorg's, would be ours. Resembling an efficiency apartment, it was attractively papered and paneled with a faux fireplace and wood trim. Pari, Esmat, and the nephews unloaded our luggage while Nas and his father settled onto a carpet with an intricate design and leaned against overstuffed cushions to exchange news. I stood in the doorway, unsure of whether to join my husband or stay with the women. Jason climbed into Nas's lap to watch television, which was showing a *Mary Tyler Moore Show* episode with Persian dubbed in for English. Jason giggled to hear Mary chatter in Farsi.

I decided to leave the men to themselves. Taking Mathew from his carrier, I used the last of the boiled water to make a fresh bottle of milk. Pari motioned she would like to feed him, and with a smile I handed her the baby. Mamanbozorg took a seat on the indoor steps that led to a second floor storage area. Smiling at us, she nodded from time to time as I tried to communicate with the little bit of Farsi I knew. No one in the house spoke English, although Pari wanted to learn. The tall, quiet sister, Esmat, brought us tea in an ornate pot with small glass cups on a flowered metal tray, accompanied by a box of sugar cubes. She first served the men, and then poured for us in the dining room, where we sat around a sofreh on the floor, as in Tehran. Here the custom of placing a sugar cube in the mouth while sipping tea became evident. I wondered if the practice resulted in a dentist's treasure cache.

Auburn-haired Pari stood nearly five feet tall. With a wiry build, she was physically strong and delighted in playing with the baby while asking me questions about the United States. Pari was overjoyed to see her older brother again and to have two little ones under the roof, as well as a new companion. She could not do enough for us, from washing baby bottles to introducing me to the neighborhood bakery or showering Matt and Jason with affection. Esmat, older by a year, also seemed happy to have us there, but she kept busy with the cooking and housework, in which she took great pride. I soon learned that her marriage negotiations were concluded, and she was promised to a schoolteacher who came monthly to converse with her father. They did not date as people do in the West. In fact, they barely spoke. Her suitor sat in her father's room where they discussed politics, the economy, and family news. Esmat blushingly served tea and perhaps exchanged slight greetings with the man she would marry in the course of time.

Praising God for her son's safe return, Mamanbozorg told me in Persian how she had wept for three days after hearing Nas had married an American. But her sorrow had turned to joy as the years slipped by, and disaster had not struck. Now that Nas had returned with his wife and children, she fully embraced me as her daughter-in-law, despite my Western fashions and lack of Islamic faith. The women were easy to talk to, and down to earth. I could not have wished for nicer relatives—or those who could be more accepting and tolerant of our Western "differences."

Bababozorg ("Grandfather") asked to see the baby, and Pari carried Mathew in to him as the elderly man lit a pipe. Inhaling deeply of the pungent opium that was dispensed at the drugstore, he patted Mathew's blanket. Alert and squirming, Mathew suddenly squalled. To soothe him, Pari waved the baby level with the mellow smoke, and his wailing ceased. I was not sure whether to protest, but trusting the family to know if it were safe, I said nothing. Privately, I decided to ask a doctor about the drug's effects and whether to avoid additional exposure.

After the tea things were cleared, we women chatted a while before Nas, the boys, and I settled into our "otaq," or room. The décor was charming, with Italian wallpaper and the aforementioned tall windows. Vibrant Persian carpets in swirling patterns graced the floors. With our window opening to the patio to admit a clear view of the starlit sky, I settled Jason onto a comfortable bedroll and adjusted Mathew's carrier into a reclining position. On a pallet near my husband, I stared out at the peaceful night. I felt very far from my Midwest upbringing, but somehow, I also felt secure.

We settled in. I picked up enough of the language to communicate our wants or questions. Nas's family members unconditionally accepted us as the "foreigners" we must have seemed to them. Within a few days, Nas got a job working for his cousin in a downtown office. Though the work was primarily organizational management of the extended family's business concerns, Nasrolah sometimes went out of town for a few days to check on regional projects. The job paid well, and we began to save money for bedroom furniture. Abdolah had shown us the site a few streets away where a duplex was being built in anticipation of our families sharing it within the year. On weekends, which in Muslim countries are Thursday and Friday, we went shopping for household items and groceries. Sometimes we visited with relatives who came from across town or outlying areas to welcome Nas home and to meet his bride and children. The dark-hued faces of those from the south reminded me of Native Americans in the States. Others from northern provinces resembled Europeans.

During our second week, I heard that government offices and commercial enterprises were hiring "foreigners" to teach English, which was recognized as the universal language of commerce. After a thirty-minute interview with the dean of nurses at Nemazi Hospital, reputably the best medical facility in Shiraz, I was hired to teach English to student nurses. This would be my first college-level teaching assignment. Using the British textbook, I pronounced a list of medical terms like "trachea" and "hysterectomy" in English, pausing after each so the students could repeat it. When I heard discrepancies in repetition, I restated the word three and four times until most resounded it correctly. Then I would answer questions about definitions, having the girls make up sentences using the words. Sometimes we discussed distinctions between words like "family" and "relatives." Their questions made me more aware of vocabulary needs of non-Westerners. I was learning a lot about English, about teaching, and about culture. The students and I enjoyed the opportunity of getting to know each other.

I soon learned that many Shirazis wanted to learn English, from the next-door teenager to the local shopkeeper. When people suspected me of being American, they would switch into English, since many had studied the basics in school. Surprised to find my native language in high demand, I slowed my speaking pace and simplified vocabulary to help listeners understand what I was saying and be able to respond.

When I was not teaching at the hospital, I gave Pari English lessons at the dining room table. In turn, she took me all over Shiraz. We found an American-trained doctor for the children's checkups and a dentist for a troublesome tooth. We shopped at the local "super" for imported foods like canned tuna or Pillsbury cake mixes, and local items like butter and tea. Esmat showed me how to make cutlet and calam polou (cabbage rice). Mamanbozorg asked questions about my family and home in the States, like whether the houses were constructed similarly and if all women held jobs. We watched American television programs that were broadcast in Farsi.

I grew fond of the in-laws. Despite occasional mishaps, our personalities meshed as I continued to learn Farsi and Pari studied English. Even old-fashioned Mamanbozorg began to say "cheek-en" and "tea" in a good-natured salute to my native language. Abdolah checked in by phone from Tehran weekly, his English conversations a welcome change from the effort to speak Farsi each day. Once, he came to visit, and gave us several hundred tomans (Persian currency) when Nas was out of town, in case we needed anything. He sometimes gave Pari spending money, since she did not have a public job, remaining at home to help Esmat care for their parents.

We stumbled through humorous language gaffes. One morning, observing Esmat on the patio as she potted roses that would be moved indoors during the winter, I sat down to watch and was soon joined by Pari and Mamanbozorg. Esmat explained her method, step by step, in slow Farsi for my benefit:

"First, I put soil in the pot, then add fertilizer. Next, I set the plant, like this."

Her gloved hands cautiously plucked a rose shrub from several sitting beside her, and she placed it in the pot.

"Now I fill the pot with soil."

I understood most of what she said. She set the plant in the pot, then sprinkled something that looked like dried excrement on it as she made a final descriptive statement that included the word "kaseef," which I thought meant "poop," since I had heard Pari use it when changing Mathew's diaper.

"Did you say you poop on these to make them grow?" I blurted without thinking.

An astonished look sprang to Esmat's face as Pari and Mamanbozorg burst into hilarity. Realizing I had made a blunder, I felt my face redden. Pari leaned on her mother's shoulder for support, she was laughing so hard. Esmat began to giggle and finally broke into whoops of laughter, a welcome change to her serious personality. In a moment, we were breathless. Pari stood, wiping her eyes, and came over to hug me. She explained that "kaseef" means "dirt" or "dirty," which could describe either a messy diaper or plant soil. My interpretation was a little coarser, but they understood.

On another occasion, several relatives and friends were invited to dine. One of the specialty dinners that Esmat prepared was khoresht "badan joon" (eggplant), a favorite with many. Seated around the sofreh, I looked for the serving dish to request a second helping. Not seeing it, I asked an aunt on my right,

"Badan joon hast?" ("Is there any eggplant?")

Misunderstanding my poor accent, she addressed the table at large:

"Nas's wife wants to know if dear Bahram [Bahram jooni] is here."

The man who was named raised his hand, waving gleefully as I blushed. The others stared curiously and then burst out laughing—it wasn't "dear" Bahram I wanted, but eggplant. Hastily correcting my mistake, I explained I had meant the stew, not the guest.

One evening after dinner, I tried to ask Pari how her English was coming along. She nodded and left the room, and to my surprise, returned a moment later with a tomato. Evidently my question had sounded like a request for a tomato! As I struggled to explain, we started laughing.

Nas's older sisters were married, and all had children. Khanum, about fifty, had married a man who now was about seventy. She had several children, most of who were grown and married or employed at jobs. Fortyish Puran had three daughters and five sons—the nephews we had met in Tehran and Shiraz. Abdolah was thirty-five; Nika's husband (then in Lebanon) was thirty-two; and another sister, Fatemah, was about thirty. She was the second wife of a well-to-do merchant who owned a pomegranate orchard near Kazerun. Next in Nas's family line was Tooran, who lived with her husband Jehan and their three children in the village of her birth, Dasht Arzhan. She often came to Shiraz to shop or visit her sisters.

Nas was then twenty-seven; Esmat, twenty-five; and Pari, twenty-three. The youngest brother, Yadolah, was twenty-two and in college overseas. Some females wore the billowing village dress, while others wore jeans or modest slacks. The women worked in the kitchen, chatting as we steamed rice, browned meat, chopped vegetables, and laid plates. After a meal, some of the women smoked the water pipe, a large bubbling device with a long spout. Meanwhile, male visitors clustered in Bababozorg's room, watching televised soccer or discussing village affairs. Men and women ate together around the vinyl flowered sofreh. Though some households segregated meals by gender—serving first the men, then the women—we ate together, which as an American I appreciated. Yet, it was fun gathering with the women for health updates like an aunt's soaring blood pressure or a cousin's birth control options. Girls painted each other's fingernails or styled one another's hair, as young girls do everywhere. Many unmarried females did not wear makeup or shave their legs, viewing cosmetic treatments as worldly or vulgar. In fact, when a close relative died, even the girls who routinely "polished" their appearance let themselves go as a gesture of mourning. Unplucked eyebrows, unmade faces, and uncombed hair reflected authentic grief, making me think of Shakespeare's Ophelia.

On weekends we browsed roadside stands and peeked into plaza stores. The two-hundred-year-old Vakil Bazaar displayed a fascinating array of sights and scents! My eyes greedily absorbed the vivid offerings at every turn, produced and sold by a variety of ethnic vendors. Leather harnesses, spices like cumin and saffron, fruit such as citron and lime, gorgeous cloth, felt caps, inlaid mosaics—whatever one might look for, it was possible to find it here. I saw inexpensive handmade infant's clothing displayed near high-priced European fashions. Regional pottery, delectable sweets, sparkling jewelry, and decorator artwork fed my appetite for Persian culture. Pari had to remind me to haggle over prices when we finally decided to purchase a book that I wanted. Then I realized that haggling itself was an art; vendors love to drive a bargain, but will let something go below market price to make a sale. A few noted my words to Pari and caught my ear by speaking in English:

"Over here, Mrs., I have very fine things for you. Your American family will love these."

We invited Nas's parents to go with us, but they usually declined. Once, we coaxed Mamanbozorg to come shopping. She held the car door handle in the back seat for dear life, fearing it would fly open or that she would tumble about. Obviously, she had not ridden in a vehicle very often! When she hovered over a lovely tulle fabric for a new skirt she wanted to make, I urged Nas to buy it for her. The smile on her face remained a long time afterward. We stopped at a teahouse after hours of wandering in the underground bazaar, and it was clear we made Mamanbozorg's day as she looked about in awe, taking in the extravagant décor while sipping her beverage and enjoying delicate cake. Pari told me that my roommate in the States had once persuaded Mamanbozorg to put on Western clothes. But that night, she switched back, unable to get used to slacks and a blouse. I liked Mamanbozorg as she was, and saw no need for change. Fortunately, she viewed me in the same light. We were as different as day and night, and comfortable to remain so.

Pari labored over an English text she had purchased from the Iran-America Society bookstore, patiently waiting for a few minutes of my time to check her answers and to practice pronunciation. Though she had not completed high school, she was bright, always reading about a host of subjects and striving to improve her communication and reasoning skills. She would listen intently when I spoke English with Abdolah or Nas, and soon tried out a word or phrase.

"Take-it-easy," she said one morning as I placed Mathew in her arms while preparing to leave for class.

Taken aback, I replied, "Thanks, Pari. I will take it easy—you, too!"

Tickled when I addressed her in English, Pari pushed herself to keep learning.

Esmat, meanwhile, gave me cooking lessons in exchange for my preparing some American favorites, like French toast and fried potatoes. Absorbed in running the house, her forte was domestic excellence compared to Pari's educational pursuits. The sisters adored their brothers and parents, but occasionally they argued, usually when Esmat wanted Pari to do more housework or Pari wanted time to study. I tried to help with the chores, though neither Pari nor Esmat liked me to. They insisted on treating me more as a guest than a family member, but I wanted to be one of them. Sneakily, I would strike up a conversation with a sister-in-law while she worked, and casually pitch in to help on the pretense of maintaining our chat.

"Ooh, these dishes are sturdy," I commented to Pari one afternoon as she washed plates on the patio. In nice weather, it was not unusual to do dishes or laundry outdoors, as had been the custom in the village where they grew up. Handing Pari a stack of bowls for the soapy tin basin, I nonchalantly picked up a dishtowel and began wiping those she had set in the drainer. After a minute, her lips turned up.

"What are you doing?" she asked in Farsi, knowing exactly what I was up to.

"Heechi," I said innocently.

We laughed and finished the dishes, side by side.

CHAPTER THREE

East and West

A T NEMAZI HOSPITAL WHERE I TAUGHT ENGLISH VOCABULARY to nursing students, I met a woman named Caroline from the U.S. West Coast, who, like me, taught English classes. Her husband was an American corporation executive who had been transferred to the company's Iranian branch. These wives frequently taught English, along with the rest of us who had been trained for the classroom, and we clustered for tea or coffee during class breaks to exchange the latest news from our home countries. One day, Caroline, along with another American named Sharon, invited me to lunch at the Shiraz Club. From her description, the Club sounded like an exclusive place, the kind I was not used to.

"Am I dressed okay?" I asked anxiously, tugging at my ankle-length cotton jumper over a white blouse. Compared to Sharon's neat business attire and Caroline's svelte pantsuit, I looked like a country bumpkin. But despite her usual remote manner with staff and students, Caroline was friendly, as was Sharon.

"You look fine," they assured me.

We hailed a taxi at the curb of the hospital compound, leaving the lush green lawn and full-bodied trees for the gray concrete of downtown. The taxi deposited us before a low brick building. There was no sign indicating the type of establishment it was, but Caroline gave our names to the doorman, and he readily admitted us. Entering the dimly lit restaurant, we were shown to a round table near a window facing the street. Covered in bleached linen, the table appeared sterile, and I was afraid to touch it for fear of leaving a fingerprint. Blinking pale blue eyes against the bright noon sunlight that peered through the window, Caroline raised her hand to catch the server's attention. Behind us, a middle-aged couple with British accents conversed in soft voices. Across the room, a blonde with her brown-haired companion prepared to leave. Our server appeared instantly.

"Yes, ma'am? What would you like today?"

Her face whitish in the anemic lighting, Caroline looked at me expectantly.

"I recommend the meatloaf," she suggested. Sharon nodded. Glancing over the menu, I saw it listed entrees both in English and in Farsi. The meatloaf would come with mashed potatoes and corn. I had not eaten American food in over a month.

"That sounds good," I replied obediently.

"My treat," Caroline affirmed lightly.

"Thank you."

Sharon ordered baked chicken, while Caroline requested a salad, and the server left to turn in our order. I glanced around the room, finding it tastefully decorated, with pastoral watercolor prints on the wall, and fresh flowers in vases on each table.

"Waiter," Caroline said sharply to a teenager filling water glasses a few tables away, "bring us fresh water."

"Yes, ma'am." He headed for the kitchen, as I marveled at Caroline's commanding manner and the teen's subservience.

"Don't Iranians like the food here?" I asked without thinking, seeing none around us.

Sharon appeared to size my words.

"Actually, this club caters to westerners. It was started by one of the original American companies with a branch here."

I leaned forward to lower my voice. "So Iranians aren't allowed in?"

Sharon offered hurriedly. "You know how country clubs are at home; you have to be a member."

Nodding, I let it go. I knew little of country clubs. Dismay filled me when our server in white jacket and black pants, towel over his arm, set plates before us. I was no longer hungry. Picking at my food, I drank the ice tea that was a change from the hot beverage we had every day.

"Thank you for lunch," I told Caroline during the quiet taxi ride back to the hospital. She and Sharon had chatted mostly about company business where their husbands worked, and there was nothing I could contribute to the conversation.

"We'll come again so you can meet more Americans," she offered.

I did not want to be part of an exclusive group. It felt awkward. After that, I did not see Caroline or Sharon much at the hospital, and I did not return to the Shiraz Club.

Those autumn days were golden, though with less foliage than I was used to in the States. The hospital and university compound trees were ablaze with orange, red, and yellow leaves that fluttered to the ground like lonely memories. The river that flowed through town had shriveled to a stream that trickled sluggishly under the ancient bridge. Temperatures stayed in the sixties and fifties by day, dropping about ten degrees at night. Jackets appeared on early morning and evening commuters, some in the traditional style of local culture, and others from the racks of import shops offering wares from England, Germany, France, Russia, and Italy.

I came home more than once to find Pari speaking a mixture of English and Farsi with Jason, as both expanded their vocabularies. Jason got sick with a bad virus that lasted two or three days. He looked so pale and wan lying in bed that I became very worried, wondering if he were dehydrated. Just when I was ready to call the doctor, he got better quickly, and soon was jumping spryly around the house in his usual manner. Except for a bad cold that he got over within a few days, Mathew remained healthy, as did I.

Jason and I lost a few pounds, due to our new and improved Persian diet minus American fats and sugars. There was no easy way to exercise, though I practiced a workout routine several mornings a week when I didn't have to teach at the hospital. Breakfast consisted of warm bread or toast with butter and jam, seasonal fruit, and hot tea. Lunch, which we called dinner, was the main meal of the day, usually prepared by Esmat and Pari or Mamanbozorg. For supper, typically a light meal, we often ate cutlet, made of grated potato mixed with raw egg that was molded into patties and fried. Fresh salad or greens would be served with kebab, almost like a hamburger when eaten on warm bread. For desserts or snacks, there were apples and melons, with the usual tea.

While the weather was still warm in early fall, Nas took us to the village to meet our country relatives, who welcomed us with kisses, compliments, and cooking. While en route we listened to the Eagles' eight-track cassette, with songs like "Take It Easy" whose rhythm perfectly fit our relaxed getaway. Upon our arrival in Dasht Arzhan, Pari introduced me to various neighbors and cousins, and we strolled the hillside on dusty goat tracks past adobe homes. Occupants parked their vehicle, if they had one, near the main road or adjacent to their houses. The tracks were too narrow to admit much traffic. There was a one-room store, more like a roofed booth or shed, where a middle-aged man with a black moustache sold pop and a few food staples. Across the highway lay a huge plain on which cattle, sheep, and other herds grazed, although the winter migration to the south would soon commence. Surrounded by tall mountains, the view was scenic and inspiring. Lions had roamed this area a generation or two before, and there were still stories of wolf packs that threatened grazing herds.

Many of the women here dressed in traditional Turkish garb with long flowing skirts, tunic, and veil. Their sun-kissed cheeks told of time spent out of doors fetching water from the stream or watching over flocks in the field. Little ones clung to their skirts or backs, while older children chased a ball in the tall grass. Husbands worked the fields or drove off to blue-collar jobs in distant towns and cities.

In a large, two-story villa near the center of the village, my husband and his siblings had been born. The place was deserted now, but it grabbed my attention each time we passed the place on our village rambles. Pari had described to me its medieval, domineering walls, multiple rooms framing a central courtyard, and pleasant vistas that allowed one to see miles across the plain or far into the distant hills. I imagined toddler feet scrambling up the worn stone steps, as busy mothers swept flagstone floors with handmade brooms. Bababozorg's commanding voice echoed in the chambers of my imagination. I envisioned his tall form appearing in the doorway with a brace of wild fowl in hand from the hunt, calling for Mamanbozorg or the servant girls to come and clean them. Now, as we hurried past, there was only the sound of drying weeds brushing against the unrelenting walls that time had not crumbled. Pari promised to take me one day to see inside.

Jason loved scampering from house to house, finding playmates and exploring new domains. Many of those he met were relatives who welcomed him with open arms. There was an ageless quality here that I liked very much, along with an air of peacefulness, although I would later learn that this was temporary. I imagined that life in Bible times would be much as it was in Iranian villages today. After dining with Nas's sister's family in their modest home, we lingered over tea before piling into the truck to return to Shiraz. I felt welcome and accepted, grateful that these gentle people and I shared similar values.

That fall, I mailed letters home, but my mom and sister had trouble transcribing my Iranian address until they asked an international student who was Becky's neighbor to write it in English on an envelope. Their accounts of everyday, mundane activities sometimes pinched me with homesickness. When I wrote back to describe our new lives, I was filled with gratitude for the experience of living in an exotic place where I saw new things every day. Although I missed home a little bit, I was happy in our new lifestyle.

In September, Mina's mother hosted us for dinner at her three-story home in the heart of Shiraz. The woman's husband, who was Bababozorg's brother, had died of a heart attack a few years previously, right after the family had moved from their village villa to this town house. Mina and three of her six sisters joined us, the married ones accompanied by husbands and children. The younger girls, fifteen and seventeen, sat close beside me, asking amusing questions in Farsi or English:

"Do you like Iran? Are you comfortable with Mamanbozorg and Bababozorg?"

The next-to-youngest girl's bright eyes reminded me of a young bird's. I heard her sister ask if Nas and I slept in the same room.

"Of course," the other whispered, "they're married."

I remembered what it was like to be a teenager exploring the mystery of marital relations.

A shady patio in front of the house, filled with potted plants and slender trees, provided a welcome haven from the passionate sunlight.

Inside, wooden floors blanketed by ornate Persian carpets enhanced the old-fashioned feel of the spacious rooms with antique wood furniture. The girls prepared a wonderful dinner, with eggplant and spinach stew, steamed rice, warm bread, salad, tea, and even a Pillsbury cake for dessert. First, the girls had opened the box and sifted dust bugs from the powder before mixing it with eggs and oil. I realized for the first time how long some imported products sat in warehouses or on shelves. Mina and Abdolah had come from Tehran for the weekend, and we were able to visit for an hour or so before they got up to leave. The sisters seemed to be suspended between old-fashioned values and progressive goals. One sister held a bank job and displayed a cosmopolitan air. Yet, in the months that followed, she was contracted in marriage to a longtime family friend rather than to someone of her own choosing. While this may seem odd to westerners, over time I saw that these arranged marriages worked. The couple wed without romantic ideals, focusing on fulfilling their marital roles in complementary fashion.

Mina's mother's home was attractively decorated, which motivated me to ask Nas about shopping for our new furniture, as savings for the hoped-for bedroom suite were growing. Soon Mathew would have a crib, and Jason could get a twin bed. If there were enough money, Nas and I would buy a queen-size bed and matching dresser. My teaching pay would be helpful, if minimal.

"They need English teachers everywhere," Nas said in response to my question about getting another teaching job one night, as he sat in our room reading the newspaper. Jason was playing a card game with Pari in the dining room, and I was writing in my journal. Mathew lay on a blanket, waving arms and legs as Nas and I took turns making faces and noises to entertain him. With further discussion, my husband agreed to help me find another part-time position. The next day, he accompanied me to the Shiraz Technical Institute. The administrator hired me on the spot, and I began teaching English to engineering students once a week beginning Wednesday, September 12. Now I kept really busy, with two types of lesson plans and occasional essays to grade. But I still had time for reading with the kids on the patio each evening, or drinking tea with Mamanbozorg and the sisters while discussing the latest family news, like a niece's engagement or a nephew's new job.

September melted into October, and the weather grew cooler. We had rain a few days, and then a temporary clearing. Mathew's medical checkup brought a good report. He was thriving, as was Jason. Soon he would be able to have powdered cereal with formula, and we would use a blender to make fresh food for him. Jason was eating plenty of fruits and vegetables every day, along with small portions of mutton, beef, or chicken. Muslims, like Jews, do not eat pork for religious reasons, and I had never been fond of it, anyway.

Sometimes, I grew bored. The change in pace from harried to moderate was hard to get used to. I enjoyed our predictable routine, yet I felt constrained. Lacking an Iranian driver's license, I was dependent upon public transportation when Nas was at work. During the evening, he sometimes went out with cousins or watched television with his father. We occasionally went shopping or out to eat, but aside from visiting, there was little to occupy my time. Perhaps if we lived in our own home, I would have kept busy with housework. We visited the local sites and shopped in downtown stores with both Nas's and Mina's sisters. At times I longed to jump in the car and head for the mall, but the closest option was the bazaar. I tried not to brood over this loss of freedom and activity. I had kept ultra-busy for so many years with a full-time job, college classes, and a family, that slowing down required an effort. I consoled myself in listening to music by Fleetwood Mac or other American groups that we had brought with us.

Looking ahead to the holidays, I told Nas we should visit the American Consulate in Shiraz so I could update my passport by adding Mathew's photo. It would be easier to do that than get him a separate passport. We had talked of taking a Christmas vacation somewhere in Europe, and we would need to get our passports ready. Nas agreed to drop me off at the consulate on his way to work on Tuesday, October 11. Warning me to expect a wait of two hours or more, he promised to pick me up on his morning job break.

As I entered the tan building with its cool, dim interior, I was dismayed to find a reception area overflowing with sitting and standing Iranians who were there to apply for student visas abroad. Telling the receptionist my name and reason for coming, I took a standing position near the door, resigned to waiting my turn. A few minutes later, she got up and took her list of names to the consular officer in the next room. I could see a redheaded man in his thirties poring over the list. A moment later he stood in his doorway, scanning the room.

"Mrs. Kamalie?" his voice boomed.

My hand shot up involuntarily. "That's me," I replied, eagerly moving forward. Every pair of eyes in the room stared at me enviously, and I felt guilty taking precedence over those who had been waiting a long time—some for hours.

The officer showed me to a seat across from him, and we sat down. I explained my passport request. He slid a form across the desk toward me, and then got up and led the way down the hall to another room at the back of the office suite, where a young man was taking photos. The young man guided me to the next waiting seat there, cutting in front of several youths in line.

"Should I go to the back?" I asked as he turned to leave.

"No," he said simply. "We're here to serve Americans first. We do the Iranians a favor in processing visa requests."

"Okay," I replied sheepishly, "thanks."

I was waiting for Nas when he pulled up.

"Done already? I thought I'd have to wait for you."

"Americans get special treatment, apparently. The passport will be ready in a month or so."

Just when it seemed as if we had settled into a routine, I developed troubling physical symptoms. We had struggled with mild intestinal bugs at various times since our arrival, which I assumed were part of the adjustment process. Flies were everywhere on warm days, and they slept at night on the ceiling of each room to begin the next day with fresh torments. Boiling our drinking water and washing fruit in chlorinated water, followed by rinsing, helped to control bacteria exposure. In my personal journal, I described some symptoms of October 1, 1977:

I was sick today. I don't know what it was, but my head and back and stomach hurt, and tonight, though better, I'm warm and sweating a lot. I hope it passes by morning.

My discomfort persisted off and on, as indicated in this October 21 entry:

Had a bad night last night, and don't feel too good today.

The weather turned cold on October 31, and it rained hard for two or three days. Then the temperature grew warm again, with sunshine a welcome reprieve from the gray skies that had dampened our spirits.

Serious symptoms returned, with steadily increasing abdominal pain, and progressed to alternating bouts of diarrhea and constipation. This lasted several days, and I developed a fever the first week of November. I began to vomit, and leaned over while walking. On Saturday, November 5, Nas insisted on taking me to the hospital emergency room where a British-trained resident performed a physical examination and ordered a lab workup. As I lay on the exam table waiting for test results, a nurse came to check me. When I asked about the cries I heard coming from down the hall, she explained that a very pregnant village woman had climbed atop the Western toilet to crouch over it, being used to those that were set in the ground, and could not get down. Fortunately, my attendant and another nurse were able to rescue the soon-to-be-mom.

My young doctor spoke good English, using slang like "yeah" and "okay" that put me at ease. Pressing first on one side of my abdomen, then the other, he theorized that I seemed to have a classic case of appendicitis. I didn't think so, given my lower abdomen discomfort. But when tests came back to confirm a high white count and serious infection, the doctor said I would need immediate surgery, and politely denied my request to go home and see Jason and Mathew first. Telling Nas not to alarm the boys, I waited for the next available surgical room that night. I wondered what would happen to the children if I did not make it through the operation. Then I wept, wondering why I had ever come to Iran in the first place.

Trying to focus my thoughts on more neutral topics, I noticed the hospital décor was plain. With pale walls and floors devoid of color or carpet, permeated by a strong smell of alcohol, the overall effect was bleak. Nurses were polite, and most spoke a few words of English, but after Nas left to go home to check on the kids, I felt very alone. Close to midnight, I was prepared for surgery. My abdomen was shaved, and I was given an IV. As the nurse wheeled me into the operating room, she mentioned that Nas had returned and was waiting in the adjoining area. My fear dissipated, and I prayed to survive the ordeal, so I could return to my children. The main thing I recalled was waking up after the procedure, and shivering with cold before being sent back to the dark realms of unconsciousness.

I awoke sore and groggy, reminded of my recent C-section delivery of Mathew. For the next several days, I was offered the same meal three times daily: red gelatin, beef broth, and tea. On Thursday, November 10, I was ready to go home after eating my first "real meal" since the surgery, which was the ever-popular chelou kebab. It tasted terrific, hospital food though it was.

With a slight case of laryngitis, I was packed up and wheeled to our car. As we drove home through light traffic, the emotional trauma of the surgery hit me, and I wept hoarsely. The doctor said that an appendage along my upper bowel had gotten twisted and developed gangrene. If I had not come to the hospital when I did, I would have died within hours. It had not been my appendix, after all, though the surgeon had removed it as a "precaution," since it was awkwardly located. A British doctor making morning rounds with his entourage of medical students mentioned that mine was just the second such case he had seen in twenty years of practice.

Leaning on Nas while making my way into his parents' house, I saw that Jason was sitting on the floor playing with one of the nephews, barely noticing my return. New tears spilled down my cheeks. I crept into our bedroom and lay down as Pari brought Mathew to me. Small as he was, the baby seemed to pull toward me in recognition—at least, I longed to think so. The girls and Mamanbozorg had made soup that I gratefully ate the next few days, interspersed with some solid food. By the end of the second week, I had lost twelve pounds. Some of our friends became alarmed. I was happy about nearing my ideal weight.

Somehow, I could not get focused after the surgery. The experience had been unexpected and unnerving, and I feared a recurrence or some other health crisis. Unable to return to teaching for a few weeks, I sat on the patio bench, relaxing in sixty-five-degree weather that felt balmy after the chill rains of October. I began to question the wisdom of our move to Iran. Why had I come? Were things any better here than in the States? What would happen to Jason and Matt if I were to get sick or die? Since Jason was adopted, would he face difficulties or perhaps even persecution?

I began to flirt with thoughts of going home. I tried to call my sister, using the neighbor's phone, since ours was out of order temporarily.

But Becky did not answer, and the neighbor seemed to be one of the few who were not eager to help Americans—or me, anyway. A week later, with Nas's help, I reached my mother's house, and Becky was there. I was so relieved to hear their voices again. All of us cried when I told them about my surgery, which sounded odd given the faint transatlantic echo that followed my voice. My sister strongly urged me to come home, at least for the holidays. I told her I would discuss it with Nas.

I broached the subject the next day. At first, he was sympathetic, but my husband encouraged me to try and get used to life in Iran, promising things would be better when we moved into the duplex with Abdolah and Mina.

But I pressed him, insisting on the need to leave right away, fearing for my health. It was not like me to whine like this, and Nas knew it. But after several minutes, he lost patience:

"Go home if you want, but the boys stay with me!" he fumed.

Perhaps Nas recalled another situation involving the American wife of a Shirazi whom she had married in the States. They had come here to live, and the girl seemed to be settling into her new life quite comfortably. Then she had decided to go home for the Christmas holidays to visit her family, taking the couple's five-year-old son. Upon arrival in the States, she had filed for divorce for unknown reasons, giving the husband limited visiting rights when he followed them to the United States to find out what had happened. The husband was perplexed and heartbroken. Nas might have thought I was planning to do the same thing. I knew he needed time to think about the idea of my going home for a visit. My husband was not unreasonable. He loved the boys, and it must have seemed as if I were trying to break up our family by suggesting we leave Iran. In reality, I longed for the comfort of my relatives and former life, and I was struggling to control new anxieties that had welled up following my illness.

In the days that followed, I cooked American recipes for Jason and played with Matt. In conversations about Pari's disinterest in marriage, I could not be sure if she truly disdained the idea of a husband, or whether she said so to cover her disappointment in not being sought. Her status as a khan's daughter should have attracted some suitors, and I thought her pretty, capable, and personable. Mina told me during one of her visits to Shiraz that Iranian men often prefer tall, slender, domestic girls rather than short, sturdy intellectuals. Is that not universal?

On Tuesday, November 22, the Iranian holiday of Eid-e-gorban was celebrated, commemorating the biblical Abraham's preparation to sacrifice his son in obedience to God's command as a test of faith. Abdolah came from Tehran and purchased the sheep that would be slaughtered on the patio, a feat that Jason found fascinating. A host of family members from near and far came to share that day with us. Esmat, aided by Mamanbozorg, Pari, and cousins from the village, outdid herself by cooking holiday dishes, using festive currants and raisins, along with seasonings like saffron and dill. Still recovering from my recent ordeal, I sat and watched the women prepare the meal. It was a good day, peaceful and reflective for me. I would learn more about this holiday's meaning later.

On November 25, I felt well enough to cook fried chicken, mashed potatoes, green beans, and salad for Thanksgiving. Nas's parents and sisters enjoyed it all on the dining room sofreh, praising my cooking skills. After dinner, Nas left for a hunting trip, returning the next day with quail, but no turkeys!

Nas hunting

As my reprieve from classroom duties ebbed, I knew that soon a decision would have to be made. Either I would resume teaching, or I would return to the States. I tried convincing Nas that the boys and I would come back in the spring if I went home temporarily, but he insisted that if I left, that would be "it," with no second chances for our marriage. Believing his ultimatum to be a bluff, I continued to pester him about my passport. Just after Thanksgiving, he grudgingly consented to pick up my passport from the consulate where I had left it for the addition of Matt's photo before my hospitalization. Using the last of my teaching pay for airline tickets, I made travel arrangements with Nas's help, though he remained cool and aloof.

Abdolah came from Tehran that weekend to talk me out of going home. Politely but firmly, I insisted on my need to leave Iran for a few months to strengthen my health and collect household items for the new duplex.

"Why you go? My family loves you. They want you and boys to stay here."

I looked down guiltily. "I know," I said finally, "but I will come back."

Sorrowfully, he gave up trying to dissuade me, but when Mamanbozorg and the sisters learned we were leaving, their tears nearly changed my mind. I did not want them to think I had lost trust in their family, or that they had done anything to disappoint me. The opposite was true—they had treated us so well that part of me did not want to leave. Nevertheless, I felt our departure was best.

Jason, Mathew, and I left Iran on November 30, 1977. The night was overcast and crisp. Our flight to Tehran would leave Shiraz at midnight, and we exchanged hugs and promises with Mamanbozorg and Bababozorg, along with Pari and Esmat, before settling suitcases in the car for the ten-minute drive to the airport. Nas said little, but I could feel the strain between us.

We filed out the door into the dark patio. Pari's tears were unnerving, for she and I had become like sisters. With a desperate clutch of a hug, we parted, and I climbed into the car. We drove along the forlorn highway that was empty of cars this time of night, and Nas's tears finally overflowed. He berated me for taking away his children. Silently, I accepted his condemnation, finally reassuring him we would return as soon as possible. He refused to be consoled and stubbornly adhered to the notion that this separation would be our final break. I understood that he felt like a failure before his family, with a foreign wife who, with his children, had deserted him.

Outside the small, empty terminal as we boarded the plane that would take us to Tehran for an international flight, I turned to see Nas's sad eyes as he kissed first Jason, then Mathew. His glance followed as we entered the plane. Then, after taking our seats, the engine rumbled into gear, and in moments we were soaring into the blackness toward distant mountains, our first obstacle in the quest for Tehran. I wondered if I would see Nas or his family again, and the sobering thought of my new single-parent status began to weigh on my conscience and my heart as the plane droned on.

In less than two hours we were touching down at Mehrabad. A Tehran cousin and his wife helped us make the connection for the U.S. flight after a few hours' layover at their apartment, where I tried un-successfully to nap, although the boys drifted off for a short time. Boarding our next plane with a thank-you to the cousins, we flew on to Frankfurt and a five-hour stopover. Finally, after another eight-hour flight, we landed at New York, where my sister Becky waited to join us on the Pan Am flight to Ohio. I was delighted to see her, but fatigue overshadowed my pleasure at being home again.

"Deb! I can't believe you're finally here." She picked up Jason and hugged him tightly. "Here, let me take the baby."

I was grateful for her assistance. After a brief rest in the women's lounge, we prepared for the final leg of our journey and boarded the plane for Cleveland.

Finally, we touched down one last time and made the hour-long drive to Akron. Exhausted after nearly twenty-four hours of travel, we entered my mother's cozy home with bear hugs. Then I collapsed in the extra bedroom for several hours of healing sleep, with Jason at my side and Mathew tucked into a portable carrier that Becky had bought. They were glad we had come back in time to celebrate Christ-mas, but I wondered if it had been the right decision, after all. We talked about our Iran experiences at dinner or while shopping over the next several days, but somehow words did not bring my memories to life. Although I was relieved to be home and get a medical checkup, as well as spend time with my parents and siblings, I missed my other family in Iran.

Jason recognized Grandma and Aunt Becky, and soon was following a normal schedule of eating, sleeping, and playing. During the second week, I found a job as a legal secretary with a salary that was barely enough to pay for a two-bedroom apartment, utilities, and food. Using the last of my savings and the promise of income, I bought a used car that I hoped would get me to work and the boys to day care. I wondered if Mamanbozorg and Pari missed us. Was Nas looking for another wife, as his Tehran cousin had hinted might happen?

A few days after our arrival, Nas called my mother's house.

"Nas?" Relief flooded my voice. He had not given up on us, after all.

"How are the boys?" he asked gruffly, all business. I knew he was hurt, and healing would take time. Soon a letter came. In it, Nas said he would come in the spring to see us. But I wondered if he would then divorce me, as he had sworn to do when we parted. Surely, that had been an angry retort, and not a promise?

I did a lot of thinking over the winter months, trying to figure out the best future for our family. My anxiety was not helped when Mathew developed chronic wheezing that required hospitalization for testing. It turned out he was allergic to some of the baby food he had been eating, and his diet was restricted to squash, carrots, and a few basics until doctors identified the symptom triggers. During his weeklong hospital stay, I felt more alone and frustrated than ever. If only my husband were here to help me deal with the stress—scheduling visits during my lunch hour, coordinating Jason's care with Matt's needs, struggling with expenses. I began to feel as overwhelmed as I had felt in Iran, though for different reasons. Would peace and contentment remain forever out of reach?

My middle-aged mother and out-of-town father were unable to provide much financial or practical help, not that I expected any. While Becky was happy to have us home, she was finishing nursing school, along with working a part-time job as a pharmacy assistant, so she kept busy much of the time. Having lost touch with my college friends, I no longer knew many people with whom to socialize. Iranian acquaintances whom we had visited before moving overseas had now graduated or relocated. As in the days before my marriage to Nas, I felt lonely and vulnerable. I wrote a few lines of Farsi to Pari and Mamanbozorg, and Pari immediately responded, though I could not understand everything she wrote. I was happy they had not forgotten us and did not seem to hold a grudge that I had left Iran.

In August 1978, after a nine-month separation, Nas returned to the States. Jason and he immediately reestablished their former closeness by sharing fruit and watching television, but I remained reserved until I could find out what Nas's plans were. For all I knew, he had come to divorce me. Mathew, now a year old, was still too young to understand much, yet he climbed readily into Nas's lap, and I was happy to see them bonding. Nas was quiet and contemplative for a couple of weeks before finally announcing that he wanted a formal separation. Jolted, I could do nothing but agree, since I had left him first.

He got an apartment within a mile of us, and enrolled in graduate courses in urban studies. Several evenings a week, he came to see the boys, after calling to make sure it was okay, and I let him visit whenever possible. I felt it was important to help him stay connected with his sons. At least I did not feel quite so alone, since he would stay with them while I ran errands or kept business appointments. In some ways, we were still a family, but in other ways we were not. This upset me, but Nas could not be pressed for a decision about our marriage. I, too, needed time to decide the best course of action.

One night, after the boys went to bed, Nas and I reminisced in the living room until late at night. Normally, he left just before their bedtime, but tonight he remained stationary on the sofa, as though reluctant to leave.

"Remember the look on Annie's face when we told her about the power outages in Shiraz?" I smiled. This had been when Nas first returned, and Annie had hosted us for dinner.

Nas laughed in agreement. Our memories rekindled latent emotions, and we allowed ourselves to be drawn to each other in a romantic interlude. Throughout the Christmas season, we spent increasing amounts of time together, cooking dinner for the kids, shopping for gifts, and visiting family and friends. It seemed inevitable after the turn of the year that Nas should ask if he could return to our apartment. I agreed, hoping we would make wiser decisions this time.

Nas was not really interested in urban studies. He preferred supervising road building, but here in the States, especially in winter, there were no jobs that fit with his experience and education. I was tired of my secretarial job. I wanted to teach again but would need a master's degree to teach college classes in America. Our budget would not support further university studies. After detailed discussion and much soul searching, we decided to give Iran another try.

As winter slipped into spring of 1979, Iran underwent a major political shift. The Shah, Mohammad Reza Pahlavi, left the country, and the Ayatollah Khomeini returned. Fundamentalist leaders crafted a conservative Islamic government. The new regime's values were not incompatible with morals that I believed in, especially since resuming church attendance after returning to the States. Surely our readjustment to Iran would not be difficult, since I had a better idea of what to expect. While my family was concerned that the political shift suggested instability in that region, Nas and I felt that we would be safe in Shiraz with his family, out of the way of national political movements centered in Tehran. I hoped our marriage would thrive in Iran's family-oriented society.

Following months of phone calls to Abdolah that revealed he and Mina already were occupying the downstairs unit of our newly completed duplex a few streets away from Nas's parents, we made plans to leave for Iran in the summer of 1979. I would apply for a teaching assistantship at the university in Shiraz to support my master's studies, while Nas had been offered the management of a road construction company. Though he would travel during the week, he would be home in Shiraz with us on weekends. Our new life sounded promising, and I was ready to start over. Jason looked forward to our reunion with Nas's relatives, and was old enough to attend school there, while Matt, nearly two, would be able to attend preschool the following year. His asthmatic bronchitis had improved dramatically over the past several months, and he did not need to take medication.

Saying good-bye was difficult. My parents invited us for a home-cooked dinner attended by nephews, my brothers, and our aunt. My father, generally a quiet man, said little, no doubt feeling helpless in the wake of our decision to leave. I would miss them all, but my immediate family goals and that innate craving for adventure drew me onward, away from my comparatively calm lifestyle in the States. I instinctively trusted Nas's family to look out for us. Having met Abdolah, my mom and sister agreed that we should be in good hands, but they were uncertain about the political implications of the regime change. I emphasized that the shift was done and over with, that things were returning to normal in Iran, and there was no need to worry.

"Be careful," my sister said in a low voice, hugging me tight.

"Don't forget to write," I mumbled the cliché, meaning it. This time I wrote our new address in English to facilitate the exchange of letters. Becky was equipped with phone numbers for Abdolah and Mina, Nas's parents, and Mina's mother.

My mother tearfully kissed us. I suppose she wondered if she would see us again. Her long-standing cough had grown no worse, though she appeared a little pale. I promised—out of Nas's hearing, naturally—to return on vacation the following summer, if possible.

"Call if you need anything," my father said gruffly.

"I will, Dad," I said, knowing I would not. What could he do, after all? I admired his courage in letting a headstrong twenty-something daughter seek life on her terms, maybe because I resembled him at that age.

Our friend Mohsen drove us to the airport. This time, Nas, the boys, and I boarded an airliner together. I realized the quest for excitement was not enough to make our relocation work. I would have to remain committed to Nas and to Iran if our fragmented family were to be successfully repaired. I was grateful for a second chance at our unique lifestyle, and had no qualms about the shift to an Islamic country. Priding myself on open-mindedness and tolerance, I expected the same from others. Yet, I soon would have to confront my own narrow-mindedness in ways I could not anticipate.

Everything should work in our favor, I told myself whenever the small voice of doubt whispered in my ear. This time, nothing would stand in the way of our success.

CHAPTER FOUR

The Return Adventure

I F NAS OR I HAD BEEN SUPERSTITIOUS, WE MIGHT HAVE CANCELED the trip following two alarming incidents. The first occurred en route to New York, when our plane lurched and tilted while cruising over the Allegheny Mountains. Passengers screamed and grabbed each other before the aircraft could right itself. Fortunately, we landed without incident, so I felt the nonfatal dip was a premonition of good fortune rather than an omen of disaster.

The second incident was more frightening. At JFK Airport, we had a layover of several hours while awaiting our overnight flight to Tehran. Nas and I took turns getting the kids something to eat or using the restroom. Suddenly, two-year-old Mathew disappeared. When I returned from buying the kids some milk, Nas was looking through a magazine while seated on a bench with Jason beside him.

"Where's Matt?" I called sharply. Looking around, Nas sprang up.

"Isn't he with you?"

"No!"

Frantic, my glance darted around the vast terminal, first one way, then the other. The airport already was moderately crowded, and the

72

pace would pick up as travelers began to arrive for the popular evening overseas flights. It was now 4:30, and our departure time was 7:00.

"You take Jason and go that way—I'll search the lower concourse."

I flew down the corridor, looking for a small boy in summer shorts and T-shirt. At the lower end of the hall, I turned left and found the major airline ticket counters.

Matt was not in sight.

Turning back, I headed for the other corridor, passing numerous boarding areas. Fortunately, no planes were boarding just then, but I wondered if someone had grabbed my child and taken him into a restroom or private office. I strained my eyes in the direction Nas had gone, but saw no sign of him and Jason. Turning to the other end of the T-shaped corridor once more, I forced myself to slow down and study each doorway and alcove that might hide a small boy.

I tried opening the first door, but it was locked. As I approached the next door to my right, it quickly opened and closed—twice—revealing a dark interior. I caught the handle and pushed it open.

Matt was standing on the other side, in a utility closet stocked with buckets, mops, and cleaning supplies. There were no signs of anyone else, and the toxic products did not appear to be disturbed. Evidently, he had wandered here and gotten caught up in playing with the door. Thank God.

I picked up my son, laughing and crying.

"Mommy was worried. Don't ever go off by yourself, okay?"

He hugged me happily.

"'kay."

I ran with him in my arms up the way I had just come. Nas and Jason were rushing toward me, and Nas's anxious expression turned to relief. Though he seemed relatively calm, I knew him well enough to see he had panicked. He would have been devastated had Mathew been hurt. The Iranian men I knew were protective of their families. Mentally, I stored this frightening episode as one more reason to hold on to my marriage.

I kept a close eye on both boys for the next two hours. Finally, it was departure time. Dozing off as the plane was enveloped in darkness, I was startled hours later by the announcement that we would soon land. I woke up the boys and took them to the bathroom in case we were delayed in customs. Nas and I took turns freshening up, as well.

We arrived in Tehran on a hot summer day. Once more we were met at the airport by adoring relatives, and again we celebrated our return over dinner, this time at a family-style restaurant with the cousins from northern Tehran. Abdolah had come from Shiraz to meet us, and we stayed for a few days with the cousins, who opened their attractive apartment to us. I looked forward to the privacy of our new home, and to decorating it in a tasteful blend of American and Iranian styles. We did not take time to see the sights of Tehran following our arrival, though I was curious about changes resulting from the new government. Within two days, we said our good-byes and set out once more for Shiraz, using a borrowed vehicle, as Nas's truck was with his parents.

Along the highway, I looked for familiar oil refineries, the solitary blacktop roads with their kilometer speed limits, and the far-reaching mountain ranges. Reaching Esfahan by noon, we found a chelou kebab restaurant for our lunch. As I peered through large glass windows into the streets, I noticed most women wearing head coverings, some in loose-fitting Islamic dress or ankle-length veils. But I also saw others in contemporary Western fashions, and decided my jeans and shirt would be acceptable public attire.

"Have things changed much since the shah left?" I asked Nas over tea as we waited for our bill.

"It's much like before. Just don't do anything crazy."

He seemed edgy since arriving in Iran. I wondered if he were concerned about his new job, or perhaps quietly worried about our safety. After all, he had not been back since the revolution and probably knew little more than I did about what to expect. Abdolah had phoned a few times, and Bababozorg's letters had arrived as before. Obviously, if anything of major significance had developed, the family would have warned us not to come. I did not expect problems. Still, what did Nas mean?

"Like what?"

He shrugged as the server returned with the bill and scooped Nas's money off the table.

"Don't make speeches about America or feminism."

"I wouldn't do that."

"Well, don't. There aren't many foreigners left to back you up."

That was my first inkling of change.

We arrived in Shiraz before 7 P.M. and were warmly greeted with hugs and kisses. I felt as close to the family as ever. It was almost as if we were returning from a weekend trip. Settling into the dining room with Nas's mother and sisters, we caught up with each other's lives. Pari had continued learning English, and she proudly demonstrated her new skills by reciting a litany of common expressions:

"How are you?"

"I am very well, thank you."

Although I had to smile at the textbook tone of her speech, I was touched that she had continued her study even after our departure and despite the new regime, for Pari was a staunch follower of Islam.

Esmat dreamed her way through housework and tea service, anticipating the new life that would come with her marriage in a few months. Mamanbozorg was the same—reliable, steady, and jovial. The boys and I hugged her generously. Nas and his father exchanged news in Bababozorg's room. As the evening wore on, Pari rolled out raktekabs, or pallets, for us to sleep on, and we settled down for the night. All of us slept soundly, fatigued from the long drive. Before closing my eyes, I wondered how our new life would work out. Before, I had come to Iran with a sense of innocence. Now, in light of recent news stories and our reassembled marriage, I wondered if unexpected trouble laid waiting in the shadowy streets.

A few days after our arrival, the local newspaper featured a headline story about three women caught running a brothel. Photos of their veiled faces accompanied their printed apologies; they were hung a few days later. The government's stand on depravity would protect law-abiding citizens. Crime was dealt with speedily. Drunkenness, fornication, and gambling not only were discouraged, but were aggressively punished. I did not know then how the government interpreted and enforced morality laws. I was not upset to learn that discos and brothels seemed to have disappeared or gone underground. What I did not realize was that westerners might become the next "criminals" of this newly laundered society, targets of anti-imperialist violence. I was naïve enough to hope that we had discovered a twentieth-century government model that might influence Western societies in taking a firm stand against immoral and illegal acts.

Abdolah and Mina, aided by Pari and the teenage nephews, helped move our things into the upstairs unit of their duplex. Mina and I arranged twin beds for the boys, along with a chest of drawers in Jason and Matt's shared room. We swept the carpet and laid down striking Persian rugs, gifts from Nas's parents. Nas and Jason went to the store for groceries to fill the refrigerator that Abdolah had gotten for us, along with a stove. Mamanbozorg sent a set of dishes and a few pans, as well as silverware and cooking utensils that Pari and I washed and put inside the powder blue kitchen cupboards. A seamstress at heart, Mina measured the kitchen windows facing the street below for chintz curtains. Jason and Matt sat on the floor and unpacked toys from a carton left with the grandparents, as well as those we had brought on the plane.

The bathroom left something to be desired. It was a dimly lit cubicle that barely separated the wall shower from the toilet, although the tile walls and drain were clean. I would try to find a way to make it more attractive. Finally, we had put away towels, set aside clothes, and arranged floor cushions around the carpets as our living room area, lacking furniture, but comfortable, nonetheless. Our first meal was scrambled eggs, fresh-baked bread, and hot tea, which we found very satisfying while sitting around our beautiful rugs. Everyone was in good spirits at being together again.

The next day, Nas took me to the university to apply for a teaching assistantship. Here I encountered another indication of the political shift.

Stopping by the languages department chairperson's office, I greeted the secretary whom I had known during our first visit. We sometimes spoke in English, and other times in Farsi.

"Good morning, khanum. I would like to apply for a fall teaching assistantship."

"Very good. Please fill this out, and bring it back with a passport-size photograph."

I stared at the letterhead of the application form. Where the university's former title had been "Pahlavi University," it now read "Shiraz University."

Pointing to it, I asked, "When did the university change its name?"

"When the Ayatollah returned."

"Oh. Well, thanks. I'll bring this back soon."

Surprisingly, the government's anti-Western stance had not diminished the Iranians' desire to learn English. A neighbor wanted to pay me to tutor her son, and Abdolah told me about several businesses that were seeking English speakers to teach employees the language. Evidently, America had not fallen completely out of favor, at least with the general population. In fact, over and over again, as the hostage situation played out, I was told that Iran's conflict was with America's government, not the American people. Many were careful to make this distinction whenever the subject entered a conversation.

I decided to focus on my graduate studies and teaching, as well as helping the kids adjust, rather than spreading myself too thin by taking another job, although the income would have been helpful. Returning my application to the languages department a few days later, I encountered the departmental chairperson outside his office and asked about my chances of getting the assistantship.

"Excellent!" he replied with gusto. "We don't have many Americans in Shiraz anymore, and the students appreciate learning English from native speakers. You can probably count on it, but I'll let you know for sure next week."

Looking around the grounds as I left, I saw everything was as neat and orderly as before. There were few students or faculty around, since it was the summer break. The campus looked like one you might see in any Western nation.

Five days later, the secretary called to say I had the assistantship.

"Mina!" I called downstairs excitedly, hurrying down the steps. She appeared at the door of her first-floor duplex and held it open to welcome me.

"I'll be teaching at the university while taking classes this fall!"

We celebrated over tea and cookies while Mathew looked at a picture book about trains. It would be exciting to take part in university life, since my previous teaching experience had been limited to the hospital compound.

Jason got reacquainted with cousins, quickly adapting to their personalities and games. Many relatives came to visit in our new home for an official welcome, and Mina and I cooked dinner or offered tea, aided by Pari. Mathew, whom the family called "Jamshid" after the famous king of old, began picking up Persian phrases that he often spoke to himself at play or to me when we chatted. Jason, at six, was proficient in English and in Farsi; sometimes he interpreted for me when I could not grasp a store clerk's description or a visitor's comment. The boys watched television with Bababozorg. This probably helped them to pick up Farsi speech patterns and vocabulary. Abdolah helped us enroll Jason for fall in the international school, which was operated by Iranian administrators and instructors who spoke English. Many had studied in Europe or the United States. The curriculum used both English and Farsi. Students included children of mixed marriages like mine, in which one parent had been born in another country but was now married to an Iranian. Some diplomats' children also attended, as their parents sought a cosmopolitan learning environment for sons and daughters. When the school held a bake sale to raise money for new textbooks, I donated a chocolate cake. It was fun meeting staff and parents, and I felt that Jason would fit in smoothly. He was bright and needed a challenging learning environment that we thought the school would provide.

When Nas left town in late June to accept the construction job he had been offered, I did not worry about staying alone in our upstairs flat. After all, Abdolah below was a police officer in Shiraz now. And criminals were punished harshly. Oddly enough, I felt safer from common crime in Iran than I did in the United States, knowing that justice was clear-cut and swift. Potential criminals knew it, too. Despite murmurs of political unrest and clashes in outlying regions, I found Shiraz peaceful and orderly. The downtown district, with furniture stores and butcher shops, reminded me of ethnic neighborhoods in my American hometown.

The summer of 1979 passed in leisurely fashion. Mina and I spent long days at her mother's house, slicing apples or sipping tea while resting in the airy, cool hall. Once, when Nas came home for the weekend, we went to visit one of Mina's sisters whose husband was an overseer at Dariush Dam, outside Shiraz. Clambering up the bank to view the basin of sky blue water, we found the sight breathtaking. Laughingly, we slid into paddleboats and whisked across the deep blue waves that gently lapped at surrounding hills. After cooling our feet in the reservoir, we descended a rocky incline to the compound of groundskeepers' homes for a delicious meal and midday rest, followed by hours of Ping-Pong and early evening walks. The two-bedroom homes were furnished Western style, a legacy from their original American owners. Resting in a cushy chair while eyeing a plush sofa for a possible later nap was like visiting neighbors at home in the Midwest. When dark descended, we exchanged thanks and good-byes with Mina's sister, the woman's husband, and their two little girls.

Those early months were an enjoyable time of rest and renewal. Free from the financial worries of single parenthood, and secure in the network of an affectionate family, I felt good about our decision to return to Iran. Though I missed Nas when he was away on weekdays, we spent weekends rekindling the romance that had brought us together on the other side of the world. Playing checkers or chess with the kids, cooking favorites like pizza or pasta, and snuggling late at night were key ingredients to the recipe I hoped would keep us together.

Organizing and maintaining our home took much of my time. The duplex faced the paved road with other recently built homes, though an open lot to the right created dust on windy days. Inside the foyer of our building, a wooden door and glass window opened to Abdolah and Mina's flat, while sixteen steps, two flights of eight each, took us upstairs to a landing outside another wooden door with its own slender window. Stepping into our apartment, visitors found themselves in a wide but short "hall" where we usually ate our meals and hosted guests. To the left of this area were three wooden doors—to the boys' bedroom, the combined bath and shower, and our master bedroom, with balcony doors facing out across the plain to a far mountain ridge. On the right side of the master bedroom, behind the hall, was the living room bordered by a wall of windows, one of which opened as a door onto a narrow patio facing the mountains that often were snowcapped in winter. The living room included an ornate faux fireplace to the right, which soon would be flanked by decorous seating cushions and mounted by framed family photographs. Oriental rugs adorned each room's floor, settled atop a forest green wall-to-wall carpet. Persian carpets are handmade by artisans who often inherit the trade. Their artistry features beauty, quality, durability, and value.

The hall was our dining area, which would hold less decorous sitting cushions and a place for the sofreh. Beyond that was the long kitchen.

Matching cream-colored Venetian blinds covered all the windows of our flat. We kept these closed during the day to shut out heat, except in winter, of course, when we welcomed Master Sol indoors. The general impression of our home was simple rather than elegant, a comfortable, open, and spacious environment. We might buy more furniture later. Or we might not.

Mina opened her home to us day and night, and we were welcome to share their television for any program we cared to watch. I listened to a shortwave radio for the news in my flat, and played American as well as Iranian music in my eight-track tape player while studying, cooking, or relaxing.

Nas took his first paycheck and me shopping for bedroom furniture. Jason and Matt already had twin beds and a dresser. We decided on a queen-size mattress with a white wooden frame, matching dresser, and large wardrobe to hold our clothes. Living room furniture like a sofa and chairs would have to wait while we used the floor cushions, accented with an attractive tea service for guests. My letters home described these living effects. Occasionally, I sent photos of the places we visited or the people who came to see us to reassure my family of our relatively normal lifestyle.

I stayed alert for possible changes in society when I went grocery shopping with Mina or book browsing with Pari. Though class-consciousness remained evident, the grasping commercialism that was so prevalent in the United States did not seem as dominant here. Appreciation for nature and family was highlighted, as before. We saw plenty of visitors at the parks and public attractions, like the poets' tombs. When the weather was nice, we would watch families with their children thronging scenic areas by the river or national monuments. Everywhere, I noticed a simpler lifestyle. But at that stage of social development, only the surface crust of society was visible. Later, I would find more complex issues below the surface.

On July 16, Mathew's second birthday, Nas's American-educated cousin Ali hosted a dinner party at the National Iran Oil Club. A socialite with considerable charm, he invited a dozen family members, mostly those who were college educated or held professional jobs. I did not see any of our village kin on that occasion. I assumed the club was nonexclusionary, unlike the Shiraz Club, since there seemed to be no restrictions on who could be invited to dine there.

The long dining table, covered with starched linen, was adorned with crystal glasses and elegant china, accompanied by sparkling silverware. Two waiters promptly attended our group, bringing ice water with lemon wedges and soft disks of fresh bread to be dotted with delicate swan shapes of butter.

The guest of honor could not keep his eyes open, as eight o'clock was late for my two-year-old's dinner. After a few bites of bread, he slid off his chair, laid his head in my lap, and dozed off. I shifted his weight onto two vacant chairs and pulled them alongside so I could watch that he did not roll off. Meanwhile, the servers took our orders. Most of our group ordered steak, but others, me included, requested jujee kebab—young chicken served on white rice alongside steamed vegetables with lemon juice.

Nasrin, a cousin's wife, appeared sophisticated and stylish. She helped host the event by making introductions and linking conversational threads. I felt dowdy next to her. The young woman's hair was smartly arranged in a becoming, chin-length style, and a pricey Italian dress graced her slender figure. Educated in the States by her wealthy, well-traveled parents, she was courteous and friendly. Her smile met mine as we glanced at Mathew's sleeping form.

"Are you two members of other clubs like this one?" I asked.

"When the shah was here, there were clubs where couples mingled. Now the government keeps an eye on public gatherings and prefers to separates the sexes. Birth control, you know!"

I nodded with a brief smile.

"Did Ashvar get engaged?"

Nasrin looked puzzled, her small nose upturned quizzically. "Oh, the village girl who is marrying her cousin. They had a nice engagement party before you returned to Iran."

"Isn't she just fourteen?"

"Here, the girls marry young, especially if they have no education. Ashvar had eight years of school; now she helps her mother take care of the house. She's ready for a home of her own. Her uncle's family will help the couple get started with a few rooms in his large villa and a share of the company business. Soon babies will come along to fill her life." The speaker looked wistful.

"You don't have children yet?" I asked. Belatedly, I wondered if my question was too personal. She was only twenty-three or twenty-four. Maybe they were choosing to wait.

"No."

"Do you like going to the village?" I asked, suspecting she did not, but recalling the times I had enjoyed walking the narrow paths between cottages or having tea with welcoming country folk. Perhaps she enjoyed occasional respites from city life.

"There's nothing there anymore. Most of our childhood friends have grown up and moved away. It's a changing social system. Before, when Nas's and Ali's fathers ruled, along with Reza's father, the people were deferential. Now they are discontented. The farmers want their own land."

"You can't blame them," I said lightly.

Nasrin nibbled a piece of bread. "Change is coming. If her husband permits it, Aktar may go to university in a few years, as the city girls do. But she probably will live and die in her village, surrounded by children and caring for her parents."

I sighed. "Maybe independence is overrated."

"Independence is expensive. Everyone is looking for freedom of one kind or another. Life is hard; I want to keep it simple. Ali will build things the rest of his life. He will be successful, and we will be happy." It was a pronouncement.

Just then a server appeared with a large, round cake studded with two lit candles.

"Should I wake Matt?" I asked Nas.

Our host interrupted with his perfect English.

"Let him sleep. The cake means more to us than him. He can have the rest tomorrow."

From the corner of my eye, I watched a large palmetto bug scurry across the carpeted floor and under a table nearby. Hoping it would not turn in our direction, I hurriedly ate my slice of white cake with gelatinous frosting and quietly coaxed Nas to announce our departure, since it was after nine and Jason was nodding off, too. We thanked everyone, and I kissed the cheeks of our women guests, who returned the gesture. As we nestled the boys in the back seat for the drive home, I hoped the celebration marked a propitious start to our new life.

By midsummer, I had begun receiving replies to my family letters. I loved those communications, reading them first to myself and then portions aloud to the boys. My sister generally wrote a page or two, often cheerful and curious, as seen in this excerpt dated July 4, 1979:

> Dear Debbie,
>
> How are you and the kids? We miss you so much. I guess I really took you for granted. I miss the kids knocking at the front door and all the other little things. How are things over there? Please write and tell me *everything* in detail . . .

My mother wasn't much of a writer, but she did manage to respond on a few occasions:

> Dear Debbie,
>
> Received your letter dated 8/4/79. We are always so anxious to hear from you. Each one of us waits for the mailman. If one of us receives a letter from you, we'll say to the other one (or even just have a smile on our faces) and then we know, and just say, "What did she say, and when are they coming home?" (8/14/79)

My aunt's letters came every two weeks at least, filled with homey details:

> Hi Debbie,
>
> Becky wanted to call so bad last night and I kept telling her she better not, unless necessary. . . . I was over to your mother's after her cookbook. That's a nice one she has. Hope you are all well, we do miss you and I think of you constantly and I say prayers. Many times I hope when you come back, Nas will come with you. . . . I hope you are all feeling better and didn't catch some kind of a bug. . . . (Friday, August 3, 7:30 A.M.)

Annie sent Jason his own letter, enclosed with mine, which made him feel special:

> Dear Jason,
>
> Hi Sweetheart. How are you and how is Matt? I hope you are o.k. Your school will be starting soon, and you will meet some new friends. That's nice. I can't wait to see that picture your mother is sending of you on your bicycle. . . . How is Matt? He will miss you when you go to school but he can play and take a nap, then you and your mommy will be home. . . . Love and kisses, Annie (Tuesday night, 10 P.M., August 29)

Before classes began that fall, Nas took us to Dasht Arzhan for an overnight visit. We cooked lamb and beef over an open fire, swapped childhood stories with his relatives and family friends, and picnicked in a rustic spot frequented by deer, fox, and other wildlife. We invited aunts, uncles, and cousins to visit us in Shiraz, where, with Mina and Abdolah, or sometimes with Mamanbozorg and Bababozorg, we served dinner or tea. Guests often brought fresh eggs from their hens, orchard fruits, or homemade preserves. Ali and the city cousins came to visit, too, especially on the Muslim holidays. I liked our country getaways, returning to Shiraz rejuvenated.

As summer ebbed, I grew excited about teaching the classes that would bring me in contact with other graduate students. My intellectual nature needed academic exercise. I had gotten a head start on the reading for my classes, which were Transformational Grammar, Modern American Drama, and Creative Writing. Inquiring about my teaching schedule at Shiraz University, I learned I would be teaching two sections of English Structure, which provided students with a basic knowledge of English syntax and sentence forms. This could be challenging, since American grammar often follows a subject+verb+object structure:

Example: I went to the store.

> I = subject
> went = verb
> store = object

But in Farsi, sentence structure can be different:

Man beh forooshka raftam.
I to the store went.
or
Man raftam beh forooshka.
I went to the store.

Using sample syllabi from the department archives helped me develop a plan that would guide students and me through the course successfully. I began to look forward to working with the creative Persian teenagers. I wondered what they thought about American teachers and ideas. Although my political side had not yet awakened, I was beginning to wonder about the effects of Islamic fundamentalism on college students, and what, if anything, should not be taught.

Despite occasional news reports of demonstrations or protests, there was no hint of approaching danger in Shiraz. Continuing to learn Farsi, I half-understood radio and television broadcasts, though I expressed myself clearly enough. In fact, with my dark looks, some of the university students accused me of being an Iranian who was trying to pass herself off as American! While I knew that Iran's new government was demanding the return of the shah for trial and probable execution, I expected the conflict to remain a stalemate, little dreaming that violence would escalate tensions to crisis proportions.

At last, the fall term began. I found my students polite and attentive, eager to learn English. They asked perceptive questions and offered correct answers to grammar problems in the textbook or on the blackboard. Some spoke English well, having learned it in elementary school. Others knew a small amount and were hungry for more. Surprised, I donated extra time before and after class to answer questions or explain complex rules, like the serial comma or semicolon use. They were good students whom I felt privileged to teach.

Sometimes, the students asked intriguing questions that I found difficult to answer. On other days, the questions were humorous:

"Is it proper to say 'a pile of people,' Mrs. Kamalie?"

Other students, when they were outside of class, asked about American customs:

"Can you arrange a marriage for me with an American girl?" (Certainly NOT!)

I was excited about taking graduate classes. With perhaps twenty or twenty-five students in each one, we used English texts and discussion except when topics went off on a tangent, especially an emotional one. The professors were well prepared and interesting. Several had earned advanced degrees, mainly doctorates, in Europe or the States, and spoke fluent English. They had published scholarly articles and books, and attended international conferences. At first, I did not pick up on political undercurrents or opinions. Later, I began to sense that some felt the Islamic regime had gone overboard in repressing individual freedoms and social progress. Little was said during class time, which kept discussions on track and safe from the spies I later learned were haunting our halls.

I shared my campus office with two female Iranian instructors. Since our schedules did not overlap, I seldom saw Miss Karaji or Miss Afsoon, whose last name I did not know. But I did get to meet several instructors of many nationalities, which reminded me of working in the International Student Office years before at home. The professors came from Iranian, German, Swedish, Mexican, American, Asian, and British backgrounds; most were married to Iranians. They rounded our diverse campus community. Occasionally, several of us would meet for lunch, and the English chairman's British wife invited me for tea one day. Christina from Sweden had been in Shiraz for several years. She coordinated English classes and volunteered information about local shops and customs. Gisele, a German lady, was plump, blonde, and good-natured. She came to campus just to teach classes and left speedily to return to her three children. George of Great Britain, whom we called "St. George" in playful reference to England's patron saint, was affable, if shy. Married to an Iranian girl, he spent the academic year in Shiraz, where both taught, and summers abroad. Then there was Zahra, who came from the Southwest in the United States, where she had met and married her quiet, slender spouse. Tall and firm of step, she exuded confidence in her newly adopted persona as Muslim convert, with changes to her name, faith, and clothing. With the convert's zeal, she took every opportunity to prove her support of Iran's Islamic government.

While these acquaintances were entertaining in their own right, I found our family circle of relatives and friends more interesting. As fall brightened in brilliant foliage, I found less and less time for family visits, instead concentrating on homework and class lessons. Perhaps it was because of my newfound busyness and disinterest in political intrigue that I failed to notice subtle social developments.

While a series of long- and short-term clashes led slowly but surely to the critical juncture that would play out behind American Embassy walls in Tehran, the fall of 1979 cast a short shadow on our private lives, which had continued to be fairly simple and seemingly stable since school had started. My university schedule remained hectic, with students attending class and submitting assignments as requested, and Jason's school followed a predictable routine. Two-year-old Mathew stayed with Mina on the days I went to campus. On monthly paydays, I gave her the amount my husband had recommended as compensation for her generous support.

Though we knew of the country's furor over the shah's asylum in the United States, we expected political upheavals to calm down. In Shiraz, we felt removed from the hub of militant turmoil in Tehran, and I did not worry that the crisis would have a direct impact on us. But with each passing week, I nervously kept an eye on news stories of protests and demonstrations that were taking place around the country.

Mina proved a good friend and role model, dressed neatly in long-sleeved blouses and calf-length skirts. Occasionally, she slipped into jeans and pulled her dark, shoulder-length hair into a ponytail, although she always covered her head and sometimes her body in a scarf or chador when in public. A prudent housewife who cleaned and shopped daily for fresh meats and produce, she taught me Persian cooking and customs, and she showed me where to buy affordable groceries and feminine products. Mina did not concern herself with politics. A moderate Muslim like her husband Abdolah, she prayed regularly and kept the ceremonial fasts in a routine rather than a zealous manner. Surviving losses of her father and a younger sister, she was a strong, stoic woman who was not easily shaken.

Pari, on the other hand, was an ardent Muslim. She lived her personal faith in Allah and the prophets, read regularly from the Koran, and readily explained the five pillars of Islam. I learned more from her than anyone else by watching her example of washing before prayer, fasting on holidays, and discussing the Koran. At times, I explained my Christian views, which occasionally contradicted her understanding of the Bible. For example, she interpreted the Gospel promise of a helper, which Christians believe refer to the Holy Spirit, as pointing to the seventh-century prophet Muhammad, founder of Islam. One of the great things about our friendship was that we shared dissenting views without rejection or criticism. These conversations met our emotional and philosophical needs, for our personalities and interests were similar. Neither of us expected to convert the other, which made our friendship solid and enduring.

Though I missed my American family and amenities like shopping malls and fast food, I was mostly content. My husband's frequent absences and my brother-in-law's protective attitude shielded us from awareness of revolutionary events that were creeping toward Shiraz. It was like being in a cocoon during those first months of our return.

Nas would return on Wednesday evenings from outlying regions in the south where he supervised road construction, arriving by 7 P.M. or so. In addition to weekend activities like shopping, we went out for dinner or visited family members in or around Shiraz. There was also the Kentucky Fried Chicken franchise or local pizza, but neither was particularly tasty, and became less appetizing when, through an open kitchen door at one neon-lit pizza parlor, I watched rats scamper over crates of empty pop bottles until a man shouted and threw something, making them scatter. We left without ordering! On another occasion, we bought kebab and leeks with warm bread from an open-air grille. Within minutes of finishing our meal at home, I experienced sharp pains around my chest and wondered if I had been poisoned. Just when I was about to ask Nas to take me to the hospital, the pain subsided. Eating out could be challenging, though most establishments we tried offered clean, safe meals.

As tensions gathered that autumn, sensed in shoppers' glances or taxi passengers' whispers, I tuned into the British Broadcasting Corporation (BBC) on the radio for global news. Waiting until the kids were asleep, I would get into my pajamas and settle on a living room cushion before turning the radio on low. As news programs increasingly reported widespread protests and anti-Western demonstrations, I dismissed some of these as propaganda. I bought news magazines like *Time* and *Newsweek* at the newsstand, while family letters and occasional phone calls supplemented my awareness of current events. I tried to remain optimistic, determined to enjoy our new life and ignore potential disruptions until I could gather more facts. On campus, life continued as usual, and no one seemed to feel that violent upheaval was imminent. Yet, students seemed to feel the suspense, too, and it began to hinder their schoolwork by keeping some out of class or preoccupied while there. Mehdi, an engineering student, remained cheerful and optimistic. One morning, he caught up with me while walking to class and noticed a newspaper I was carrying with a headline about a protest march in another city.

"Oh, that's nothing. We are safe here!"

Mehdi sat in the front row and invariably raised his hand with the correct answer. His friend sitting beside him also was a dedicated learner, and the two, along with others, earned high marks. The girls were shy but often smiled and stopped to say "thank you" or "good-bye" after class. They tended to sit in the back rows but remained attentive, and sometimes asked questions or offered answers, as the boys did.

In late October, the autumn rains came. The kids and I played checkers after dinner or visited Mina and Abdolah downstairs, giggling over Farsi-dubbed episodes of *Little House on the Prairie,* one of the few American programs that was still broadcast on Iranian television. Jason and I made plans for Christmas, wondering if we would be able to find a real or artificial evergreen tree. Christian Iranians, a small portion of the population, naturally celebrate Christmas, so there would be token symbols in public places. Some Muslims celebrate the birth of Jesus, considering him a prophet, but not God's son. Shopkeepers decorate store windows with lights and feature special gift purchases. Jason and I speculated on the fudge and cookies that my mom, Becky, and Annie would send, as well as the affordable gifts we could mail home. It would have to be soon, since shipping could take several weeks. I planned to buy leather or silk wall hangings outlining traditional Iranian garden scenes, or small decorator boxes that could be purchased from the bazaar or a downtown shop.

In her letter dated October 23, 1979, my sister Becky began to plan a two-week visit at Christmas, bringing her five-year-old son, John.

Though we had discussed a possible visit before my departure from the States, her plans now swung into high gear:

> I went and got our passports. I put a rush on them. She said 10–14 days. I'll send it to the Iranian Embassy as soon as I get it back. . . . What clothes are appropriate over there? I only want to bring the necessities. . . . Tell the kids I love and miss them. . . . God bless you.

Mamanbozorg and Pari assured me Becky would be welcome and could stay with them, though I explained I hoped to have her at our house. Mina and I chatted after dinner, since we shared most meals, and I helped with the dishes. Sometimes we went shopping for new shoes or groceries, and often we stopped to visit her mother, brothers, and younger sisters in town. She could be opinionated, and I was stubborn at times, but for the most part we got along like sisters, bickering and all.

Happy to be in graduate school doing something I enjoyed, I had no time for fundamentalist marches or televised speeches, and I largely ignored the gathering momentum that continued to threaten the West with the growing demand for the shah's return. I did not realize that Iranians regarded the United States' acceptance of the shah in October for cancer treatment as continued interference in the country's internal affairs. A major outcry was heard across news media, but I assumed that some protests were more rhetorical than action-oriented. I probably would not have left Iran even if I had foreseen subsequent events. But I would have been better prepared.

A couple of incidents caused me to question my son's school and our status as Iranian Americans. One afternoon when Jason got off the school bus, he handed me a note from the principal. It asked me to come in for a conference the next day. Abdolah agreed to drive me so I would not have to catch the bus.

At the meeting, Mrs. Abadi shook hands and motioned me to a chair. In a firm but polite tone, she explained that Jason had kissed a little girl, also a first-grader, on the playground after catching her in a game of tag. Momentarily, I was embarrassed, until I reminded myself he was only six years old. Then I was at a loss to understand the principal's concern. She added that the girl had cried, since children are taught to have no physical contact with the opposite sex. When she came in from the playground, the child told her teacher, and the mother was called. She had insisted that Jason be disciplined. Explaining to the irate parent that Jason was new to Iranian culture, the principal promised to speak to me. Taken aback, I assured her I would rebuke Jason and insist he avoid girls, even in play. We parted with a courteous handshake.

On our drive home, Abdolah reassured me that Jason's behavior was normal, and he was sure Jason would have no further problems at school. Nevertheless, the incident shook me up.

A second event occurred a few weeks later. This time the school nurse called and asked me to meet with her. Curious about Jason's health or safety, I went the next day, escorted by Mina this time, since Abdolah was out of town. The bespectacled nurse appeared prim and tense. She explained that Jason had brought an inappropriate lunch to school—a foil packet of cooked fish that contained small bones. I explained that Nas's mother had handed me the packet after dinner the day before, telling me it was for Jason's lunch. I had refrigerated it before packing it in his lunch bag. In retrospect, I should have checked the contents, but since Mamanbozorg had raised numerous children of her own, I assumed the lunch would be satisfactory. I apologized, telling the nurse I would take greater care with future lunches.

"Does your son eat breakfast?" she asked in a serious tone.

"Yes. Sometimes I make scrambled eggs or French toast. If he gets up late, he has peanut butter toast with milk and fruit."

The middle-aged nurse's expression was skeptical. Adjusting her glasses, she said Jason had told her he did not eat breakfast. That was a shock! I had not missed cooking a single morning meal. Would Jason lie? Had someone misunderstood?

"You can ask my sister-in-law," I offered. "She can smell our cooking downstairs when Jason gets on the bus at 7 A.M."

The nurse blinked behind thick lenses, looking like a fish questioning the bait. Suddenly I was angry, feeling as though I were on trial for a crime I had not committed.

"I assure you, khanum, that nutrition is an important concern for my family. I make sure my children eat three healthy meals a day."

With suspicion shadowing her face, the brown-haired woman suggested I telephone her if I did not know what to pack for lunches. I left politely, hiding my irritation. Did school officials consider me an unfit parent? Would these events have raised doubts about Iranian parents, or was I under close scrutiny because I was American? Shaking off this paranoia, I forced myself not to doubt the school's good intentions. They seemed to want what was best for Jason. That is one of the nasty by-products of political unrest, as people begin to doubt each other and themselves.

CHAPTER FIVE

November 4, 1979

O N QUIET TALEGANI AVENUE IN A FASHIONABLE TEHRAN
suburb, a walled complex of buildings on twenty-seven
manicured acres stood ominously still. November 4, 1979,
was cool and overcast. Though embassy officials were conducting business as usual, despite several days of street demonstrations, neither sound
nor movement could be detected behind the protective walls that were
defaced with anti-American threats in Farsi and in English. Some op-
erations had been cut, but the embassy remained functional, which
these days meant mostly processing Iranians' visa applications.

For months, tensions had been mounting against the westerners
who remained entrenched in Iran's capitol, following the flight of Shah
Reza Pahlavi in January 1979. The shah had benefited from U.S. support and military aid that continued through eight American presidents.
In return, Pahlavi ensured a steady oil supply to the United States. Between 1963 and 1979, the shah spent oil profits in the billions of dollars
on military weapons while economic progress declined. Meanwhile,
the general population clamored for oil revenues to build more structures and roads. The shah lost popular support, and the regime collapsed.

Claiming to take a short vacation, Pahlavi and Empress Farah left Iran with their children on January 16, 1979. They would not return.

The Ayatollah Khomeini arrived a few weeks later to an enthusiastic welcome from those who were disillusioned by the shah's pro-Western machinations and the failure of democracy to bring real freedom to the masses. Clerics and nationalists hoped that Khomeini would lead a regime shift based on conservative values and stop Western nations from plundering Iran's resources.

To more fully understand the implications of these events leading up to the climactic 1979 embassy takeover, readers should examine the twentieth-century framework from which they emerged. Following years of political unrest, land division, regional clashes, and invasions, Iran's national identity was dramatically forged in a dynamic coup led by Reza Khan Pahlavi in the early twentieth century. Pahlavi freed women from the veil and urged men to wear Western attire. Promoting suffrage, literacy, jobs, and communication, Reza Khan, the civic chief, led Iran into the modern era with a view to improving the quality of life and standard of living while repressing dissenters' freedom of speech. Utilizing a puppet Majlis (parliament), Reza Khan became Reza Shah, or supreme chief, and implemented a tax system that favored the wealthy, disenfranchising landlords and clergy. But over time, his strong-arm governing strategies came under increasing criticism and denouncement both within and outside of Iran.

Religious faith played an important role in the country's political history. While the Pahlavis were Shiite Muslims, father and son pursued visions of authority built on secular, rather than spiritual, principles. It was not until the cultural revolution of the late 1970s, when the Ayatollah Khomeini assumed the rule of Iran, that the Islamic faith took a leadership role in the shift of authority to a fundamentalist state. Under the Pahlavis, Iran regained much of its former national glory, but also alienated potential supporters who would later embrace fundamentalist Islam.

In 1941, Britain and the USSR invaded and occupied parts of Iran to maintain a balance of power they feared would be compromised by Reza Pahlavi's alliance with Germany. Petroleum had been discovered decades before, leading to the formation of the Anglo-Iranian Oil Company in 1918, with Iran holding a 16 percent share. Despite commercial mergers like this, Eastern and Western cultures remained distinctive, with neither fully understanding the other. Britain and Russia had worked behind the scenes to gain control of Central Asia in the nineteenth century; during World War II, the two countries manipulated Iranian interests, including initiatives like Russia's efforts to establish Azerbaijan as a satellite. Iran's leaders appealed to Washington for nonpartisan intervention to support Iranian independence. Throughout most of the century, foreign interests played a key role in Iran's economic and social development, including its limitations and failures.[1]

Britain offered a treaty that affirmed Iran's independence while attempting to create a protectorate. Reza Khan abdicated, and the Allies permitted his twenty-two-year-old son, Mohammad Reza Pahlavi, to assume power as sovereign and head of state over Iran's constitutional hereditary monarchy. Amid food shortages, dissensions, and economic instability, the new shah took steps to continue his father's reforms.

In January 1943, the U.S. State Department supported a policy claiming that to "build an independent Iran . . . it is to the advantage of the United States to exert itself to see that Iran's integrity and independence are maintained, and that she becomes prosperous and stable."[2]

The Big Three Conference was held in December 1943, with Churchill, Roosevelt, and Stalin meeting in Tehran. The war had fractured Iran's economy, and a declaration was issued to preserve Iran's unity and freedom. American troops were in Iran by 1945, with both positive and negative results. On one hand, Iranian leaders were grateful for nominal support provided by the United States to protect the country from outsiders' control. On the other hand, some American troops behaved poorly, causing problems like vehicle accidents and property damage. Many Iranians got their first close glimpse of Western culture through this negative lens, raising questions of whether any outside country could be of real assistance in protecting Iranian interests. Over the next thirty-five years, the United States exchanged a saintly for a satanic image: in the late 1970s, descendents of those who had first witnessed American intervention in World War II called America "the great Satan."

Iran's Constitution emerged in 1906, with amendments in 1925, 1949, 1957, and 1967. The last one named the Shahbanou (mother of the Crown Prince) as regent if the prince became shah before age twenty.

Many applauded this amendment for recognizing the value of female leadership. The prime minister headed the government's executive branch. His handpicked cabinet, approved by the king, was made accountable to parliament. A national consultative assembly, called the Majlis, with 280 members, directed the legislative process, with a minister of justice overseeing the judiciary. Every four years, a national vote of men and women age twenty or over elected deputies to the Majlis. Religious minorities like the Armenians, the Assyrians, the Jews, and the Zoroastrians elected representatives. The shah appointed half of the senate's sixty members, with the other half elected by common vote. Ostensibly, the monarchy operated under democratic principles, but with time it appeared the shah grew reluctant to share authority with the prime minister or other cabinet members.[3]

Mohammad Pahlavi faced dissenters from his earliest days on the Peacock Throne. In 1949, an assassination attempt by a member of Iran's Communist Tudeh (masses) party resulted in the banning of Communists from Iran. Confronted in an uprising led by supporters of nationalist Mohammad Mosaddeq in 1953, the shah and his wife fled the country. James A. Bill points out in his book, *The Eagle and the Lion,* that at this juncture the United States adopted European tactics to become involved in Iran's internal affairs:

> There is little doubt that petroleum considerations were involved in the American decision to assist in the overthrow of the Musaddiq [sic] government. . . . Thus both the politics of oil and the preoccupation with the communist threat were major reasons for the American policy change.[4]

Subsequently, the American government took an active role in advising and supporting the Shah of Iran, as explained by Barry Rubin in his book, *Paved with Good Intentions:*

> American strategists saw Iran as a chess piece on the international political game board: capable of making potent military and diplomatic moves in support of the grand strategy without reference to its own internal tensions. . . . The road to the hell of the hostage crisis was often paved for the United

States with good intentions, coupled with exceedingly bad judgment.[5]

The year 1953 proved a pivotal point in determining not only the course of the Pahlavi dynasty, but also the nature of U.S.-Iran relations for the next twenty-five years. By many accounts then and now, it has become evident that the American government took an active role in supporting the shah and stifling Iranian nationalism, as indicated in the following summary from the National Security Archive's website:

> On the morning of August 19, 1953, a crowd of demonstrators operating at the direction of pro-Shah organizers with ties to the CIA made its way from the bazaars of southern Tehran to the center of the city. Joined by military and police forces equipped with tanks, they sacked offices and newspapers aligned with Prime Minister Mohammad Mosaddeq and his advisers, as well as the communist Tudeh Party and others opposed to the monarch. By early afternoon, clashes with Mosaddeq supporters were taking place, the fiercest occurring in front of the prime minister's home. Reportedly 200 people were killed in that battle before Mosaddeq escaped over his own roof, only to surrender the following day. At 5:25 P.M., retired General Fazlollah Zahedi, arriving at the radio station on a tank, declared to the nation that with the Shah's blessing he was now the legal prime minister and that his forces were largely in control of the city.
>
> Although official U.S. reports and published accounts described Mosaddeq's overthrow and the shah's restoration to power as inspired and carried out by Iranians, this was far from the full story. Memoirs of key CIA and British intelligence operatives and historical reconstructions of events have long established that a joint U.S.-British covert operation took place in mid-August, which had a crucial impact. Yet, there has continued to be a controversy over who was responsible for the overthrow of the popularly elected Mosaddeq, thanks to accounts by, among others, former Shah Mohammad Reza Pahlavi and Zahedi's son, who later became a fixture in the

Shah's regime. Those versions of events virtually ignored the
possibility that any outside actors played a part, claiming
instead that the movement to reinstate the Shah was genuine
and nationwide in scope.

. . . Iranians and non-Iranians both played crucial parts
in the coup's success. The CIA, with help from British intelligence, planned, funded and implemented the operation. When
the plot threatened to fall apart entirely at an early point,
U.S. agents on the ground took the initiative to jump-start
the operation, adapted the plans to fit the new circumstances,
and pressed their Iranian collaborators to keep going. Moreover, a British-led oil boycott, supported by the United States,
plus a wide range of ongoing political pressures by both governments against Mosaddeq, culminating in a massive covert
propaganda campaign in the months leading up to the coup,
helped create the environment necessary for success.

However, Iranians also contributed in many ways.
Among the Iranians involved were the Shah, Zahedi and several non-official figures who worked closely with the American and British intelligence services. Their roles in the coup
were clearly vital, but so also were the activities of various
political groups—in particular members of the National
Front who split with Mosaddeq by early 1953, and the
Tudeh party—in critically undermining Mosaddeq's base
of support. . . . The "28 Mordad" coup, as it is known by its
Persian date, was a watershed for Iran, for the Middle East
and for the standing of the United States in the region. The
joint U.S.-British operation ended Iran's drive to assert sovereign control over its own resources and helped put an end
to a vibrant chapter in the history of the country's nationalist and democratic movements. These consequences reso-
nated with dramatic effect in later years. When the Shah
finally fell in 1979, memories of the U.S. intervention in
1953, which made possible the monarch's subsequent, and
increasingly unpopular, 25-year reign, intensified the anti-
American character of the revolution in the minds of many
Iranians.[6]

Shortly after the 1953 coup, the royal family returned with Western support. Those who bewailed the tyranny of his rule blamed the United States for helping Pahlavi regain control of the country in the face of increasing popular dissent.

It was at this point that many Iranians began to seriously distrust Americans and suspect that the various kinds of economic and social support that were offered favored U.S. interests over those of Iran. Although uncertainties about Iran-U.S. relations had existed since World War II or even before, many viewed the downfall of Mosaddeq as the pivotal event that revealed the self-serving motives underscoring so much of the aid that came from the West. Iranian fears intensified in the decades that followed, as the Shah solidified a number of investment opportunities that opened the floodgates to American enterprise in Iran. Although the Shah received military aid and arms in exchange for Western trade and infiltration, many Iranians, especially the conservative Muslim sector, viewed the Shah as granting the West a large stake in Iran's resources that would shortchange the country's people of their entitlement to these things.

The ongoing Arab-Israeli conflict contributed indirectly to the problem. In 1948, the American government recognized the state of Israel, which received a significant share of U.S. economic and military support. United Nation resolutions calling for a Palestinian homeland did not receive U.S. endorsement, which angered Arab nations and Islamic cultures, as well as Iranians. Many Muslims felt the United States had proven itself more of a foe than a friend to Islamic and Arab interests.

U.S. support to Iran's monarch continued when in 1963 the shah initiated the "White Revolution," which proposed redistribution of land (some taken from clergy), massive construction projects, increased literacy, and women's rights. Iran's Islamic clergy criticized these objectives as pro-Western, and outspoken oppositionists were exiled, including the Ayatollah Khomeini. Parliament honored the shah in 1965 with the title "Aryamehr" (Light of the Aryans). The king's official coronation as Shahanshah, or "King of Kings," and Emperor of Iran took place on his birthday—October 26, 1967. The celebration featured opulent public displays, perhaps as symbols of authority and grandeur.

In 1971, the shah commemorated Iran's official founding by Cyrus the Great. A 2,500th anniversary was celebrated in a dazzling display at historic Persepolis, attended by numerous international heads of state including Princess Anne and Prince Philip of Great Britain. Maxim's of Paris catered the $200 to $300 million affair. Marble and gold adornments accented furnishings provided for the event, while famine raged in other parts of the country. Excesses like these caused the public to question the shah's fiscal management of state funds. The royal family's image as jet-setters and fashionmongers outraged clerics and nationalists.[8]

During the Arab oil embargo of the 1970s, Iran's oil business boomed. The shah funneled profits into building the military and supporting construction projects, but progress was slow, and discontent grew. Dissenters began meeting at mosques (where secular police could not interfere) to plot against the shah's regime. Pahlavi's replacement of the Persian calendar with an "imperial" calendar in 1976 solidified complaints against his allegedly anti-Islamic stance and further incited the clerics' displeasure. Political pundits used terms such as "megalomaniac" to describe Pahlavi's increasing absorption of political authority, while Iran's intellectuals and legal authorities claimed the shah had overstepped the monarch's constitutional boundaries and was limiting social progress by focusing his attention disproportionately on military matters.

Others lauded Pahlavi's reforms as transporting Iran from feudal to modern times. During the 1970s, many intellectuals and academics left Iran as part of the Asian "brain drain" that attracted great thinkers to the West in pursuit of unfettered self-expression and political freedom. To entice educated Iranians to return, the Pahlavi government offered Iranian students a year's paid tuition for each year of government employment after graduation. This financial aid could be renewed annually. Jobs awaiting the graduates included teaching, banking, and business.

Relying on military training bolstered by an autocratic style to suppress opponents, and aided by Iran's security and intelligence organization, SAVAK, Shah Pahlavi led Iran's military forces to a position of regional superiority. Despite his goal of improving people's lives and leveling social inequities for the Iranian people, the reality was that Pahlavi also restricted political freedoms. Critics claimed he failed to adequately address public concerns. The gulf widened between rich and poor while corruption incited anti-shah fervor. Anti-Western sentiment fueled by the United States' support of Israel fed Islamic and nationalist rage, evidenced in uprisings during 1978 and 1979 in several Iranian cities.

In the late 1970s, the American government sent General Robert "Dutch" Huyser, deputy commander in chief of the U.S. European Command, to evaluate Iran's political situation and bolster the military. He learned of the cultural divisions that separated groups like the Kurds and the Turks within Iran, further limiting the shah's dwindling authority. Iran's military leaders were angry that the United States allowed anti-Pahlavi broadcasts in Farsi to undermine the besieged ruler.[9] At about the same time, the shah's abuse of power was questioned and condemned in the U.S. Senate when Congressman Donald Fraser "exposed SAVAK brutality and asked why the United States embraced a regime that used torture to maintain power."[10] Inside Iran, Islamic visionaries saw their chance to topple the shah's administration and replace it with an Islamic fundamentalist governing structure that would purify the country of Western influence and political excesses. In January 1979, the Pahlavi family fled Iran once more, leaving the country in the hands of the Islamic vanguard that welcomed Ayatollah Khomeini from exile in February 1979.

Iran's intellectuals, nationalists, and Muslim clergy endorsed the idea of a supreme leader who would head a regime built on Islamic principles, returning Iran to an earlier state of religious rule and a simplified society untainted by external influences. A new government would replace corruption and pro-Western ideologies with Islamic fundamentalism arising from the dictates of a theocratic state. Iran would once more come into its own as an imperial Middle East power, this time based on Islamic precepts instead of a political platform modeled on the might of classical rulers like Cyrus and Darius.

Under a supreme leader, the proposed Islamic state would oversee the election of a president for a four-year term by the general public. The Majlis, now to be called the National Consultative Assembly, would comprise members elected by commoners and resemble Western-type parliaments. The ayatollah's cabinet, to be termed the Council of Guardians, would ensure that the government followed the tenets of

Islam and responded to the people's primary needs. Islamic clerics stepped into leadership positions vacated by civil authorities.

The Ayatollah Khomeini was the supreme leader, of course. Ruhollah ibn Mustafa Musawi (Mousavi) Khomeini was born in the town of Khomein (c. 1902). His family descended from Imam Mousa al-Kazim. Preceding generations were devoted to religious scholarship in eighteenth-century Neishapour, in Iran's Khorasan province. Migrating eastward to minister to the religious needs of northern India's Lucknow Shi'i population, Khomeini's grandfather Seyed Ahmad left India on a pilgrimage to the tomb of Hazrat 'Ali in Najaf before returning to Khomein. As an infant, Khomeini lost his father, and when a teen, his mother and aunt died. His religious education began with the memorization of the Koran at a religious school before he acquired a public school education in Qom.[11]

Young Khomeini followed the spiritual leadership of Ayatollah Haeri, who, despite growing concern about Iran's secularization, did not engage politically with Reza Shah's reforms of the 1920s and 1930s. During a national campaign against the Baha'i faith in 1955, Khomeini tried to recruit Ayatollah Boroujerdi's support (following Ayatollah Haeri's death), without success. In the early 1960s, the shah's government rescinded a law requiring elected officials to be sworn in on the Koran. Khomeini telegraphed the shah and the prime minister to warn them that the growing alarm of the "ulama" (Islamic scholars) would lead to increased protests if such reforms continued. They did increase, culminating in Khomeini's denunciation of the Pahlavi government, with its rumored links to the United States and possible secret arms deals with Israel. Khomeini's speech announcing to the shah that people would one day give thanks for Pahlavi's departure from Iran was followed by Khomeini's arrest on June 3, 1963. Khomeini again was arrested in the fall of 1964 after publicly criticizing the shah's acceptance of a $200 million loan from the United States that the Ayatollah claimed compromised Iranian sovereignty. The clerics also labeled as traitors the Majlis supporters of the agreement and claimed the government had lost legitimacy. In fall 1964, commandos raided Khomeini's house and took him directly to Tehran's Mehrabad Airport for exile. He settled first in Turkey, but, forbidden to wear his Muslim scholar's cloak and turban, in 1965 he moved on to Iraq for thirteen years.

In 1975, students supported by a crowd demonstrated at Iran's Fey-ziyeh School. Three days later, the military attacked the group, causing several casualties. Ayatollah Khomeini issued a message announcing that "liberation from the bonds of imperialism"[12] was in progress. On January 7, 1978, a newspaper article in *Ittila'at* calling Khomeini a trai-tor who was working against the Pahlavi regime touched off a mass protest in Qom and led to a series of anti-shah demonstrations through-out the country. The Iraqis informed Khomeini he would have to leave the country if he continued to stir political controversy.

In October, the Ayatollah Khomeini moved to Paris, France, where he built a following of the shah's opponents and continued to blast the Pahlavi regime in the global press. Anti-shah messages were recorded on music cassettes and smuggled into Iran for duplication and wide-spread distribution. Radio broadcasts doubled Khomeini's impact from abroad and awakened in the minds of Iran's Muslims the image of the "occulted Imam" who had disappeared in the tenth century A.D., but was believed to be waiting for the right moment to return and rule with justice. Khomeini adopted the title of imam, which is the highest title of Shiite Islam. Upon his return to Iran, the ayatollah's mystical image grew, supported by his semireclusive state at Qom, which he punctuated with periodic international speeches to the media.

On February 14, 1979, fundamentalists and leftists attacked the American Embassy in Tehran, and the Americans surrendered. The Ayatollah issued an apology that things had gone too far, and the mat-ter was quickly resolved with the assailants' departure. On March 30 and 31, 1979, a majority of the population voted support for the estab-lishment of the Islamic Republic of Iran, and on April 1, the new gov-ernment began its rule.

On November 4, 1979, the extremists who mobbed the American Embassy had been planning a "sit-in" demonstration. This time the Ayatollah Khomeini did not intervene, presumably pleased with the students' aggression due to the fact that the United States had not re-turned the shah for trial.

Termed the "Leader of the Revolution," and then "Supreme Spiri-tual Leader," the Ayatollah Khomeini assumed Iran's leadership for life. Duties included the approval of government candidates and spiri-tual guidance. Reforms implemented under the new regime retracted freedoms granted to women under the shah's rule, and a public dress code dictated acceptable appearance for both men and women, with modesty the prevailing objective. As with the Pahlavis, opposition to Khomeini or his government resulted in severe punishments that included torture and execution, especially of those believed to support the Pahlavi regime. Settling into his new role, Khomeini issued a call for surrounding Arab nations to return to fundamentalist Islam. Concerned about the possible spread of Shiite influence, Saddam Hussein invaded Iran in 1980. Thus began a ten-year Iran-Iraq war that resulted in as many as 450,000 to 730,000 Iranian casualties, compared to 150,000 to 340,000 Iraqi victims, by 1988, according to one report.[13] These severe losses are still keenly felt in Iran today. Khomeini's influence on Iran specifically, and the Middle East generally, is undeniable.

The long-standing friction between Iran's secular and spiritual factions represented polarized ideologies that brought contrasting philosophies to bear on successive periods of rule. Mohammad Reza Pahlavi, son of a king and friend to the West, linked arms with modern culture to bring Iran, with its classical past and turbulent present, to the twentieth century. Based on study abroad and military training at home, the shah's reign was characterized by efforts to emulate Western culture's social, economic, and political advances. Improved highways, schools, and hospitals fostered a sense of progress and well-being in Pahlavi's reign.

Empress Farah Pahlavi and her children portrayed a modern family prepared to take their place among the ruling heads of state throughout the world. Farah dedicated her energies to social welfare as patron of twenty-four education, health, culture, and charity organizations. The king's twin sister, Princess Ashraf Pahlavi, supported human rights and women's emancipation, and served as Iran's delegate to the United Nations General Assembly. The official impression projected by the royal family was moderation and sophistication. Reminding the world of Iran's past glories and referencing classical touchstones to support his right to rule, the shah absorbed his country's political authority to retain autocratic control of divergent groups and vocal dissenters. Rumors of abuses and secret police patrols marred the image of aristocratic royalty, as Mohammad Pahlavi grew increasingly concerned about threats and criticisms articulated by human rights organizations like

Amnesty International. Though the Pahlavi regime sought to ease suffering by improving Iranians' lives via economic and social advances,
Mohammad Reza Pahlavi relied heavily on his own judgment and
failed to delegate budgeting and governing processes to others with experience in those areas.

Ayatollah Khomeini projected an image of a scholarly ascetic
whose religious plan to turn Iran into a fundamentalist regime was
viewed as an escape from and response to the problems of the Pahlavi
administration. A Western correlation might be the Puritan movement arising from outcries against Europe's sixteenth-century Catholic
Church. Colonies such as Boston and Salem were founded on Protestant Christian values. A church-state political structure governed behavior including worship, business, and personal dress by biblical principles. However, that theocratic experiment ultimately failed.

The Ayatollah Khomeini's return to Iran and acceptance of government rule ended 2,500 years of monarchy. In efforts to dispel immoral influences and to reestablish spiritual ties with Allah under a
central government, the Ayatollah sought to purify Iran of twentieth-
century corruption. Khomeini's goal was to unify Iran internally, not
extend linkages outwardly to non-Muslim nations. His Revolutionary
Guards replaced the Shah's Imperial Guard. "Komitehs" searched for
evidence of nonconformance to Islamic dress or political/gender dissi-
dence. Polygamy returned, and moral lapses such as adultery, drug use,
or prostitution resulted in swift judgment that included public repentance
and televised whipping or private execution.

As Iranians struggled to shift from a political to a religious government, some left Iran while others returned after years abroad. Following
the shah's departure and Khomeini's return, celebrations bred demonstrations as religious activists cheered the Ayatollah and protested Pahlavi's admittance to the United States for cancer treatment. Iran remained an unstable entity with an uncertain future.

In the months leading up to the autumn of 1979, American concern over growing Middle Eastern instability required ongoing efforts
to maintain diplomatic ties with Iran's government; hence, the American Embassy in Tehran remained staffed and functional. Yet, there were
immediate indications of the Islamic regime's reprisals against pro-shah
factions. Several members of Pahlavi's government had been executed

or jailed following the ayatollah's rise to power. Westerners left voluntarily, if reluctantly. But some Americans, mainly those married to Iranians or serving intermediary organizations, remained in Iran, trusting longstanding relationships and a nonpolitical stance to ensure their safety.

On February 1, 1979, the Ayatollah Khomeini returned to Tehran to an enthusiastic welcome by fundamentalists and conservatives. On February 11, he accepted the position of becoming Iran's Supreme Ruler. His chief supporters were those who desired to improve Iran's economic and social progress, and religious extremists who were determined to rid Iran of Western influence while implementing a fundamentalist Muslim culture. Ninety percent of Iran's fifty million people are Muslims belonging to the minority Shi'a sect (rather than the Sunni denomination). Unlike governments that separate civil rule from religious practice, the Islamic regime welded the two in a move to consolidate secular interests and spiritual authority.

Through October 1979, Revolutionary Guards, tentacles of Islamic rule, incited crowds to protest outside the American Embassy. When the United States permitted Mohammad Reza Pahlavi to enter the States for cancer treatment, demonstrations became urgent, frequent, and violent, evidenced in screaming, posters, graffiti condemning the United States, and missiles hurled at the compound. Each day the crowd grew more frenzied, fed by government broadcasts decrying U.S. support of the shah. Finally, tensions accelerated to propel an uncontrollable mob toward the only available American target: the U.S. Embassy.

On November 4, 1979, a chanting crowd of thousands surged toward the embassy's unsuspecting staff secured behind the brick façade of safety. Ostensibly, U.S. Marines had been posted at the barred gate. At least one marine had predicted the attack.

A few streets from the compound, ten to fifteen thousand protesters picked up volume and speed. A swell of outraged voices rumbled nearer the compound, bubbling over into angry shouts:

"Marg bar Emrika!"

"Death to America!"

"Death to Carter!"

A core group of five or six hundred militants in khaki jackets and young women heavily veiled in chadors called themselves the Muslim Students Following the Line of the Imam. Wearing red armbands, the group burst onto the street by foot and vehicle as several Pekan autos raced to the curb near the compound gate, spilling radicals from all four doors. Armed with zealous fervor and weapons, the furious mob stormed the compound, seizing security personnel and breaking into the main building. Women used bolt-cutters hidden in their long skirts to snap the chains at the gate.

Behind the barricaded door, American guards worked quickly to destroy documents hastily pulled from file cabinets. Pounding feet echoed on the pavement. A blow sounded on the door.

"Everyone on the floor! They're coming in—there's tear gas down here!"

Another blow was struck. The door splintered as hundreds of bodies broke through the wooden panel. Groping hands thrust through the opening to find the lock. Hand-to-hand combat ensued as the guards fought to protect the lives entrusted to their defense.

A moment later, it was over. An Iranian yelled brutally in accented English, "Give up, and you won't be killed!"

The marines were outnumbered. Clawed, slapped, hit, and beaten with clubs and tools, they fell quickly, leaving the upper floors unprotected. Extremists milled around the room, saving documents from the impromptu fire and opening drawers to seize files that were passed to others, including the veiled women. Two militants spied the open door leading to the stairs and screamed in Farsi,

"Eenjoori—bereem!" ("This way—come on!")

Dozens poured through the entrance and raced for the stairs. Taking two or three steps at a time, they reached the second floor quickly and glanced down a deserted corridor.

Revolutionary Guards rounded up clusters of Americans, male and female, of various staff positions and ethnic backgrounds, threatening them verbally and with physical gestures as they tied their hands with phone cords and rope. Marines, code clerks, and secretaries were herded into groups of five or six and separated from each other. Veiled women blindfolded the females and pushed them down the hall into another room as the deafening roar settled into an excited buzz of voices. The wall clock read 4:00.

On that day, the Iranian militants took sixty-six staff members captive:

Thomas L. Ahern Jr., 48, McLean, VA. Narcotics control officer.

Clair Cortland Barnes, 35, Falls Church, VA. Communications specialist.

William E. Belk, 44, West Columbia, SC. Communications and records officer.

Robert O. Blucker, 54, North Little Rock, AR. Economics officer specializing in oil.

Donald J. Cooke, 26, Memphis, TN. Vice consul.

William J. Daugherty, 33, Tulsa, OK. Third secretary of U.S. mission.

Lt. Cmdr. Robert Englemann, 34, Hurst, TX. Naval attaché.

Sgt. William Gallegos, 22, Pueblo, CO. Marine guard.

Bruce W. German, 44, Rockville, MD. Budget officer.

Duane L. Gillette, 24, Columbia, PA. Navy communications and intelligence specialist.

Alan B. Golancinksi, 30, Silver Spring, MD. Security officer.

John E. Graves, 53, Reston, VA. Public affairs officer.

*Kathy Gross, 22, Cambridge Springs, PA. Secretary.

Joseph M. Hall, 32, Elyria, OH. Military attaché with warrant officer rank.

Sgt. Kevin J. Hermening, 21, Oak Creek, WI. Marine guard.

Sgt. 1st Class Donald R. Hohman, 38, Frankfurt, West Germany. Army medic.

Col. Leland J. Holland, 53, Laurel, MD. Military attaché.

Michael Howland, 34, Alexandria, VA. Security aide; one of three hostages held in Iranian Foreign Ministry.

*Sgt. James Hughes, 30, Langley Air Force Base, VA. Air Force administrative manager.

*Lillian Johnson, 32, Elmont, NY. Secretary.

Charles A. Jones Jr., 40, Communications specialist and teletype operator. (State of origin unknown. Only African American hostage not released in November 1979.)

Malcolm Kalp, 42, Fairfax, VA. Position unknown.

Moorhead C. Kennedy Jr., 50, Washington, DC. Economic and commercial officer.

William F. Keough Jr., 50, Brookline, MA. Superintendent of American School in Islamabad, Pakistan, visiting Tehran at time of embassy seizure.

Cpl. Steven W. Kirtley, 22, Little Rock, AR. Marine guard.

Kathryn L. Koob, 42, Fairfax, VA. Embassy cultural officer; one of two women hostages.

Frederick Lee Kupke, 34, Francesville, IN. Communications officer and electronics specialist.

L. Bruce Laingen, 58, Bethesda, MD. Chargé d'affaires, one of three hostages held in Iranian Foreign Ministry.

Steven Lauterbach, 29, North Dayton, OH. Administrative officer.

Gary E. Lee, 37, Falls Church, VA. Administrative officer.

Sgt. Paul Edward Lewis, 23, Homer, IL. Marine guard.

John W. Limbert Jr., 37, Washington, DC. Political officer.

Sgt. James M. Lopez, 22, Globe, AZ. Marine guard.

*Sgt. Ladell Maples, 23, Earle, AR. Marine guard.

Sgt. John D. McKeel Jr., 27, Balch Springs, TX. Marine guard.

Michael J. Metrinko, 34, Olyphant, PA. Political officer.

Jerry J. Miele, 42, Mt. Pleasant, PA. Communications officer.

Staff Sgt. Michael E. Moeller, 31, Quantico, VA. Head of marine guard unit.

*Elizabeth Montagne, 42, Calumet City, IL. Secretary.

Bert C. Moore, 45, Mount Vernon, OH. Counselor for administration.

Richard H. Morefield, 51, San Diego, CA. U.S. consul general in Tehran.

Capt. Paul M. Needham Jr., 30, Bellevue, NE. Air force logistics staff officer.

Robert C. Ode, 65, Sun City, AZ. Retired Foreign Service officer on temporary duty in Tehran.

Sgt. Gregory A. Persinger, 23, Seaford, DE. Marine guard.

Jerry Plotkin, 45, Sherman Oaks, CA. Private businessman visiting Tehran.

*Sgt. William Quarles, 23, Washington, DC. Marine guard.

**Richard I. Queen, 28, New York, NY. Vice consul.

M. Sgt. Regis Ragan, 38. Johnstown, PA. Army noncom, assigned to defense attaché's officer.

*Captain Neal (Terry) Robinson, 30, Houston, TX. Administrative officer.

Lt. Col. David M. Roeder, 41, Alexandria, VA. Deputy air force attaché.

*Lloyd Rollins, 40, Alexandria, VA. Administrative officer.

Barry M. Rosen, 36, Brooklyn, NY. Press attaché.

William B. Royer Jr., 49, Houston, TX. Assistant director of Iran-America Society.

Col. Thomas E. Schaefer, 50, Tacoma, WA. Air force attaché.

Col. Charles W. Scott, 48, Stone Mountain, GA. Army officer, military attaché.

Cmdr. Donald A. Sharer, 40, Chesapeake, VA. Naval air attaché.

Sgt. Rodney V. (Rocky) Sickmann, 22, Krakow, MO. Marine guard.

Staff Sgt. Joseph Subic Jr., 23, Redford Township, MI. Military army police officer on defense attaché's staff.

Elizabeth Ann Swift, 40, Washington, DC. Chief of embassy's political section; one of two women hostages.

★Terri Tedford, 24, South San Francisco, CA. Secretary.

Victor L. Tomseth, 39, Springfield, OR. Senior political officer; one of three hostages held in Iranian Foreign Ministry.

★Sgt. Joseph Vincent, 42, New Orleans, LA. Air force administrative manager.

★Sgt. David Walker, 25, Hampton, TX. Marine guard.

★Joan Walsh, 33, Ogden, UT. Secretary.

Phillip R. Ward, 40, Culpeper, VA. Administrative officer.

★Cpl. Wesley Williams, 24, Albany, NY. Marine guard.

Of these, thirteen women and African Americans whose names are denoted by ★ were released on November 19 and 20, 1979. Richard Queen, whose name in the list is denoted by ★★, was freed on July 11, 1980, due to an illness later diagnosed as multiple sclerosis.

Six other Americans eluded capture and were sheltered at Tehran's Canadian and Swedish embassies until January 28, 1980, when they fled Iran using Canadian passports:

Robert Anders, 34, Port Charlotte, FL. Consular officer.

Mark J. Lijek, 29, Falls Church, VA. Consular officer.

Cora A. Lijek, 25, Falls Church, VA. Consular assistant.

Henry L. Schatz, 31, Coeur d'Alene, ID. Agriculture attaché.

Joseph D. Stafford, 29, Crossville, TN. Consular officer.

Kathleen F. Stafford, 28, Crossville, TN. Consular assistant.[14]

The hostages, who included civilian and business visitors, could not have expected to become international currency between two feuding nations, one an Islamic theocracy and the other a democratic super-power. Their arena was so novel, the contestants so unusually matched, that the world turned its collective gaze in wonder to the drama that was unfolding.

The captors soon issued Communiqué Number One, the first of a series of messages. It became clear that those involved in the takeover felt securely in control. Although they were not instructed directly by the government to attack the embassy, neither Ayatollah Khomeini nor other leaders attempted to defuse the situation by ordering the captives' release. It is possible that no one expected the confrontation to escalate as it did, including the militants. David Farber writes:

> [The militants] saw their real battle as against secular mod-
> ernism and they recognized, correctly, that the United States
> was the major force spreading this cultural and political creed
> throughout the world. . . . The student hostage takers, while
> no angels, killed no one, tortured no one, and generally (with
> some exceptions) treated their hostages reasonably well.[15]

What also should be pointed out is that the embassy takeover was an unprecedented violation of international law.

On the night before the embassy assault, alone in my bed, I slept dreamlessly, little expecting the cataclysmic events that would shake my world when I awoke.

The next morning, I rose at six as usual. Cooking scrambled eggs for Jason's breakfast, I watched until Abbas Agha braked the aging yellow school bus outside our front door at 7 A.M. We were fortunate the driver lived just a few streets away; otherwise, the bus never would have come out to the suburbs so far to pick up Jason, as the school was located on the far side of the city, and I did not have a car. The driver had just been reinstated after inadvertently driving over a four-year-old girl who had come running to meet her brother as he got off the bus. Jason had been on the bus and heard the child's final screams as her father tearfully cradled her broken body. Police took away the mournful driver, though by all accounts the child's death was accidental. On this particular morning, Jason boarded as usual. Unaware of the takeover in Tehran, I turned on the radio as I put on jeans and a pullover sweater. Alarming phrases caught my attention:

". . . more rioting in Tehran . . ."

". . . President Carter . . . urgent contact . . ."

". . . embassy prisoners in groups . . ."

". . . militants demanding shah's return . . ."

With a growing sense of foreboding, I grabbed a corduroy jacket and gathered Mathew, still sleeping, into my arms as I made my way down the steps to Abdolah and Mina's flat. Abdolah was in Tehran again. His expertise often was in demand for training police recruits, though he now had a full-time job working for the Shiraz police force. Nas was supervising a highway construction crew in a rural district southwest of Shiraz.

I entered their unlocked flat as usual, laying Mathew on the large bed that was neatly made with a chenille bedspread. Mina liked Western décor and used a gingham tablecloth with matching curtains in her kitchen. She had been feeling under the weather lately and planned to see a doctor. Handing me a cup of tea, she poured one for herself as I sat down beside her at the sofreh, on the floor of the hall adjoining the living room, with its modern, light-oak furniture that was reserved for formal entertaining.

"Did you hear anything about the American Embassy in Tehran?" I asked, sipping the hot brew. Her practicality was a blessing. Seldom flustered, Mina took each day in stride. Seeing her usual calm demeanor, I figured things must not be too bad.

Mina related the basic facts, that a mob of militants, many of whom might be university students, had attacked the U.S. Embassy and rounded up dozens of American hostages. Although she downplayed the seriousness of the incident, I wondered if she knew all the facts or simply did not wish to alarm me. What would happen to the embassy staff? Would "foreigners" such as my sons and me become the next targets to be captured or slaughtered by rebels? I forced myself to stay calm.

"They want to clear out the spies," Mina explained, pouring more tea. Our demitasses were small, though the tea was strong; we usually had two or three cups at a time. Mina added that the militants were demanding that President Carter release the shah for trial on charges of misconduct during his twenty-five-year rule.

"What did he do?" I asked, stirring sugar cubes into my cup.

"They say he was corrupt. His secret police, the SAVAK, kidnapped and tortured protesters. Many people believe the embassy is 'a nest of spies'," she explained.

"Who thinks that?"

"The clerics. They resent American interference in Iran's national affairs."

Their resentment was understandable. I would dislike other countries tinkering with the U.S. government. In fact, I doubted whether Americans would stand for it.

"Are the embassy staff really spies?" It sounded like James Bond.

"No one knows."

"Why don't they expel the embassy workers to the U.S.?" I scraped bread crumbs into my hand as we cleaned up.

"The militants want to find out what the Americans were doing in Tehran."

I got up to leave. She followed me to the door.

"What will happen to Americans living here?" I asked anxiously, pulling on my jacket.

"Nothing." Mina's voice was soothing. "This is between the governments, not the people. You will be safe."

Yet, already people were involved—the hostages. Of course, they were U.S. government employees. But where would it end? I counted on getting more information from campus colleagues. Surely, they would know of the takeover and perhaps have details. I wondered how the intelligentsia would respond to the hostage situation. Most were outspoken in their views; some favored westernization, while others resented the corruption that came with industrialization. As I waited for a bus at the highway edging our development, I thought back to recent days, searching for clues that might have hinted at the uprising, and realized I had been flung more than one crusty comment or critical glance. Dismissing them as insignificant, I wondered now if they reflected a growing intolerance for westerners. Did neighbors or shopkeepers disapprove of my presence? Despite my looks and citizenship, I was still considered an outsider by some. As I stood in the chilly morning air, troubled thoughts wove a conspiratorial web around my agitated mind.

On campus in recent weeks, I had heard rumors of classroom spying and stoolies reporting instructors who taught anything that could be construed as subversive to Islamic doctrine. It was said you could catch glimpses of faces in the small, rectangular windows above classroom doors. I had seen a youthful male peering in once, just after class started, but chalked it up to a juvenile prank. Now I wondered if he were a spy. Evidently, I had not made objectionable statements, since I had not been called in for questioning. There was the odd case of the French instructor who had suddenly disappeared amid rumors of Revolutionary Guard roundups. Though he might have left of his own volition, no one seemed to know what had really happened.

Since February 1979, anti-imperialist texts had been added to American and European literature courses, though for the most part we carried on business as usual. I had ignored rumors and warnings against nonconformists because I believed I was doing nothing that could be interpreted as counterculture. Now, I recalled colleagues' occasional comments about incorporating Islamic ideology in classroom teaching, whereas in 1977 there had been an open teaching policy on course materials as long as the shah's regime was not publicly condemned. Even then, there had been reports of suspicious arrests, illegal imprisonments, and secret torture. But many people had downplayed accounts of government abuses, perhaps because they enjoyed the privileges of a Western lifestyle or because they did not wish to be taken in for questioning.

Boarding the bus that would take me to campus, I questioned our family's safety. Who could be trusted? It was easy to identify fundamentalists. Women wore long, black veils or Islamic uniforms of neutral fabric designed as baggy slacks, tunic top, and bulky headscarf. With men you could not tell as easily, though younger males sometimes wore jeans and khaki army jackets, while Revolutionary Guards had taken up camouflage. Not all women wore veils, of course, and not all veils were dark. Some were made of lightweight fabric, imparting a feminine quality. Other women wore simple headscarves like those seen in Europe. When I came to Iran, I assumed my "foreignness" would be understood and accepted, so I wore no covering of any kind except a headscarf when we visited a mosque and the tomb of Hafiz, and that out of respect, not compulsion. Something like pride or individualism kept me from adopting cultural values that would hide my identity or convert me into someone else. Would a disapproving neighbor report me to authorities?

During the twenty-minute bus ride, I wondered how Jason and Matt would fare. I hoped our ignorance of social mores would not cause Jason to be ostracized at school, where we already had drawn administrative censure. And I wondered if university students would point me out as an imperialist threat. Surely, my students would not, since they appeared to be responsible and fair-minded.

Glancing around the bus, I scanned faces for judgmental expressions or contemptuous looks in response to my uncovered head and unveiled form. Most of the women wore veils or Islamic dress. Squirming, I faced forward once more. Maybe I should try harder to fit in, not stand out.

Minutes later, the crowded bus groaned to a halt at the campus curb, and I stepped out to join students thronging toward the humanities building. Buttoning my gray corduroy blazer, I passed several buildings on my way to the languages department and answered polite greetings, some in Farsi, some in English.

"Good morning, Mrs. Kamalie. How are you?"

"Good morning, Mashid. I'm fine, thanks."

"Sobh beheil, khanum Kamalie."

"Sobh beheil!"

Inside, I headed for the chai or "tea" booth to my left, where a young Iranian, perhaps twenty, sold cups of tea and slices of spice cake. He was always friendly. I wondered if that were about to change. Indeed, it seemed as though my world had shifted abruptly and was beginning to spin on another axis.

"Good morning, khanum Kamalie."

"Good morning, Masoud."

I smiled, pulling a toman from my pocket. He handed me a cup of tea with two sugar cubes on a saucer, the way I always requested it.

"I speak good English now, yes?"

"Yes, you're coming along, Masoud. Keep up the good work!"

He handed me a few rials in change. "You Japanee, yes?"

"Nope. Not German, Japanese, or Mexican."

This was a game we played. When I stopped for tea, Masoud would guess at my nationality. I had told him I was American, but he seemed to believe I was from a different background.

"You speak English, but you no look like American. You look like Iranian."

"Trust me—I'm American!"

Immediately, I chastised myself for emphasizing it. Tucking the change into my shoulder bag, I climbed a flight of stairs to the modern languages department. Near the top, I met Christina, our resource person for local and foreign news. She had an array of connections, and everyone seemed to trust her—Iranians as well as foreigners. Tall and slender, with short brown hair and wire-rim spectacles, she wore an ankle-length skirt and a long-sleeved blouse in a passing salute to Islamic dress. Her expression was somber.

"You heard about the embassy?" She spoke in a low voice.

"How bad is it?"

"The militants are holding fifty or sixty staff members. They're saying it's Carter's fault because of the shah."

"You mean they're angry because of a humanitarian gesture? Doesn't the Koran preach forgiveness?"

Christina sighed. "You know who to ask about the Koran."

I shook my head.

"It's like she had a transfusion, replacing American blood with Persian," I said in reference to our American-born colleague who had converted to Islam. Looking around, I lowered my voice.

"Do you think they'll kill the hostages?"

I wondered if we would be targeted as well. Would there be a massacre to "cleanse" Iran of foreigners? I had heard of ethnic purifications. Goosebumps prickled my arms.

"I think the hostages are more valuable alive as bargaining chips. Even fundamentalists understand the need for civil relations to gain respect for their position."

Her expression grew thoughtful. "But you never know. People get carried away. Some complain the U.S. exploited Iran by manipulating oil trade. Iran was a longtime pawn in the global arena."

I thought about my stay in 1977, and Caroline from California who had taken me to the exclusionary Shiraz Club.

After a quick glance around to be sure we were not overheard, Christina continued, "Lots of countries use espionage. But the ayatollah's regime probably will expel spies and government plots. Good-bye to the modern era."

She paused to greet two male students on their way to class. I reflected on how I would feel if world powers infiltrated the United States or manipulated our president to demand a share of natural resources, leaving a trail of cultural debris. It was hard to imagine. Yet, Iranians had experienced such treatment for decades.

"I'll be glad when Nas gets back this weekend. Abdolah should be home by then, too."

"Who watches your boys when you're on campus?"

"Jason's in school, but my sister-in-law keeps Matt. Nas's sister Pari tells them Persian fables, like the famous Scheherazade."

"Didn't you say Pari's a faithful Muslim? Is she turning them into mujahadeen?"

I grinned. "Pari would do anything for the boys, and for me, too, I believe. And even if she weren't fond of us, she won't get on her brother's bad side."

"So Nas doesn't side with the militants?"

"He's not the easiest person to live with, but he has few political or religious convictions."

Glancing at my watch, I saw that my class was about to start. Christina offered a final comment as I started to move on.

"Don't worry about this embassy thing. The hostages might be freed in a few days."

I nodded before heading off to class. Taking my customary place at the blackboard, I noticed most of the girls had covered themselves with headscarves or chadors, and realized this had not caught my attention before. Or had they just started wearing coverings? I wondered if they expected me to do the same. So far the students had tolerated my American fashions, even when sleeves did not fully cover my arms, or skirts exposed my ankles. Later, I would realize that veiling is a cultural as much as a religious practice. I should have covered myself to show respect for the people who felt it was important, even if I did not share the government's convictions about feminine modesty. I was young and idealistic. Yet, how long could I maintain personal independence—and at what price?

Preoccupied, I did not give much thought to the short, squat man who waited beyond the classroom door. I wrote examples on the blackboard to introduce a discussion of personal pronouns. But then I grew nervous, pondering reasons for his presence and wondering if he were there to observe me. Mistakenly, I wrote "their's" for theirs. Catching my error, I hurriedly corrected it, hoping the students had not noticed. I wanted to finish quickly and get home. Maybe the hostage stand-off would be over soon. I had to keep a low profile and watch for possible threats until Nas returned on the weekend.

CHAPTER SIX

The Ordeal of Uncertainty

THAT EVENING, MINA AND I WATCHED TELEVISION NEWS and switched radio stations for the latest updates. More than sixty embassy personnel had been rounded up, though the captors' plans were unclear. By some accounts, there was a possibility of imminent release if the Ayatollah advised it, as he had the previous spring, on March 17, 1979. Marxists had attacked the American Embassy that time. Khomeini denounced the takeover, and advised his follower Ibrahim Yazdi to organize hundreds of students to free the embassy officials. What would happen this time? Later, I would learn that the leaders of the November takeover had planned a brief occupation of the embassy, and then became unsure of how to proceed when the Ayatollah refused to issue clear commands regarding the hostages.

Over the next few days, I wrote letters home, mailing them at the small neighborhood store where we collected our mail. I reassured family and friends in the United States and England that we were safe and that the country seemed relatively stable. Cheerfully, I tried to dispel their worries, which undoubtedly were fed by inflammatory headlines and broadcasts that raged in daily media. I emphasized positive things—that Jason had adjusted well to his school, and that Mathew remained healthy, without a recurrence of his asthmatic bronchitis. My version of the embassy siege was brief and hopeful. If only I could believe my own words.

I refrained from mentioning an alarming news story. A local radio station reported the curbside whipping of two college girls without headscarves at the campus where I taught. Two men on a motorbike had pulled to the curb, striking the girls repeatedly with chains. The girls required hospitalization. I do not know if they survived. Viewing the beating as a random assault, I foolishly continued not to cover my head, stubbornly clinging to my sense of invulnerability. Surely everyone could see that I was American; there was no need to pretend to be a Muslim. I had nothing to hide behind the veil. The new republic would protect religious freedom, wouldn't it?

After November 4, I grew increasingly uneasy about my redefined role. On one hand, I wanted to believe that social mores were the same as before, and that I could carry on with no compulsion to hide or reveal my American background. On the other hand, I witnessed mounting evidence that Islamic law had begun to turn the spotlight of judgment on the furthest corners of Iran. Still, some women appeared in public with bare heads, and I insisted on being one of them. I did not understand the dangerous game I was playing.

A few days after the hostage taking, Mina invited me to go to the tailor's with her to have some shirts made.

"You need new clothes for the university," she said in her practical manner.

I had never worn tailor-made clothes before, and it seemed a privilege. The tailor and his assistant cheerfully measured my arm length and waist. I was urged to select sturdy fabrics in dark or neutral colors. Mina pointed out that her sisters and she had chosen solid tones, suitable for winter. I selected forest green and burgundy as becoming shades for my new shirts, which would be long-sleeved, tunic style, with a button-up collar. They would be ready within a week. Studying my reflection in the dressing room mirror, I caught the resemblance to Islamic fashions.

Only later did I realize that Mina was trying in her tactful way to protect me by encouraging the adoption of a style of dress that might pass as "Islamic" to critical eyes. She and her sisters wore the same kind of shirts, along with headscarves, if not chadors. I thought the shirts looked smart with tailored slacks or straight-leg jeans, and I wore them to campus or on shopping trips. In this way, my sister-in-law prudently drew me away from objectionable Western styles and helped me choose stylish, yet "safe," clothing that would avert unwanted scrutiny by local Revolutionary Guards, or "komitehs."

There was still the matter of covering my head. When Nas came home that weekend, I asked his opinion.

"Do I need a headscarf?"

"I don't know," he snapped, tired from the two-hour drive. Surely, if it were dangerous not to wear one, he would tell me. Gradually, I realized the implicit problem of trusting in men's fashion sense, and realized Nas would not recognize the need for veiling, since he was working with an all-male road crew in an isolated region. I continued going to campus with a bare head. Of all public places to do so, the university probably was safest, I thought, since people expect college campuses to foster liberal behavior.

Deciding that I needed the latest news magazines to supplement the BBC and Iran television newscasts, I arranged to go downtown one day. After class, I would hop a bus and meet Pari and Mathew at our favorite newsstand. We would have lunch at a sandwich shop before coming home. Jason would be in school, and Mina had errands to run.

The day dawned gray, suggesting the possibility of rain. A temporary power outage kept us from hearing morning news and a weather report. I got a taxi to campus and taught my class, noting fewer students than usual in attendance. Shortly after 10 A.M., I caught the bus at the corner, noticing that the wind had picked up and was swirling dead leaves and pebbles in every direction. Preoccupied with recent events, I did not notice how dim the daylight had become, or the debris-littered sand that was blowing stiffly all around, until I got off at the downtown stop. Suddenly it was obvious that particles had darkened the sky. I felt grit in my teeth, and watched as it pelted my coat. Pulling up my collar, I rushed toward the newsstand a few blocks away, carrying the useless umbrella, praying that Mathew and Pari were safe. A sandstorm was building to full force.

Through the haze, I saw them approaching. Pari was carrying Matt, his face buried in her shoulder, her long scarf pulled sideways to cover his head. I was grateful for her self-sacrifice. Revolutionary Guards in other parts of the country had been known to harass women whose scarves did not cover every inch of hair. Devoutly religious, Pari followed the Islamic code to the letter, yet now she could face prosecution for protecting her nephew.

Embracing them, I yelled into her ear against the wind that had picked up volume and velocity.

"We have to get Mathew out of this—where's a taxi?"

We wrapped arms together to shield my two-year-old from the biting sand as we fought our way to the curb. Sand snarled our hair and made it nearly impossible to speak. I was fearful the debris whipping at my son's nose and mouth would cause breathing difficulties stemming from his asthmatic history. Pari signaled a taxi that stopped abruptly to let us tumble into the back seat. A businessman had the front seat. I hoped the driver would not pick up more passengers, following the common practice of stuffing five or six people inside to earn more fares. Thankfully, the driver headed toward our neighborhood without stopping.

Brushing sand from our coats onto the vinyl seats, we settled into our places. I checked Matt. Blinking at me without speaking, he was breathing normally and gave a quick smile. Pari and I looked at each other, grinning with relief. Reaching into the large bag she used for downtown shopping, Pari pulled out two newsmagazines and handed them to me.

"Oh—thanks! I thought I'd have to go without this week."

Feature stories displayed anti-imperialist demonstrations in other parts of the third world. I pored over the words, as the taxi jostled against the forceful wind that was whipping the sand before us. I wondered if traffic would come to a halt.

"Look at this," I showed Pari, in response to her curious expression.

A mob stormed and set fire to the U.S. Embassy in Pakistan, killing two Americans. In Turkey, angry crowds threw rocks through the windows of the U.S. Consulate. And in Bangladesh, a crowd chanted, "Down with American imperialism!"

In Calcutta, demonstrators stoned the U.S. Consulate and burned President Carter in effigy.[1]

"Why all this violence against America?"

Pari took the magazine with interest and studied the photos, while trying to make out English headlines and sentences. Finally she replied, "Maybe they learn from Iran."

At home, we dashed into the house, shaking off our coats before hanging them in the closet. I swept up the two-inch piles of sand that had accumulated inside my windows and balcony door, despite their having been closed and locked. Sand particles dusted the bedspread, dresser, and carpet. I was amazed at how invasive the tiny grains were, though to look at them lying inert on the plain beyond Shiraz, one would never expect the ferocity we had witnessed as the wind gathered force and swept them through town, battering pedestrians, vehicles, and buildings.

I hoped the rebel forces holding the hostages would not behave in similar fashion, expanding in reach and force by collecting in numbers and solidifying their impact. Reminders of the sandstorm would be visible for days to come in the small piles that had accumulated inside doorframes and windowsills. If the militants could be compared to the natural force we had encountered today, I hoped it would be in the storm's short duration.

Abdolah came home the following day, and helped me dial my mother's telephone number in the States, but we could not get through; the overseas line was "shulukh," or busy. That weekend, Nas was unable to get home from his job.

With time on my hands, I listened to news stories, anxious for the hostages' speedy release. I felt sorry for them, especially with the holidays coming. As difficult as it was for me to get an international line to call home, it must be awful for them not being able to reassure their families. If I were one of the wives or mothers in the States, I would be crazed with worry. Somehow, I did not think the captors would kill the prisoners, but I could not understand why the Americans weren't allowed to leave, which would have solved everyone's problems. Some of the university professors believed the takeover had been a gaffe, conducted on a whim, without forethought. Now that the militants had sixty-plus prisoners to look after, they did not know what to do with them, some surmised. I just wanted it to be over, before the situation grew increasingly volatile. I worried that my American identity would be studied under the microscope of Islamic inquiry, and then what would happen? Somehow, I related to the hostages' plight. If they were freed, my chances of a safe sojourn in Iran would improve. But if something happened to them, would it have a domino effect on my children and me? My sister's hoped-for Christmas visit would have to be postponed unless negotiations for the hostages' release were quickly successful.

Boarding the bus after class the next day, I relaxed in my seat for the ride. Leaning back, I observed feeble rays of sun reaching between clouds to touch buildings and streets. I closed my eyes in mental exhaustion. Would the tensions in Tehran soon cease, or was this the beginning of a long, drawn-out conflict? Since the takeover, I had become more alert to my surroundings. Opening my eyes, I glanced around cautiously. Did that middle-aged villager's basket hold a whip for chastising nonconformists? Would the policeman at the corner accost me for not wearing the veil? Impatient with these fancies, I forced myself to switch mental gears and enjoy pleasant memories.

I recalled the fun times we had enjoyed since returning to Iran. Browsing bookshops with Pari was a special treat, finding classics in English and in Farsi. Friday afternoons with family were relaxing. Nas's father and mother would regale us with lighthearted tales of their youthful wooing, the stuff of legends. When Mamanbozorg's father refused to let Borzu marry her, the suitor threw an oxen yoke over the old man's neck. Pulling his intended to the back of his horse, Borzu and young Talat fled to the mountains. Later, they returned as a married couple for reconciliation with Talat's father. They built their home in the village, and Borzu took up the reins to rule. I subsequently learned that these "abduction marriages" were not uncommon. Perhaps that is where we get the romantic notion of a girl being "swept off her feet"!

Once, Bababozorg caught a pair of thieving rascals who were troubling a neighboring warlord. Presenting the two to the ruler, Bababozorg was given the man's youngest daughter as a gift of gratitude. Riding home on horseback with the fifteen-year-old girl mounted behind him, the young hero found his wife fuming at the gate, brandishing a hearth iron. Apparently, news of his "reward" had preceded Bababo-zorg's return.

"If you bring that girl here, it will be the last thing you bring home," Mamanbozorg warned as he approached.

Without dismounting, Bababozorg turned his horse and retraced the eight miles they had come, contriving to explain the situation to the girl's father without offending his benefactor, besmirching the girl's virtue, or losing his dignity. We passed around old photos of a slender Mamanbozorg with flaming eyes, dressed in decorous Turkish skirts. Bababozorg's youthful image revealed a tall, sturdy young man with light eyes and brown hair. Though now in his seventies, Bababozorg was still tall and straight, but he used a walking stick. His blue eyes were clear. When he spoke, his tone showed that he meant business, and yet I knew him to be fair and generous. Many men would come to see him at home, bringing gifts and news. I knew he had formerly kept a personal driver. He would issue orders, and things would get done, even from the privacy of his suburban home. There were other tales of Borzu's youthful forays. The best story told of his hunt for the wolves that had been attacking village flocks. Descending into a steep ravine where sightings had been reported, Borzu found himself face to face with a lion. Exchanging baleful looks, the two turned tail and fled in opposite directions.

The village had since come under government control as a wildlife preserve famed for lion sightings—the last one in the 1940s—as well as for leopards and other exotic creatures in the surrounding mountains. Leafing through the photo albums, I found a more recent picture that showed Nas in hunting gear kneeling behind the carcass of a wolf, rifle in hand, with a stack of dead wolves beside him. Nas explained that he and a friend had shot them for stealing sheep.

With these soothing memories, the rhythmic motion of the creaking bus lulled me. There was much I liked about Iran's people, the pace of life, and my university classes. Jolted to the present as the bus hit a bump, I stretched briefly. We were passing the street where the Shiraz branch of the American Embassy was located. Straining to see the building I had visited in 1977 for a passport update, I saw with dismay that it was abandoned and boarded. Anti-American slogans, spray-painted or written in chalk, defaced the walls. Turning my eyes away, I settled into a reverie about finishing my master's degree.

As the bus slowed to release a young man at the next stop, I noticed three women veiled in full black chadors sitting in the rear of the vehicle. One whispered to the others, evoking a sharp reply. I saw their eyes shift to me, and I turned quickly to face forward as my face reddened. The women's robes covered all but their faces.

At the Faisal Abad stop, I got off, followed by the three veiled women. Turning onto the road that led to the newer section of the community where we lived, I quickened my step. It was nearly one o'clock, and Esmat would have dinner waiting at her parents' home. She had promised sabsi made of spinach, dill, and parsley with leeks, if these greens were available from the grocer's. The savory combination would be cooked in a stew to which beans and beef chunks were added, and ladled over steamed rice. Warm flat bread and Coke would finish the meal. But first, I would stop at home and change into more casual clothes, for comfort.

The women trailed me into the road leading to our neighborhood. They must have lived in the area, though I could not recall seeing them previously. Just before I turned into the first adjoining street, one called:

"Khanum! Boro khaneh o chador bepoosh."

("Mrs., go home and put on a veil.")

Without thinking, I shot back,

"Cherah, choon Islami neestam?"

("Why, when I am not Islamic?")

With a disapproving look, the women pulled their chadors closely around them and muttered together as they scurried around the corner into another narrow street.

Grappling to master my anger, I looked left and right to see if anyone had heard. Seeing no one, I hastened the last few steps and turned into the next road on the left. As I passed a nine-foot orchard wall, blood-red words that seemed to flash fire blurted a threat in huge Persian letters that I could just make out:

Women who don't wear veils are whores.
Men who don't make them are pigs.

My breath stopped momentarily, and then my pace quickened to a trot. Like the Old Testament ruler confronted by prophetic writing on the wall, I felt terror rising within me. I couldn't afford to dawdle, but I did not want to draw attention by running. I wondered who had written those words—someone in the neighborhood or transients? In moments, I was at our duplex entrance. Quickly, I unlocked the door and slipped inside, pulling the door shut tightly behind me. I checked to be sure it locked. Why did Nas have to work out of town? I wondered how much longer it would be safe for me to go out alone. How dare these people try to force me to convert to their belief system—a system that even now held dozens of Americans prisoner without cause, and perhaps without hope?

The downstairs apartment appeared dark through the narrow window. Mina was gone, and Abdolah would not be back until Thursday. Kicking off my loafers and slipping into house shoes, I darted up the steps and unlocked the second-floor flat, closing the door firmly after entering. Matt was with Pari at her parents' house, and I would join them. But first I slipped into the bedroom and tossed my purse and books onto the neatly made bed, grateful the blinds were closed.

Sliding out of my jacket, I reached for the customary jeans and sweater. Pausing before the mirror of our white wooden dresser, I studied my look: American or European, with shoulder-length dark hair and brown eyes. Freckles spotted a medium complexion. My figure was neither heavy nor slim. I looked quite ordinary—and unIslamic.

Sweeping aside perfume and hairbrush, I pulled up a silk runner that decorated the dresser top and draped it over my head, checking the effect in the mirror.

Now I looked Persian.

But it wasn't me.

I was too enlightened to retreat to the Middle Ages and cover myself in an alternate identity to pacify extremists.

Was it my Irish stubbornness, my Russian temper, or my Native American stoicism that led me to throw the scarf on the dresser and grab my purse? Maybe it was just the universal selfishness of the human spirit. Letting myself out the front door, I clattered down the steps, stopping to step into loafers once more. With a hand on the door latch, I paused. Should I cover myself? A simple headscarf would suffice.

Frozen with indecision, I paused as seconds ticked by. If I gave in now, I would lose myself. I would become another Zahra who had exchanged her American identity for an Islamic persona. Why should I become a victim by succumbing to Islamic pressure? If the government did not want to become westernized, why should I turn Islamic? I would not become another casualty of the U.S.-Iran conflict.

I was reminded of a recent event. A few days before, Mina had called me downstairs and pointed through the front door to the street where Jason was standing, looking first one way and then the other.

"What's he doing?" I asked.

"Watching for cars," Mina replied, semi-amused.

"What do you mean?" Panic gripped my heart. Surely he would not get into a vehicle with strangers.

Mina explained that Jason was playing chicken with passing drivers. As a car approached from either direction, he would jump in front of it and wait to hear screeching brakes before whirling out of its path. My heart was beating wildly as my sister-in-law finished her account.

Grabbing the door, I pulled it fully open.

"Jason! Get in here now!"

"He's just a child," Mina reminded me in a mild tone, undoubtedly surprised by more emotion than she had ever seen in me. I roundly scolded my son, reminding him of the foolish dangers of trying to outwit a multiton vehicle.

But was I likewise challenging those who could easily crush me? Perhaps it was the same rebellious streak that ran through my son's blood and beat in my husband's heart that propelled me through the door that day, head uncovered. It was either that, or a death wish.

I hurried down the road, looking left to right as I crossed the main thoroughfare before turning onto the next street in my haste to reach the safety of Mamanbozorg and Bababozorg's house. I was playing chicken with the authorities, dodging spies and surveillance that might mean whipping, imprisonment, or worse. Maybe another day I would cover myself, but not today.

Esmat had dinner waiting, though the others had eaten already. Pari was finishing her meal, having arrived shortly before I did. I gave Mathew a kiss and settled him to play on the floor again. Pari and I sat at the tablecloth and listened as the radio bristled with breaking news. Esmat joined Mamanbozorg to nap in their room; Bababozorg was in his sitting room facing the sun-drenched patio. Catching bits and pieces of the fast-flowing radio broadcast from his room, I heard phrases like "Carter lied" and "the shah's return." Matt played with building blocks at my side while I ate.

"Was Jamshid good today?" I asked Pari in English to help her practice.

She nodded enthusiastically while finishing her salad, grasping the basic idea.

"He good every day," she said, proud of her sentence.

In halting phrases, she told me he had used the toilet (a thumbs-up for potty training) and eaten lunch with Mamanbozorg and Esmat. Dipping fresh tomato slices in creamy yogurt dressing, I asked in Farsi, "What have you heard on the news?"

"Heechi," she replied. Knowing my concern, she gleaned information from any available source—neighbors, shopkeepers and their customers, or friends in other parts of the city. Had Pari been married, a husband might not have approved her wanderings, but freedom of this sort was one of the few blessings accorded a "spinster" in her mid-twenties. Since she always wore a veil when she left the house, Pari could move freely in public without fear of inciting governmental censure.

Bababozorg overheard my question, and called out a stream of explanation drawn from recent news stories. I understood most of it, but Pari translated into simpler Farsi the report that President Carter was meeting with cabinet members to address the crisis. It did not seem likely he would release the shah. I would listen to the BBC later for more information.

"Should I wear a veil?" I asked Pari bluntly.

In her self-deprecating way, Pari did not like to give advice. She merely said, "Many women wear the chador."

She probably thought I should, but did not want to be pushy. In retrospect, I can see now that I was selfish. I should have bowed to the social norms that held religious and political significance for all of us. But rebellion had ushered in a society that reacted against Western influence by erecting solid Islamic boundaries. I literally did not know my place. Should I maintain my American heritage or adopt an Iranian identity? A sense of danger seemed to elicit the determination to be my own person. Yet, personal freedom could be costly, as Iranian Azar Nafisi, author of *Reading Lolita in Tehran,* has since written:

> The government didn't take long to pass new regulations re-
> stricting women's clothing in public and forcing us to wear ei-
> ther a chador or a long robe and scarf. Experience had proven
> that the only way these regulations would be heeded was if
> they were implemented by force. Because of women's over-
> whelming objection to the laws, the government enforced the
> new rule first in the workplaces and later in shops, which were
> forbidden from transacting with unveiled women. Disobedi-
> ence was punished by fines, up to seventy-six lashes and jail
> terms. Later, the government created the notorious morality
> squads: four armed men and women in white Toyota patrols,
> monitoring the streets, ensuring the enforcement of the laws.[2]

But more compelling than physical danger was the concern that individuals did not matter, that we were merely part of the design in a tapestry, woven through a pattern not of our choosing, and forced to blend with a backdrop that was largely indecipherable. Striving to find myself, I could not extinguish my identity under a piece of cloth that would cover all that I was. Right or wrong, that is how I felt.

Matt fell asleep on the dining room sofreh, and Pari excused her-self to take a nap, after offering to sit with me if I wanted company. I thanked her, but said I would rest, too. Settling onto the dining room floor with my back to a cushion, I dozed in the cozy, quiet room. An hour later, I awakened to the clink of Mamanbozorg's kettle for after-noon tea. Devoted to daily prayer and family needs, Mamanbozorg was simple and dear. I never heard her argue, nor did I hear anyone speak a critical word against her. Brewing fresh tea was her way of pro-viding domestic nurturing, the primal blaze that keeps at bay the cold and fear of the outside world.

As we gathered around the sofreh for tea, I helped Pari with an English lesson on articles like "the" and "an" from her grammar text. Jason got off the bus at four, deposited by the driver at the patio gate per my morning request.

Esmat assumed we would stay for supper, called "shom":

"I made spaghetti for you," she smiled from the kitchen doorway, knowing how much we appreciated her baked pasta.

After dinner, I helped clear the dishes. By now the sisters accepted me as a full family member, and I was permitted to help, if marginally, with basic chores. Afterward, the boys and I went home before dark, with me looking nonchalantly around each corner to be sure we were not followed.

Mina was home by then, but feeling unwell; she had gone to bed early. I herded the boys upstairs and helped them get ready for bed. I wished someone would call—Nas, Abdolah, my sister Becky—anyone to talk to. I felt very alone as I settled the kids in bed after their showers. Kissing them good night, I turned on the radio and sat on a cushion in the living room to listen to the BBC. I caught a newscaster's report of the militants' communiqué demanding the United States return the shah to Iran for trial. This was followed by an announcement from Prime Minister Mehdi Bazargan assuring the United States that remaining citizens would be shielded from attack.

Attack? I was shaken to learn such assurance was necessary. There was no further word on the hostages' condition. The newscaster rambled on with information about meetings, plans, and demands. I wondered if U.S. government officials were frenzied or calm. Later, I would learn President Carter called the early days of the crisis "the worst" of his presidency. As the long day ended, I longed to talk to my family. I would try to get a call through soon, though I knew from experience it could take days.

In frustration, I pulled on a nightgown and slid under the sheets an hour ahead of my 11:00 bedtime. As I shut my eyes and turned on my side, I heard the sound I had come to dread: a dull gnawing from the depths of the wall behind the bed. It had been there for days, like a guilty memory refusing to be suppressed.

The sound conjured a horrific sight from a few days before.

Mina had driven me to the supermarket that day, with the boys in the back seat. Passing the edge of the development a few hundred yards from our recently completed street, we glanced at new homes under construction.

"Look!" Jason pointed to a huge garbage dump where neighbors had added their refuse to a mountain of construction waste.

Rodents swarmed the pile. I was shocked to see so many horrid creatures in plain view during the day. Farmers say the actual number of rodents is a multiple of those seen in daylight. Mina said the garbage collectors killed rats periodically, shooting or poisoning them en masse. I shuddered, hopeful the new structures would eliminate this problem as buildings replaced garbage and soil.

But that night in my bed, hearing the persistent drilling of sharp incisors, my hope turned to fear. Rats were eating through the walls. It was just a matter of time before they tore through the wallpaper. I had heard of rats attacking small children. Under the warm blanket, I shuddered. *Please, God, don't let them get in.*

Could safety be found anywhere—at home, in faith, or by citizenship? Within a few short days, it felt as if the solid world I had naively trusted was quickly starting to crumble. How long would it offer any vestiges of protection? Closing my eyes, I pulled the blanket around my ears and willed myself to fall asleep.

That weekend, Nas had little to say about the hostages except that embassy personnel should have left Iran months ago. Oversimplification was both his strength and weakness. When I questioned him about our safety, he reminded me this was a government conflict, not a war between nations. Yet, I had to wonder if it would escalate.

We went to a movie downtown—an Anthony Quinn film titled *The Prophet,* about the seventh-century Muhammad who had founded Islam. There were not many, if any, other films playing in public theaters at the time, and this one was shown for obvious thematic interest. Responsive to the Islamic belief that Muhammad's face should not be replicated, the film camera avoided a view of the Prophet. The movie was interesting and informative.

A few weeks later, I heard that extremists in another city had locked movie patrons inside a theater and burned it. That was the last theater we visited, as another social pillar of my world came crashing down in flames.

The weather turned colder. Nervously, I left the house each day, watching for suspicious-looking individuals. Neighbors greeted me politely, but there seemed to be a furtive look in their eyes, or so I thought. Each night, I listened to news reports for information about U.S. efforts to free the hostages. I couldn't wait for the crisis to be over so we could resume normal lives. I did not realize then that Iran never would be the same, nor would I.

The next day I stopped at a newsstand for *Time* and *Newsweek,* although Zahra had termed these publications Zionist propaganda. Features included President Carter's briefings at Camp David and meetings with world leaders to seek U.S. support. Restraint was urged to protect the hostages' lives as well as the global economy. But the American public showed less self-control. I read of students torching the Iranian flag and burning Khomeini in effigy, while in some U.S. cities, anti-shah demonstrations by Iranian students created riot conditions.

At Shiraz University, rumors surfaced about the possible release of female and African American hostages at Thanksgiving. But then, news reports from the BBC and the Iranian media reported demonstrations and clashes across the United States and Europe:

"The shah is an American puppet—send him to Iran!"

"No way, camel jockey! He's in the U.S. where people believe in freedom—not feudalism!"

In New York, the United Nations Security Council convened in closed session. At Columbia University, Iranian students staged a campus protest as university security officers struggled to restrain furious Americans. A college student hurled insults: "We're gonna ship you back, and you're not going to like it! No more booze, no more Big Macs, no more rock music. No more television. No more sex . . . you're gonna be back in the thirteenth century!"[3]

The following day, I left the boys with Pari so I could accompany Mina to her doctor's appointment. She wore a pretty silk headscarf. I thought about wearing one for our outing, but since we could park at the curb and only a few patients would see us inside the doctor's office, I decided to forego it this time.

The doctor gave us exciting news: Mina was pregnant!

Her seven-year marriage had produced no children, a crushing disappointment for both her and Abdolah. She came from a family of eight, and Abdolah, nine. Their married sisters all had borne children, but my sister-in-law was forced to manage her keen disappointment after doctors told her she most likely would not be able to have a family due to blocked fallopian tubes. Now that she was expecting, my attention expanded beyond hostages, rats, and students to include concern for her. I hoped the pregnancy would be safe and successful.

"I'm late, too," I joked. "Maybe I should get tested."

"Do it," she urged.

"It's probably stress," I suggested. But as she continued to persuade me, I decided it would not hurt to take a test and asked the nurse for a specimen cup. I was shocked a few minutes later when my result came back positive.

Mina was thrilled, as were Nas's mother and sisters when we told them later that day. Though using birth control pills, I had missed a couple days around the time of my husband's last weekend visit. Surprised but pleased, I decided not to tell my family right away to avoid worrying them. With a prior miscarriage, I also would wait to tell Jason and Matt.

I was able to telephone Mom and my sister Becky a few days before Thanksgiving, and I reassured them that our situation was stable. They were relieved to hear from me and promised a Christmas package of cookies and gifts. Becky was disappointed she would not be able to come for a visit.

"Maybe the hostage situation will be over soon," she sighed, after explaining recent news stories she had heard on television or read in the paper. "Have you heard anything more?"

"Not really," I replied with reluctance. Becky told me about her son John's preschool progress. She was in a study group of nursing students that helped each other prepare for tests. My sister added details about a recent shopping trip for a new coat, and a Halloween party where she had worn a Pocahontas costume. Exchanging a few more bits of information, she handed the receiver to my mom.

"When are you coming home?" my mother asked expectantly.

"Not for a while, Mom. The government tolerates non-Muslims, and I have dual citizenship. It's the radicals we have to worry about, and the U.S. has its share of those. Besides, I'd like to finish my master's degree first."

I told funny stories to amuse them, like visiting a Kentucky Fried Chicken restaurant where cooked chicken smelled worse than a dead one. I did not mention that I had been sick for two days. And I kept quiet about my pregnancy. We ended the conversation with a promise of letters.

Nas made it home that weekend; I was relieved to see him, grateful for his tall, solid form at my side when we went out shopping or visiting. He always seemed glad to get home, take a hot shower, and relax. On that Thursday night, when I told him about my pregnancy, he said little. I suspect my miscarriage had bothered him more than he let on. I decided to put the pregnancy out of mind for now. After turning off the bedside lamp to sleep, Nas soon was snoring. Lying beside him, I heard the hateful rats again. Like worries, the faint drilling through wood and concrete would not let me forget the dangers that gnawed at us. I would have awakened Nas to see if he could do anything, but he was so tired that I let him sleep. I hoped the nosy rodents would go away of their own accord. When Saturday morning came and he had to leave, both of us were a little sad.

"Be careful," he said, kissing my cheek, and then opening the door to leave.

I began taking a head scarf along in my purse—just in case—and I stopped going out alone much, instead waiting for Pari when possible, and wearing a beret and long tweed jacket in my own version of Islamic dress. I would bend for the sake of Nas's family and my sons, but I would not break.

Bababozorg discussed current events with male guests in his room. Mamanbozorg shook her head at news of extreme violence. Pari remained cheerful, insisting things would be all right. Preoccupied with her upcoming marriage, Esmat gave little thought to the hostages. She had grown up devoid of political orientation and now had little interest in public matters. She bought and packed towels, clothing, and dishes, along with blankets and linens that Mamanbozorg had given her. Soon, she would have a traditional wedding in the village where she had been born. So, at least we could look forward to a celebration. Not all weddings were traditional, of course. At one of our summer get-togethers, a cousin had told me of the civil ceremony and hotel honeymoon she and her bridegroom had enjoyed before embarking on a two-week European honeymoon. This was before the Ayatollah returned.

Since phone calls were infrequent due to cost and access, family letters provided an emotional lifeline. Becky's humor, my mother's worries, and Annie's reminiscing set the tone for their writing styles. Mom expected the worst, and, when it didn't happen, she predicted it soon would. Happily, she often was wrong, and then would start worrying about the next thing that might go bad. My sister made light of difficulties and replayed them in funny ways that made us laugh, while Annie emphasized the practical needs of everyday life.

My family understood little about Iran, as did most Americans. They were concerned about our safety, wondering if we would join the hostages in a makeshift prison or face murder and mutilation by midnight radicals. In each letter, I unveiled a little more about our lifestyle, such as what we ate, where we went, and the kindness of Nas's family, as well as the attentive respect of my college students. Their return letters showed that my loved ones gradually were becoming more aware that people in other places lived much as Americans do.

Sometimes I could not resist the urge to tease. One weekend, while enjoying a country drive with Nas, we took pictures of a few outlying adobe houses and nearby donkeys. I planned to send a picture to Mom, telling her the adobe hut was our new home, and the donkeys, local transportation. Given the hostage tensions, though, I decided against it. She might send the Red Cross after us!

Letters took anywhere from two to four weeks to arrive, so I was always catching up on old news. Becky said that Annie became fretful, while Mom sat before the television night after night, chain smoking. Eleven months apart in age to the day, Becky and I wrote back and forth like friends as much as sisters:

> Iran is the main topic of all the news broadcasts. I wish they would make some progress to reach an agreement. How are things over there? . . . Try to keep me posted and current on whatever happens. . . . How many more credits do you need after fall semester? Couldn't you transfer here if you wanted to? (November 14, 1979)

I pictured blonde Becky writing in her scrupulously neat two-bedroom apartment. Or maybe she had written at Mom's house while her son John lay on the floor watching television, as the letter included a "7:30 P.M." time reference. I recalled the small hurricane lamp on its old-fashioned stand that cast a warm glow in Mom's comfortable living room. An older-model nineteen-inch Zenith television would be playing across from the sofa. A simple wooden cross was hanging on the wall above the television, as though competing for attention. The mental scene tugged at my heart.

Becky's mid-November letter contained a newspaper clipping and photo of a newscaster with the words "Iran Crisis" in bold letters behind him:

> Iranian captors have issued Communiqué Number One demanding the U.S. release former Iranian ruler, Shah Reza Pahlavi. The Shah fled Iran last January and is currently being treated for cancer at NYU-Cornell Medical Center. Iranian militants blame him for the deaths of thousands of Iranians through his secret police, the Savak.[3]

Becky added she would continue trying to call us. But it would be several weeks before we would talk again, and many things would happen before then.

CHAPTER SEVEN

The Crescent and the Cross

THE NEXT DAY I SAW THE SUSPICIOUS MAN LURKING NEAR my classroom again. Wondering if he were too shy to inquire about a son or daughter who was a student, I approached to ask if I could help. As I stepped into the hallway, he abruptly turned and left. Had I frightened him? Or should I be frightened? I began to harbor suspicions that the man was not an innocent observer. He was there for a reason; I needed to find out what it was.

Several days into the hostage crisis, my students remained polite and studious. They seemed eager to learn English. I was touched by their dedication. Mehdi still sat smiling in the front row. Mashid scribbled quick notes beside the window. Hamid pored over the textbook as though trying to memorize it. The others faced me rather blandly, but without rancor. Occasionally, they would raise their hands to answer a question, if Mehdi had not already done so. Maybe the teens were wary of me, now that Americans had become suspect, or maybe they were tired as we approached the semester's end. Given our unstable political situation with its potentially frightening implications, I questioned even small changes in the daily routine.

Between classes, instructors exchanged information and traded rumors, the popular currency. Over tea, while grading papers in our offices or in the faculty lounge, with its long table where we could spread things out, we pondered Carter's plans for freeing the hostages, wondering if he would take the advice of hawkish advisers and launch a military initiative. Some instructors sympathized with his helpless plight, while others sided with the Iranians. Zealous ones suggested that the Americans were finally reaping what they had sown for decades. Although there was truth in these sentiments, many of us still were unfamiliar with the big picture or the long-standing history. We discussed media images showing a haggard president with loosened tie and rumpled shirt, in earnest discussion with cabinet members. It struck me that he really did not know what to do, just as the embassy captors seemed confused about their options. This was a unique situation demanding patience and finesse. One wrong move could have fatal consequences, and I didn't believe even the militants wanted that. The United States had never been more vulnerable. Iran's ancient power had reawakened in the posture of Islamic militants under the ayatollah's authority.

We learned through press reports that President Carter, working with Secretary of State Cyrus Vance and press secretary Jody Powell, was earning mixed reviews from Americans by staying calm in those early days during a situation that threatened dozens of lives and millions of oil consumers. As an Iranian citizen, I was grateful for U.S. restraint; as an American, I wondered how the hostages would fare if tensions should escalate. Would I be viewed as American or Iranian? Which passport would be demanded before I was assaulted, captured, or exiled by American or Iranian forces? What would happen to Jason and Mathew?

The Iranian news media buffeted the president, with photographs and film footage showing demonstrations of thousands calling for Carter's death. On campus, I overheard students in small groups criticize my homeland for protecting the shah and flouting Iran's demands. There were rumors that revolutionaries guarding the hostages taunted them that the United States would not intercede for their safety. Allegedly, the captors were planning to move hostages from place to place to avoid discovery and defy rescue attempts.

In her next letter, my sister included a newspaper clipping from the secretary of defense's speech:

> It is a time not for rhetoric, but for quiet, careful, and firm diplomacy. The State Department has warned 300 U.S. citizens in Iran to leave the country as expeditiously as possible. James Schlesinger told *TIME* Magazine this crisis is "a cataclysm for American foreign policy—in fact, the first serious revolution since 1917 in terms of world impact." But rest assured that President Carter and his cabinet are working day and night to bring this situation to a peaceful conclusion.[1]

The report did nothing to reassure me. Were Americans with Iranian passports like me expected to leave? I doubted Nas would agree to our departure.

A few days later, we learned via the campus pipeline that militants had allowed a handful of hostages to meet with diplomats from Sweden, Syria, and other neutral countries. According to reports, the hostages had appeared tired, though one was smiling. We learned that even though thirty-three captives had signed the militants' "petition" supporting Shah Pahlavi's extradition, none would be set free. Hope for a speedy resolution was evaporating.

Despite this political upheaval, the kids and I tried to look forward to the holidays. I offered to cook Thanksgiving dinner for Nas's family and planned to blend American and Iranian menus to suit everyone's tastes. I would roast a chicken and add the trimmings. On a mid-November Wednesday, I dismissed class as usual and moved down the brightly lit hall, where I encountered Zahra, my teaching colleague who had converted to Islam, emerging from the women's restroom. Her tall, solid figure was draped in a tunic over matching slacks, hair shrouded in a cream-colored scarf. An American native, like me she had become Iranian by marriage. Her Southwest twang gave Persian words an amusing lilt. I had not warmed to Zahra much over the past few months. Her attitude toward newcomers was more condescending than caring.

"Sobh beheil, khanum Kamalie," she greeted me breezily. "Chetoreh?"

Falling into step, we continued down the hall toward our faculty offices.

"Don't you speak English anymore?" I asked.

"Why should I?" she smiled sweetly. Pushing a wisp of hair under her scarf, she continued, "When in Rome . . ."

I wanted to remind her this wasn't Rome, but held my tongue. "What does your husband say about the hostages?"

"He thinks it's time for Iran to put the screws to the United States. They've had it coming for a long time," she replied with half a smile.

Pausing outside my office, I fumbled for the key. "Have you heard from your American family? Are they worried?"

Zahra's manner grew cheerier. "I called them last night. Behrooz has connections with the phone company."

"Nice."

I pushed open the office door and set my books on a crowded desk. Shelves filled with grammar and literature texts lined the walls. A large window peered over the campus's late fall landscape of tan buildings and naked shrubs. A few scattered glimpses of color, remnants of the near-empty trees, tumbled over the brown grass below.

"Do you think Carter will return the shah to Iran?" I turned to face her.

"I don't think he'll betray his old friend and admit U.S. policy in Iran was a mistake, do you?" She paused before continuing. "I hope he doesn't underestimate Iran's military might."

I glanced at her sharply. "Why? Is Iran buying arms from the Soviet Union? There are rumors that Iran supplies weapons to terrorist groups."

"Forget it." She started to move away.

"Zahra—wait! Why do you hate the U.S.? Learning English will open up a new world for them."

Zahra snorted. "A world of greed and manipulation."

"Iran and the U.S. can learn from each other. Even if the shah exploited the people, he also built roads, schools, and hospitals."

"Sure—roads to Western decadence, schools teaching imperialist materialism, and hospitals for the protesters."

"Do you really believe that? Or have you been listening to revolutionary rhetoric? There are two sides to every story."

She shot me a skeptical look and continued down the hall.

"The word is someone's spying around campus to find out who's teaching counterculture stuff. Know who it might be?" I leaned against the doorframe.

She glanced back with an uneasy expression but kept walking. "Of course not."

"Maybe it's the same people responsible for whipping girls without head coverings or the mob that burned the Bahai meeting hall. Or it could be the murderers who slit the priest's throat to shut down the Christian church."

Zahra froze momentarily and turned one last time, blue eyes glaring. "Don't be paranoid. Khodah hafez."

She hurried down the hall. I locked my office door before heading for the stairs. A graduate student, Amir, stopped to warn me about the mustached man I had seen waiting in the hall.

"That guy outside the classroom yesterday? He's been hanging around—he listens to what we say."

"What will happen if we say something he doesn't like?"

Amir leaned forward, displaying dramatic humor. "He'll report you. And then you'll disappear."

"I thought they only did that during the shah's reign."

Amir shook his head. "Militants do whatever they want to. Be careful."

"I will."

Uneasiness welled up. When would the next axe fall, and on whose neck? Was this a political or a religious crisis? Having little familiarity with either, maybe it was time to examine my beliefs in both areas.

The next day after lunch, Pari and I lounged in the dining room, looking through an Italian fashion magazine. Casually I asked, "Do the neighbors say anything about me?"

Since the painted warning on the orchard wall, I was on the lookout for suspicious looks or probing questions. Had the threat been intended for all women in our area? Or did someone have me in mind? Maybe I had become the target of a rhetorical sniper.

Pari shook her head. She liked to believe the best of everyone.

"They like you."

Putting away the magazine, I settled on the dining room sofeh to read Arthur Miller's play *The Crucible* for my drama class, while Pari retreated to her bedroom for a nap. The 1692 witchcraft trials were a fascinating study of a church-state society where religious hysteria ran wild, leading to the arrest and trial of dozens of innocent victims as a result of young girls "crying out" neighbors they claimed were guilty of witchcraft. As I read Miller's adaptation of factual records, I began to see correlations to Iran's theocracy. While the Iranian government had not spearheaded a search for U.S. agents, it had condoned the militants' embassy assault. Perhaps it was ironic that the Islamic Republic referred to the United States as "the great Satan," since Puritans had believed that Satan was active among their numbers, too. I scribbled an outline that would form the basis of my required research paper.

Bababozorg snorted as he turned in his sleep in the next room. Grinning, I recalled the time when Nas and I were staying with his parents during our first trip to Iran and got into an argument in our bedroom. Overhearing us, Nas's mother paused in the doorway as my husband snarled, "Go home if you don't like it here."

Though his parents knew little English, Mamanbozorg understood "Go" and her son's tone. In an angry voice, she berated him in Farsi,

"YOU go if you don't like it. Your wife and the children will stay with us."

Nas and I were so shocked by her bold words that our argument disintegrated into laughter. Bababozorg had joined his wife at the door, bewildered by the commotion. Now, I hoped my presence would not put the family in jeopardy for harboring an infidel if the community decided to view me as such.

That evening, after we returned home, Mina and Abdolah hosted a married couple from Bushehr, a city in the south. I helped serve dinner and tea afterward, and then cleared the dishes so Mina could visit with their friends. The men and women talked separately awhile, and then we mingled over tea and watched television news. A public beating of an adulterous couple in a city square was replayed, and I ushered Jason and Matt away from the television as clerics stripped the man and woman to the waist before whipping their backs to the cheers of thousands.

A news announcer, appearing sophisticated and calm, reported the latest hostage developments. Mohammad Pahlavi's chemotherapy was almost finished. Would he remain in the United States, or would Carter exchange him for hostages? As the announcer emphasized that the U.S. government must admit its wrongdoing and Carter should be hung, I felt annoyance at what sounded like a violent response to a delicate situation. I muttered under my breath in Persian, "Go hang yourself," not really meaning it, but needing to vent my emotional overload. Our male guest overheard and laughed, and I realized I must watch my words. Who knew what might be reported to authorities? While I had no reason to distrust these people, I didn't want to slip and say something I should not. I had to be careful—at home as well as on campus. This was different than anything I had ever experienced. Life in the States might be mundane, but it was not cloak-and-dagger.

In my Creative Writing class, Dr. Fahrnaz urged us to craft stories from everyday life. As the only American student, I knew my perspective was unique, but I could not find a topic. I began drafting a paper about the differences between Eastern and Western culture: food, hygiene, and housing. It was boring. The professor echoed my thoughts.

"Surely you have something more interesting to say!"

Back at my desk, I pondered recent events. What had moved me most? Then I remembered. Quickly, I dashed off line after line, capturing the essence of something that jarred my memory. Pari had strolled into our apartment a few days before, leading Jason and Matt by the hand. Settling them to play after removing their jackets, she joined me in the kitchen, where I was peeling potatoes.

"Did you have fun?" I asked her in Farsi.

"Sure," she replied cheerfully. "We went downtown for a parade."

"That's nice. Did you have a good viewing spot?"

Pari grinned. "We marched!"

"In the parade?" I stopped peeling. What kind of parade would be taking place? There was no religious festival that I knew of.

"We marched for Ayatollah Khomeini," she replied in exultation.

"What?" I turned in dismay.

"Marg bar Emrika!"

Death to America?

"Pari, did you and the boys demonstrate against the U.S.?"

She shifted uncomfortably.

"Not against everyone in the U.S., just Carter."

Pari knew little about President Carter's policies.

"Next time, please ask before taking the boys downtown. They could have gotten hurt if someone found out they're American."

"Not these boys," she sniffed with pride. "They're Iranian."

I retorted, "They're Iranian *and* American, and we must be careful."

"Nothing will happen," she protested, "but I will ask you first."

"Thanks." I hugged her.

When Nas got home that weekend, I told him about the incident after we had loaded the kids into his truck and were headed out for the evening. He grinned with delight at the irony and began chanting as he thumped his right hand on the dashboard while holding the steering wheel with his left, "Marg bar Emrika . . . marg bar Carter . . . marg bar Emrika . . . marg bar Carter!"

Jason picked up on the rhythm and beat time on the back seat while chanting along. Even Matt was chiming in on some syllables as he smacked a small hand against his knee.

"Nas, what are you doing?" I protested.

Ignoring me, he continued loudly, "Marg bar Emrika . . . marg bar Carter . . ." as the boys accompanied him. I gave up, knowing Nas cared nothing for politics.

Describing this event, I showed the story to my professor before the next class.

"Much better!"

I continued revising the paper the rest of that week, realizing that my role in Iran was both unusual and precarious. I sometimes felt more like a spectator than a participant. Would I eventually have to choose sides? Could I not be part of both cultures?

The hostage buzz increased as Thanksgiving loomed, and we wondered if some of the captives would be freed. A goodwill gesture could stabilize tensions and facilitate negotiations. My sister wrote of the American government's recommendations for conserving energy by lowering thermostats and driving less. As facts about Iran's oil exports to the United States became public, I learned that energy needs added pressure to resolving the hostage crisis. The National Iran Oil Company was then shipping 700,000 barrels of oil to the United States daily, about 3.7 percent of the national need. Since January 1979, gas prices had risen 45 percent in the States. Surely, Iran's leaders must realize the impact of their actions on the Western economy. Why not let the hostages go, and focus instead on the business of global oil exports?

In my American Drama class, I presented an oral summary of my plan for the research paper. I would compare Arthur Miller's *The Cru-*

cible, a social commentary on the 1953 Communist witch hunt in the United States as well as a factual account of the 1692 witchcraft trials, to the 1979 Islamic Republic's accusations against the United States, as demonstrated by the embassy takeover. The instructor appeared thoughtful and suggested I carefully review all sources for accuracy and nonbias. The other students listened with interest but said nothing to challenge my plan. Later, I would wonder if their nonresponse was a veiled warning.

A public announcement came that Iran's Assembly of Experts was creating a new constitution to make Iran a theocratic state. I wondered how a theocracy would function in the late twentieth century, amid a plethora of third-world democracies and monarchies. My research into Arthur Miller's play revealed the problems inherent in a church-based state like that of seventeenth-century Massachusetts. Was the world ready for another theocratic experiment three hundred years later?

Meanwhile, President Carter arranged for Iranian expert Bill Miller to jet to Iran for negotiations with the Ayatollah Khomeini. The two, however, did not meet. In another move, Zbigniew Brzezinski, a member of President Carter's cabinet, questioned whether to deport fifty thousand Iranian students, but the president urged restraint. Becky's next letter told me that Americans were wearing yellow armbands to show support for the hostages, based on Tony Orlando and Dawn's pop music recording, "Tie a Yellow Ribbon," about a prisoner's release. Patriotism swelled as the American flag flew from numerous locations and church congregations prayed for the hostages' safe return.

In Iran, I began to understand that appearing in public as a non-Muslim could be construed as antigovernment and perhaps label me a traitor. An unexpected encounter at my in-laws' house emphasized this possibility. Arriving at noon following class one day, I opened the gate and entered the patio. At first, I did not see the visitor who was leaving until he passed through the front door, followed by Mamanbozorg. He was a bearded sheikh, dressed in turban and robe—a Muslim cleric. I wondered why he was here.

As he passed, I smiled and said "Salaam," the customary greeting that means "hello" or "peace," but the older man's eyes did not so much as swerve toward me, and his expression remained fixed as he passed without a word. Puzzled, I watched as he left by the front gate.

Then I turned to Mamanbozorg, who stood in the doorway, seemingly embarrassed. As we went indoors and sat down to eat with Pari and Esmat, while Bababozorg took his meal in his room as usual, I realized the cleric had not spoken to me because I was American and unveiled.

Glancing at Pari in jeans and sweater, and her mother in the usual tribal skirts, I could see from their expressions they sensed my awkwardness. But they were Muslims, after all, and I was the interloper. Perhaps my nonconformist appearance embarrassed them. The sheikh might question their tolerance of my views, if not my presence; perhaps he would report them for harboring an American spy! I realized I must consider their safety as well as my own. I would have to wear a headscarf or perhaps even the veil to protect the innocents who were trying to protect me.

Those early weeks of the crisis stirred remnants of my Christian faith. Attending church sporadically as a teen and seldom after marrying, I now realized something important was missing from my life, especially as I witnessed the significant role that Islam played not only in the lives of people I cared about here in Iran, but in the lives of thousands around the world. I had studied Islam in college, and Pari and I often discussed our divergent beliefs. I also had seen the militant side of Islam in the embassy takeover, and in Zahra's adopted identity. But I felt it was not right for me. I believed in Christianity, though I was not sure what to do about it, especially in an Islamic country. I began thinking more about my spiritual state. How ironic that my soul should awaken in an Islamic culture! Even earlier in Iran, during our first visit, I had been impressed by the devotion of simple people like Mamanbozorg, Pari, and Abdolah, who washed ceremonially, recited daily prayers, and kept the fasts. The most ardent Christians I knew at home did not display their faith as consistently. Now, responding to the religious underpinnings of the hostage conflict, I reached for spirituality and found my Christian beliefs at hand.

One night after Jason and Matt were asleep in their room, I crawled under the covers of my bed and reached for the Bible I had stashed in our bedside stand. Pulling it out of the drawer, I leafed through several pages, skimming verses, until I found Psalm 7 (NIV):

O LORD my God, I take refuge in you;
Save and deliver me from all who pursue me,
Or they will tear me like a lion
And rip me to pieces with no one to rescue me . . .

Though I did not feel pursued, I wondered if it was a matter of time until I did. Perhaps extremists would hunt and destroy us. The government might exile us. Carter could send troops who would shoot or imprison citizens indiscriminately. I had no idea from which direction hostility might come: "Keep me safe, O God, for in You I take refuge" (Psalm 16, NIV). I prayed before closing my eyes to sleep, beginning with confessing my sins and concluding with a plea for protection for my children and me. Ironically, I would try to live a Christian life by following the example of Muslim family members.

After dinner the next day, Pari and I urged Mina to rest while we did the dishes. As we worked side by side, I asked in my tentative Farsi, "Pari, how do you know what Allah wants you to do?"

"I read the Koran," she said simply.

"But how do you make personal decisions about everyday life?" I prodded.

She shrugged. "I pray and fast sometimes, and help the poor. How do you get close to God?"

"Well, we pray, too. Christians are supposed to read the Bible."

"Do you?"

"Sometimes. It says Jesus is the son of God."

Pari smiled indulgently. "God does not have a son. He doesn't even have a wife. Jesus was a prophet."

"But He performed miracles."

Pari nodded. "I know. He brought a dead chicken to life."

"What?"

She restated her claim, adding another odd statement or two that I had never heard.

"But Pari, the Bible doesn't say that."

Her smile was serene. She stood faithful to her source, whatever it was. I was puzzled. Iran was geographically and historically closer to Israel than was the United States or Europe. It seemed implausible that

Pari should know more about Jesus than I, as she clearly believed during these conversations, but did she? Her stories were incredulous, but so were biblical accounts to someone unfamiliar with them, like Jesus's withering of the fig tree or calming of a storm. I had heard of apocryphal accounts that were not included in the original biblical canonization. Maybe Pari's beliefs came from those obscure sources.

"I'll look into it further," I said. But more important things competed for my attention.

As hostage updates broke each day, it became clear the situation would not end soon. What had the militants gotten themselves into? The U.S. government was not meeting their demands, and there was no easy way to release the hostages without losing face. What if there were an uprising and mass killings, like China's Boxer Rebellion? Then common sense once more took control. I could not believe the generous people I lived among would harm us. As my flickering spiritual faith began to blaze, I read the boys Bible stories, and taught them how to pray at bedtime, using the well-known verse, "Now I lay me down to sleep . . ."

On campus, I asked trusted professors about the location of Christian churches in the region. Christina told me of a few abandoned sanctuaries throughout Fars province. Someone knew of an Orthodox church, but I was not familiar with its doctrine. Then Christina remembered a Catholic church that had been without a priest for almost a year. Extremists had beheaded the former cleric. When his replacement heard of the manner of his predecessor's death while en route to Shiraz, he turned around and returned to Tehran. Apparently, there was a small group of Christians in Shiraz who met clandestinely, and I got the address.

That afternoon, I asked Pari about the church's location, after showing her the written description.

"It's in town, not far from khaneh Reza." (This was Mina's mother's house. Widowed women are called by their eldest son's name, as in "the mother of Reza" or "the house of Reza." Reza was Mina's brother, the oldest surviving male, though he was just fifteen years old at the time.) "We can go to the church when they meet."

Startled, I replied, "You don't have to go with me. If you give me directions, I can get there myself."

With her stubborn grin, she insisted, "You might get lost."

Pari worried about us. Maybe she was curious about the church, too. We would go this weekend, but I would leave the boys at home with Mina. There was no point in endangering them. I hoped Pari would not get in trouble with the government for visiting a church.

On Sunday, Pari and I left after breakfast, telling Mamanbozorg our destination.

"Be careful," she said as we headed for the door.

We caught the bus at the highway and rode downtown. Pari wore her chador, while I had put on a long skirt that covered my calves and a beret on my head, unsure of church decorum and unwilling to attract public attention. If I had worn the chador, would I be perceived as Islamic and denied admittance? I wore a knit cap everywhere now to avoid problems. Pari led me down a side street along a high stone wall. Pausing before a massive, ancient wooden door, she banged the knocker twice before an older man called in Farsi, "Who's there?"

I stated my name, and added in Farsi, "I am a Christian. I would like to see the church."

The door creaked open a few inches. A grizzled face keenly peered at us. Finally, a short fellow in work clothes stepped aside and motioned me to enter.

"Ba'fam."

"My sister must come, too!" I protested gently. The man refused, apparently identifying her as Muslim. "Faghat baraya massehi," he said firmly, meaning only Christians could come in.

"Please," I asked, "she just wants to see what it's like."

He opened the door a few inches more.

"Hurry," he muttered, closing it swiftly behind us.

We entered a peaceful compound surrounded by the fortresslike wall. There were trees and shrubs, now without leaves, that gave the place a monastic air. I peered into the window of a large stone structure to our right. The cozy room was full of books on shelves, along with others lying on a large library table in the middle of the room.

"Church library," the old man said in response to my unasked question. Perhaps I could return sometime to browse.

He led us across a patio strewn with dead branches of ferns and flowers that must be pretty in spring. Gesturing toward a huge stone edifice to our left, he said, "Go on."

But to Pari, his tone was stern. "Wait here."

"But—"

"She will wait for you." He pointed to a bench, where my sister-in-law seated herself.

"Go on. I will stay here," she agreed patiently.

Heading toward the door that opened into the back of the church, I saw perhaps a dozen men and women seated in the pews. None looked up as I entered, and I sat near the back to remain unnoticed. Surprisingly, the girls wore dark headscarves or veils, just as the Muslim women did. Apparently, veiling was cultural as much as spiritual. The men wore suit jackets or sports shirts with trousers. An older woman in a long-sleeved black dress and bulky headscarf was playing a prelude with a faint Russian sound on the organ. Another ten or twelve congregants entered without speaking and found seats quickly. I was used to greeting other worshippers in church in the States, and the silence here was a little unnerving.

After a moment, a man in a dark suit stood and, carrying what looked like a Bible, made his way to the front of the church. As the organ music died away, he asked the group to stand as he led us in prayer. I caught Farsi phrases that included the names of God and Jesus, as well as expressions of petition or gratitude. Following the prayer, he called out a number, and everyone opened hymnals as the organist played a tune I recognized but could not name. These people were the remnant of a previous congregation and seemed to follow an established worship pattern.

After the hymn concluded, everyone sat down. The man in front opened the Bible and read a short passage from the book of John, as I was able to determine from his speech. He spent about twenty-five minutes expounding on the scriptural reading, emphasizing God's love for humans through Jesus. Following a final prayer during which we were asked to stand once more, we were dismissed, and everyone filed out without speaking, though I would have liked to exchange greetings or names with others. I suppose everyone was distrustful, given current tensions. Disappointed, I felt as though I were leaving a surreal experience.

Pari still sat on the bench, looking around. Thankfully, the day was nice, though maybe the caretaker would have let her wait in the library in the event of rain or cold. Once more, I was reminded of her absolute devotion and unconditional love.

"How was it?" she asked, standing to greet me with a smile.

"Good," I replied in a low voice. Leaving through the ancient entrance, I thanked the caretaker who had emerged from a nearby shed. As we headed for the bus stop, I began telling Pari about the service.

The roar of a motorcycle made me jump, causing Pari to look at me curiously. Pulling the beret low over my eyes, I hurried her to the main street. We passed a legless beggar lying on the steps of a municipal building. Crying for donations, he did not see us. He had scraggly hair and an unkempt beard, and was covered with ragged clothes that appeared long-worn and dirty. I felt sorry for him. Were there no disability services? Would not someone hire him to do piecework? Glancing at each other, Pari and I reached into our purses and gave him a few tomans. In Iran, there was no whitewashing of pain, loss, and death, as we attempt to do in the West. Here, I encountered intense human misery, which forced me to come to terms with my own good fortune and standard of living.

That visit was my first and last to the Shiraz church. Two weeks later, Pari and I stood outside the medieval-looking door once more. But knock as we would, no one answered. I made inquiries, but all Christina could say was that the group must have disbanded until the hostage crisis ended. My regenerated faith would have to be nurtured some other way.

Not long after that, Mamanbozorg came to visit at our apartment after her siesta. Since I did not often have guests, I was surprised and pleased. Putting the copper kettle on for tea, I brought out a plate of shortbread cookies. Settling herself on the floor at the sofreh that I spread for our snack, my mother-in-law asked about the boys, who were napping, and then inquired about my pregnancy.

"I'm hardly sick at all," I announced happily.

She smiled cautiously. "Women get sick when they are pregnant. That means the baby is healthy. You lost the other baby? You must protect this little one." Reaching into the pocket of her voluminous skirts, she pulled out what appeared to be a necklace.

"This will keep the baby safe," she said, handing it to me.

Taking it, I noticed a tiny Arabic inscription on the suspended silver plate and smiled my thanks. I felt uncomfortable wearing a Muslim amulet, but I did not want to hurt Mamanbozorg's feelings. As I unclasped it and reached both ends around my neck to fasten it, she stopped me.

"No, wear it here." She lifted my shirt and pointed to my abdomen.

Surprised, I laid the jewelry aside with a smile, and she nodded, probably assuming I would put it on later. I wondered to what degree she believed in the amulet's protective properties. I doubted whether a Christian or Muslim piece of jewelry would help. But I would not tell Mamanbozorg that. I was touched that this baby meant something to her. After all, she had numerous grandchildren, and I was the foreign wife.

Mamanbozorg did not mention her special gift again. The shiny pendant lay undisturbed atop my wooden jewelry box on the bedroom dresser.

CHAPTER EIGHT

Hope and Holidays

IRANIAN SHIITES CELEBRATE EID-E-GORBAN, THE FEAST of sacrifice. I had first observed this celebration during my recovery from abdominal surgery in the fall of 1977, shortly before returning to the States. Now I learned a little more. The holiday commemorates the obedience of Old Testament Abraham (called "Ibrahim" by Muslims) in preparing to offer his son on an altar to God. The son was spared by God's substitution of a sacrificial ram:

> "Do not lay a hand on the boy," he said. "Do not do any-
> thing to him. Now I know that you fear God, because you
> have not withheld from me your son, your only son." Abra-
> ham looked up and there in a thicket he saw a ram caught
> by its horns. He went over and took the ram and sacrificed it
> as a burnt offering instead of his son. So Abraham called that
> place The Lord Will Provide. . . ."I swear by myself, declares
> the LORD, that because you have done this and have not
> withheld your son, your only son, I will surely bless you and
> make your descendents as numerous as the stars in the sky,

and as the sand on the seashore . . . and through your
offspring all nations on earth will be blessed, because you
have obeyed me." (Genesis 22:12–18 NIV)

Muslims, like Jews, trace their ancestral descent from the biblical pa-
triarch Abraham/Ibrahim. The Arabic line from which Islam emerged
in the seventh century A.D. comes through Ishmael, born of Ibrahim's
Egyptian concubine Hagar, while Jews descend from Isaac, born to
Abraham's wife Sarah. Some Muslims believe Ishmael is the son who
was to be sacrificed, while others accept the story of Hagar and Ishmael's expulsion from Abraham's camp, due to Sarah's desire to protect
Isaac's inheritance. On this holiday, Muslims commemorate Abraham's
obedience to God and God's provision for Abraham.

Bruce Laingen, chargé d'affaires and senior officer at Tehran's
American Embassy during the militants' siege, noted that Eid-e-gorban
took place on November 1, 1979, just before the embassy takeover. After
purchasing a sheep, Muslims have a Shiite clergyman come to their
home to bless the sacrifice. The animal is killed on the patio and cooked
for family and guests. It was on this holiday in my husband's family,
where numerous relatives were celebrating, that the animal's testicles
were borne directly from the patio bonfire to Bababozorg on a silver
platter, as a restorative delicacy.

The Iranians have a saying of "gorbonnet," sometimes paired with
a hand placed over the speaker's heart as a respectful gesture and an
expression of humble courtesy. Perhaps an English equivalent would be
the nineteenth-century "your servant," in a letter's closing. This Iranian
expression moved me on several occasions, because people's actions
frequently echoed their spirit of self-sacrifice. So it was an ironic twist
of fate that after celebrating Eid-e-gorban in 1979, three days later
on November 4, the militants in Tehran captured dozens of American Embassy staff as hostages who would become sacrifices for U.S.
interests.

Ramadan, another well-known holiday, commemorates the Muslim belief that the angel Gabriel passed the first verses of the Koran to
seventh-century prophet Muhammad. For a month each year, Muslims
pray, attend mosque services, and read the Koran while fasting daily.
At night, they feast. The final three days of the event are filled with

parties and gift-giving. It was enlightening and inspiring to watch family members observe these holidays with joy and generosity.

Events like these increased my understanding of Islam and helped me appreciate the interconnectedness of the three main world faiths: Judaism, Christianity, and Islam. As my spiritual needs took root, I pored over the Genesis account of the patriarchs. I pondered twentieth-century conflict between Arabs and Jews, and the ceaseless wars that riddle the Holy Land. My political interest in the Middle East was awakened, as faith and politics coalesced in my new understanding of the Muslim world.

I learned that Iranian Muslims are mostly Shiites, followers of Ali, the Prophet Muhammad's son-in-law who had married the Egyptian daughter, Fatimah. The Shiites number one hundred million in contrast to the Sunni sect, which has eight hundred million adherents. Sunnis follow the line of Abu Bakr, the father of Muhammad's favorite wife. Successors are called "caliphs" generally, and later were known as "sultans" during the era of the Ottoman Empire. Medina chiefs who elected Abu Bakr as leader soon witnessed the demise of three caliphs, after which they asked Ali to assume Islamic leadership. His consent to do so led to the ongoing schism between the two succeeding lines. There are other distinctions, as well, including the fact that Shiites reside mainly in Iran, Iraq, and Israel, and tend to follow more militant and orthodox practices. Some compare these differences to the contrasts between Catholic and Protestant Christianity. I developed great respect for active Muslims, who faithfully practice their spiritual beliefs each day through washing, prayer, and service to others. Yet, it was the call of Christianity, through salvation in Jesus Christ's substitutionary death for my sins, that brought me peace and hope. Living in that Muslim culture where everyday I witnessed devout service to Allah reawakened my dormant Christian beliefs. Had I never left America's shores, I still might be unregenerate.

The Muslims' holy scriptures, the Koran (or al Qu'ran), is similar to Jewish and Christian teachings: "Before this, we wrote in the Psalms, after a message (given to Moses), 'My servants, the righteous, shall inherit the earth.' (Sura 21:105) We have decreed in the Psalms, as well as in other scriptures, that the earth shall be inherited by My righteous worshippers."[1]

Muslims believe in an afterlife, with the faithful sharing a garden feast and unbelievers suffering in fiery torment: "Their reward at their Lord is the gardens of Eden with flowing streams, wherein they abide forever. GOD is pleased with them, and they are pleased with Him. Such is the reward for those who reverence their Lord" (Sura 98:8).[2]

Some passages in the Koran acknowledge Jesus as a prophet, but scholars debate whether Jesus is given messiah status therein.

Confirming earlier rumors, media reports revealed that several hostages would be released at Thanksgiving. Nominally, the gesture would reflect the humanitarian notion of freeing representatives of oppressed U.S. minorities—women and African Americans. This would suggest that Iran empathized with exploited Americans more than the United States did, in sending them to meddle in Iran's affairs in the first place. I hoped the release would set off a chain reaction that would send all hostages home by Christmas.

To offer insight to race issues in the States, I took my high school yearbooks to campus to show my students photographs of African American and Caucasian students cheering together at sports events and celebrating at homecoming and prom. Their eyes brightened as I explained integrated education and improving race relations. I described the value of minorities' literary and political contributions, like Martin Luther King's "I Have a Dream" speech, along with accounts of scientists like George Washington Carver. I added that problems persisted, but they were less extreme than before, and leaders continued working to resolve them.

A few days after I had showed them my yearbooks, one of the front-row boys, Ahmad, asked a question just after everyone had taken seats and the class had become quiet.

"What do you think about the embassy situation in Tehran, Mrs. Kamalie?"

I saw Mehdi's eyes brighten in anticipation of a lively discussion, while Mashid lowered her head as though to escape resulting tensions.

My brain stalled as I pondered whether to open a class discussion and allow students to air their views, or avoid this daunting controversy.

"The hostage situation is a political issue. I will be happy to discuss it with those of you who would like to stop by my office after class. Now, let's talk about pronouns and apostrophes."

No one came to my office afterward. By the next class, two days later, the topic seemed to have been forgotten. As our class time ended, I packed books and leftover handouts into my satchel and began erasing the blackboard. A female student wearing a dark chador paused by my desk. Surprised by her overture, since she sat in the back of the room and seldom spoke, I finished erasing quickly and turned to her with a smile.

"Do you have a question, Mariam?"

"I want to thank you for teaching our class. It is exciting to learn from an American. Iranian teachers have accents."

We giggled, before she continued, gesturing toward the doorway. For a frantic moment, I wondered if she were somehow connected to the loitering man in the hall. She resumed speaking in imperfect English.

"My friend Shirin wants talk to you, but she does not understand. She thinks you are imperialist. I tell her you are very nice."

A tall girl wearing eyeglasses and a heavy black chador stood in the doorway, like the angel of death.

"Why doesn't she come and see for herself?" I asked.

Mariam looked down before continuing. "Shirin is registered for our class, but she says she will not learn from American woman."

I turned and smiled at Shirin, but her scowl remained fixed.

"Well, it's up to her. I would love to talk to your friend, but I cannot force her." Part of me was relieved by Shirin's standoffishness. What if she came in and assaulted me or incited other students to rebel?

The shrouded girl in the doorway took a step or two into the classroom as Mariam and I spoke, as though she could not restrain herself. I glanced her way briefly but Mariam continued as her mouthpiece.

"Shirin thinks Americans want to destroy Iran. She say they take Iran's oil."

I turned to the other girl, speaking in English and wondering if she were a victim of propaganda. Then again, for all I knew, she could be one of the extremist ringleaders.

"Shirin, I am here to teach Iranian students how to speak English. This will not help America in any way, but it will help Iranians do business with countries where English is spoken. Do you want to learn English?"

The girl edged another step toward me despite herself, as resistance flared from her eyes. Possibly she saw me as a predator, fearful as well as fascinating. A few more steps brought us face to face, and I caught a note of appeal in her voice. She was angry, but she wanted me to understand her point of view.

"America supports the shah. He took everything from us and made himself rich. Americans stole our oil."

I believed there was some truth to this, yet the girl seemed to base her impressions on emotion more than fact. Wondering whom she had been talking to, I willed myself to stay calm.

"This is Iran's opportunity to rebuild. Ayatollah Khomeini's government will provide new freedoms and opportunities. There aren't many Americans left in Iran."

At this she broke into excited chatter in Farsi, until Mariam grabbed her arm to calm her. Slowing her speech, she switched into English.

"Come to library and see our montage about Vietnam. Americans destroyed that country also, and killed many innocent people."

"Montage?" I looked at Mariam.

"Yes," she confirmed. "Some of the students made a demonstration—no," she caught herself, "a display of Vietnam. Come and see."

I looked at Shirin. "If I do, will you come to class?"

She fidgeted, wanting to say no, but Mariam nudged her.

"Maybe," the taller girl said reluctantly.

"Then I will go see the montage," I answered.

Shirin threw a triumphant glance at Mariam as they turned to leave. At least this time the proud young woman left with a courteous "Khoda hafez," echoed by Mariam, who followed her, with a gentle smile of gratitude for me. Afterward, I realized these two teens were like those who had been social protesters in the United States in the late 1960s and early 1970s. Young people view themselves as harbingers of political change. The challenge was to take a stand that was firm enough to draw the desired response without putting someone into danger.

Though I meant to go see the Vietnam display, I did not make it to the library that day. Mina was waiting at the curb in the Pekan after class. Shirin arrived demurely at class the following week and again before the end of the term. The young women had been respectful in presenting their concerns. This dialogue helped me see that the Iranians had serious questions about U.S. foreign policy, past and present, that deserved answers.

Finally, the much-anticipated release of some hostages came when militants in Tehran let thirteen prisoners go, female secretaries and African Americans.

"See?" Zahra exclaimed triumphantly in the teachers' lounge, pointing to the newspaper lying on the table between us. She had just arrived, removed her coat, and sat down to open her thermos of tea. A Mexican instructor, also married to an Iranian, exchanged a quick grin with me and left.

Zahra kept her hair covered, even with no men present. She poured a cup of tea and sipped it before continuing in a patronizing tone.

"The students don't mean any harm. They just want to make a point."

She persisted in referring to the hostages' captors as "students," though many were in their thirties, carried weapons, and had been trained in military camps.

"And what point is that?" I asked.

"You know," she smiled, "to teach the U.S. a lesson about meddling in Iran's affairs."

Returning to the newspaper, I shot her an absent smile before turning the page.

"My in-laws came last weekend," she offered, to fill the stiff silence.

"How did that go?"

"My mother-in-law asked who I will love more—my baby or my husband."

"What did you tell her?"

She giggled. "I made her happy. I told her, 'My husband, of course.'"

Nodding lamely, I got up. "My class is about to start."

Zahra had gleefully announced her pregnancy the week before. I had not mentioned mine yet.

The days passed in slow motion after that, although news trickled in, with letters from my family and daily radio reports. The Carter administration pursued a nonviolent reaction to the crisis and avoided tactics such as naval blockades or mining Gulf ports. Instead, the president and his advisers were seeking European support to develop peaceful ways of negotiating the hostages' release. One of the president's first actions had been to stop Iran's oil imports. The next step was to freeze Iranian bank accounts in the United States by suspending them in escrow against future hostage lawsuits. I felt these actions were not likely to bring about a speedy resolution, but I could not think of another strategy that would, either. I understood that Iranians holding the hostages believed they had been greatly wronged by the American government for many decades. They felt their control over the hostages gave them a global voice that would finally make the world listen to their charges against the United States. Obviously, President Carter's government did not feel the same way. After all, his administration had inherited generations of problems between the two countries. The situation had not evolved overnight, and it would not be solved overnight.

Over the weekend, Jason and I shopped for potatoes, lettuce, tomatoes, apples, and other dinner staples at the nearby supermarket. Iranian housewives shopped there, enjoying opportunities, and possibly prestige, associated with buying foodstuffs from abroad. I shopped there to get items we had enjoyed before, but I also bought at the local grocery stores, since I was learning to cook more Persian dishes.

When Thanksgiving Thursday came, I was up by 7 A.M. to make apple pie and homemade bread. By 10 A.M., Mina had returned from the butcher's with two large roasting chickens, plucked and cleaned, ready for the oven.

At noon, our guests began to arrive: Nas's parents with Pari, two cousins and their husbands from the village, and an unmarried, middle-aged male friend of Abdolah's. Pari set plates and silverware on the sofreh and filled glasses with cold water that we had first boiled and then cooled, as always, to protect against diseases like cholera and dysentery. Mina and Jason filled serving dishes with steamed rice, mashed potatoes, warm bread, chicken with gravy, and buttered corn.

"Een khaleh khoob!" ("This is very good!") exclaimed the fortyish cousin, dressed in swishing skirts and netlike headdress, as her husband emptied his plate. The other cousin was dressed similarly, though Pari and I wore jeans, while Mina wore expandable slacks. Her abdomen was not very large, and was unlikely to become so in pregnancy, given her slender frame. My pregnancy was not showing yet, and we would not mention it today, in mixed company. Gynecological and reproductive topics remained in the women's circles when visiting or entertaining.

Everyone ate quickly, their usual way at meals, with few words. After Pari and I had brought out the platters, we sat down, and I bowed my head for a silent prayer of thanks. This was something new I had started as a result of my spiritual journey, and I was helping the boys get used to saying "grace" over meals. Jason caught my glance and bowed his head, while Mathew was too young to catch on. I decided not to make a scene about it.

Pari, attentive to detail, saw my gesture, and asked in Farsi, "You pray?"

Feeling a bit uncomfortable that she had mentioned it in front of the others, yet determined not to be embarrassed, I nodded.

Curiosity brightened her features. "Why do you pray now instead of after eating?"

A couple of the others heard her low voice and looked at us while they ate.

"Well, uh, there are special days, like today, which we call 'Thanksgiving,' which is a day for giving thanks to God. So we pray before the meal."

Pari nodded, her mouth full.

A moment later, she asked, "What about other days, when there is no holiday?"

I knew she was analyzing the differences between Muslims' five daily prayers and the Christian practice of praying whenever one felt like it. Grabbing at my limited theology, I mumbled something about the Holy Spirit living in someone's heart, urging believers to pray at certain times.

The two cousins looked at each other as Mina and Mamanbozorg glanced our way from the other side of the sofreh. The men shot us glances between bites of food, their interest stoked by my reference to the supernatural.

"He lives in your heart?" Pari asked as though to be sure she had understood correctly.

I nodded briefly, hoping to make light of it.

"Do you feel it?" She meant in a tactile rather than a spiritual way.

Everyone was watching now.

"Uh, no, you can't feel someone inside."

I tried to keep my tone casual while buttering a piece of bread. "The Holy Spirit is more like a feeling that makes you want to pray."

I wished I knew more Farsi to make better sense of things. I did not want to confuse them by using phrases like "someone you cannot see" and "ghost," since I didn't have the vocabulary for "Holy Spirit" or other Christian terms. I saw one of the cousin's husbands say something to his wife as Pari replied, "Muslims pray many times every day."

She was being informative, not competitive.

In a light tone, I said, "I know—and that is great! Would anyone like apple pie with tea?" I stood to clear the dishes and change the subject.

Expressions turned gleeful as Mina cut slices of dessert that Pari passed around. I put on the kettle and brought cups for everyone. I felt my dinner was a success, as there were few leftovers, and no one was in a hurry to leave. Later, as we finished the leisurely tea, Mina invited our guests downstairs to spread mats for the siesta, urging me to use the quiet time to give the boys a nap. I agreed, thankful for the rest that my pregnant body was demanding more frequently. Two hours later, we went downstairs for tea with the relatives before sending them off on the evening drive home.

That weekend when Nas came home, I told him how we had spent Thanksgiving. He knew of the partial hostage release, though he said little, as was his way. We spent a quiet weekend with Mina and Abdolah, joined by Nas's parents and Pari for Friday afternoon dinner at Mina's house. She made chicken vegetable soup in tomato broth, with stuffed squash, similar to stuffed peppers. Mina was my favorite cook, though most housewives I met prepared excellent meals.

On that quiet afternoon, we settled into a discussion of village life. I asked about poisonous snakes, and Pari explained that larger villas were built above the stables where domestic animals were housed. Each morning, she and her sisters had gone to the stable to milk cows and goats or take them to pasture. One morning, upon opening the large wooden door and approaching the first cow, they had seen a poisonous serpent hanging from the rafter. With a shriek, she had fled to get her brothers, who came running with their guns and killed it. She told of trudging nearly a mile for household water on mornings when the nearby stream had run dry. She and Mina, who also had grown up in the village, called autumn the ugly season, because its cruel winds and cold temperatures dried women's skin, aging them, sometimes prematurely. Tales of Mina's father's unexpected heart attack, her niece's club-foot that was probably due to the parents' close marriage (cousins on both sides of the family), and Mamanbozorg's baby that had been overlaid reminded us of the frailty of life, sobering our moods.

I appreciated the Iranian people's struggle for survival that sur-passed anything I had faced. My admiration grew as I reflected on their clinging to a lifestyle that foreigners had tried to change. It was not about religious beliefs or political competition; these people had largely lived the same way for thousands of years. Some were ready for change; after tasting Western culture, they longed for its comforts and opportu-nities. But others enjoyed the simple pleasures of caring for family and home. There was a peaceful rhythm to life that did not run ahead, leav-ing us to catch up, but rather ambled along, with the chance to muse on distant vistas and savor friends and family. The closest thing I can compare it to is life in the rural South of the United States. In Iran, a visit might last all day, to everyone's satisfaction. Guests stayed for weeks, relatives shared all they had, and we received royal hospitality wherever we went, as do all guests.

Nas climbed into the truck to return to his job site at six o'clock Sat-urday morning. Feeling a little down at watching him leave, I turned my thoughts to holiday plans and asked, "Can we get a Christmas tree?"

He closed the door and unrolled the window to answer. "Trees are expensive. Anyway, I don't know where to get one."

Disappointed, I waved as the Isuzu pulled away. I would find a way to make Christmas cheerful for Jason and Matt. It was a season of hope. Later that day after lunch, I asked Mina about evergreen trees. She had never known anyone who had one, though she had met other Americans in previous years that had talked of Christmas decorations.

"We'll ask Ahmed—he'll know," she assured me.

Ahmed was a family friend who came to visit from time to time. Unmarried, he had his eye on Mina's younger sister. Ahmed knew Shi-raz inside out, and he was willing to do me a favor, perhaps to make a good impression on Mina's family. He agreed to look for a tree at the modest price I stipulated—about one hundred tomans, or fifteen dollars.

With that task in process, I turned my attention to decorating our flat. Jason and Matt colored pictures of Christmas trees, snowmen, and a manger with a baby. We cut them out and pasted them on doors to the kitchen, bedrooms, and bathroom, as well as the living room windows. While some families strung electric lights of white, blue, yellow, orange, or red around their patios to commemorate Muslim holidays, I found a few stores and families who likewise hung lights for Christmas, because Muslims view this a minor holiday as the birth of Jesus, whom they consider a prophet. I decided to forgo the lights. Maybe next year, Nas would be around to help.

In early December, I came home after class and made cutout sugar cookies in the shape of Christmas tree bulbs and Santa Claus faces, and decorated them with homemade frosting after I found a bakery that sold confectioner's sugar. The cookies were popped into the freezer for Christmas, after the boys and I snitched a few. I also made no-bake cookies from a recipe sent by Annie. Growing up during the Great Depression, she had learned to make tasty things from almost nothing.

Letters from home revealed family concerns despite efforts not to upset us. One from Annie, dated December 6, 1979, evidenced her worry:

> I sure hope they settle things peacefully and soon. I am so afraid for you and the boys. Are you still a citizen of [the] U.S. and can you get back over here? There are no planes out now, are there?

My sister tried to stay upbeat:

> I wish I could spend Christmas with you but things look dim. I'm really gonna miss you at Christmas. It's really gonna be hard, without the kids upstairs and all. It'll be like something just isn't complete. I'm sure you'll feel about the same. . . . Tell the kids Merry Christmas for John. I'll call you Christmas Day. . . . Tell Nas skiing is fantastic here. (I'll pay for a membership for him if you guys would come.) I'll send a letter saying, "Congratulations, you've won a free skiing trip to Vermont!" Think it will work? . . . You're giving Annie ulcers and me a sore ear. She calls 2–3 times a day to discuss your future. (December 12, 1979)

They were unable to send a package due to postal restrictions. Pari and I took Jason and Matt shopping downtown, where we stopped in stores that were decorated with colored lights or cotton (as snow), with a few old-fashioned-looking Santa decorations. I urged the boys to point out something they wanted Santa to bring.

"He won't find us in Iran," Jason protested.

"He'll find us, honey. Santa knows where everyone is."

Jason picked out a shiny metal fire truck with an extension ladder and wrapped fire hose. Mathew excitedly climbed onto a dark green tricycle.

"What do you want Santa to bring you?" I asked Pari.

"Heechi," she replied with a shrug.

I saw her eyeing some pretty silk scarves in one of the store windows we passed. As we paused before another shop, a surly-looking attendant came out to stand on the stoop, cynically surveying the street. His fly-stained window and frowning face were not welcoming. Before I could stop him, Jason sidled up and asked in English, "Are you selling anything for Christmas?"

"Krees-moss?" the man grunted, eyeing Jason as though he were a disgusting insect.

"Jesus's birthday . . ." Jason began.

"F— Jesus Christ!" the unshaven man bellowed.

Snatching Jason's hand, we darted down the street. Glancing at Pari, I saw her ill-controlled laughter as she contoured with her hand the man's large belly. My anger turned to laughter, too.

The weather turned colder the next week, and work was suspended on Nas's road project. He came home the week before Christmas for a few days' reprieve. The boys tackled him at the door, and he carried both up the steps to our apartment.

"Ma'am, bring tea," he called in his commanding tone that had become a joke with us over the years. Sometimes I verbally sparred with him to flex my feminist muscle by saying things like "Get it yourself" or "Sorry, can't hear you," which would make him laugh. But tonight, compliancy ruled as Christmas approached; I had favors to ask.

"It'll be ready in a minute."

Bringing samples of my refrigerated holiday cookies, I served tea the way he liked it—very hot, so that no "clouds" formed on the surface. We turned on the radio and listened to the BBC while he ate.

Nibbling a cookie, I asked, "What should I get your mom for Christmas?"

The question presupposed a few things. First, I did not know whether he would agree to celebrate Christmas in Iran, though we had done so in the States. Perhaps his Muslim conscience would awaken, or maybe he would be concerned that neighbors would find out we were Christians and cause trouble.

The second potential problem lay in the holiday spending budget. While we had set money aside for household needs, I was not sure Nas wanted me to use it for gifts or decorations. Related to this question was the third, of whether we should buy gifts for his family or restrict them to the kids, since Christmas is not a universal Islamic holiday.

"My mom doesn't need anything."

Not a completely unexpected answer.

"No one buys her anything the rest of the year. And she cares so much about you—about all of us. This is an opportunity to show our appreciation."

Nas's hand made a dismissive gesture.

"I'll get something useful, not too costly," I bargained.

He ignored that, which I knew from experience meant he would not oppose me. On to the next battle.

"Here, have another cookie," I urged, handing him one. "Jason saw a fire engine he just loved, and Matt picked out a tricycle. I told them I'd let Santa Claus know. Well, Santa?"

Nas grunted, the closest thing to an assent in his vocabulary. Mentally, I celebrated victory on all fronts!

Leaving the kids with him the next day, Pari and I took the bus downtown, my hair discreetly covered by a bulky knit cap. Today Pari wore both a headscarf and a chador for warmth. Hurrying along the sidewalk, we found the stores we had recently visited. I purchased the truck and the tricycle in boxes that were awkward but manageable. Then I treated us to lunch in a popular hotel restaurant. Cloth tablecloths and hothouse blossoms confirmed Pari's claim that this was one of Shiraz's better eateries, and our meal was delicious and surprisingly inexpensive. Afterward, we headed for the bus stop.

Shiraz is located in a semiarid zone and does not get much moisture, except during the rainy season. Snowfall is uncommon. Our day became perfect when snowflakes coated our jackets as we waited for the bus. We gazed into the heavy clouds, and when no one was looking, caught flakes on our tongues, like schoolgirls, laughing as they dissolved. Pari shared my contagious holiday enthusiasm and excitedly discussed gift ideas for the boys, as well as decorating possibilities for home. She wanted to hang silver paper throughout the house, until we realized there was no practical way to do so. Her camaraderie and shared excitement were gifts in themselves, since there was no one else with whom I could make holiday plans.

I had arranged to go shopping the following day with my campus colleague, Lily, who hailed from the Pacific Northwest. Like me, Lily was married to an Iranian she had met in the States. This trip, I brought Jason along. Lily and I caught up with the latest news from our personal lives and stopped for a snack at the teahouse. At the downtown shops, I picked out a silk scarf for Pari and French perfume for Mamanbozorg, with gold earrings for Esmat. Jason insisted on spending his long-saved allowance to get me a Bee Gees eight-track cassette. I was proud of his desire to buy for others when he could have spent the money on himself.

Besides the kids and Nas's mom, along with his two unmarried sisters, there was no one else I needed to shop for, since shipping had slowed to the point where it was futile to send anything to the States. Bababozorg probably would not come to our house for the holiday, since he seldom went out unless necessary when it was very cold, so I got him warm socks. I bought Nas a shirt at one of the boutiques. Lily found a wooden decorator box and gold earrings for her husband's mother and sister, and a tie for her spouse. Blonde and good-natured, my new friend wore a perky beret instead of a veil over her flowing locks, and I self-consciously glanced at passers-by to see if they were staring at her eye-catching fair features. With coat collar pushed up around my ears, and a neck scarf wrapped over my hair, I hoped my covering was adequate to avoid criticism.

Before parting ways at the bus stop, Lily promised Jason to have us over for homemade pizza. A few days later, I purchased gift wrap at a shop where I had found Oriental-style holiday cards for my American family a few weeks earlier. The wrapping paper was thinner than the kind used at home, with a simple design based on cartoonlike figures. With a bit of ribbon, it would dress our presents nicely. We were ready for Christmas.

CHAPTER NINE

Merriment and Memories

AHMED DID NOT DISAPPOINT US. ONE COLD EVENING AFTER Nas had returned to his road-building job a few days before Christmas, we sat around a propane heater, drinking tea in Mina's flat. A furtive knock was heard at the door, and Abdolah got up to answer it. In came Ahmed, hat pulled low, bundling a six-foot pine that he had covertly removed from the trunk of his car under cover of night's darkness. He set the tree before us with a triumphant smile.

"Here it is."

The boys and I jumped up to admire the evergreen. It was gorgeous, full and tall, without defect. I ran upstairs to get the hundred tomans as promised payment. Ahmed protested, as is common in Persian culture, but I insisted on paying, despite Mina's efforts to dissuade me, as she reminded me of all the things Abdolah and she had done for their friend. Since the tree was for us, though, I wanted to pay him fairly. Finally, Ahmed took the coins with a satisfied grin.

"Where did you get it?" Jason asked.

"In the mountains," Ahmed replied, without elaborating.

I wondered who would sell pine trees in the countryside. But I figured our friend must have gotten someone to part with one of their many trees. Minutes later, he left, and Abdolah helped me carry the hefty tree upstairs. I had not thought about a stand for support, but we set it in a bucket and buoyed the trunk securely with bricks from the next-door construction site. While Jason and Mathew colored ornamental pictures that we tied to the branches with thread, Mina whispered,

"You shouldn't have paid Ahmed. He probably got it for free."

"Really?"

"No one sells pine trees."

"Well, I can't make him take it back. Besides, he deserves payment for chopping it down and bringing it here."

We hung our few paper ornaments and a couple of rosy apples. The effect was festive, if not beautiful, but the kids were thrilled, and I was pleased. Mina, Abdolah, and Pari admired the first real Christmas tree they had seen.

Hostage news grew more positive as Christmas approached. Three clerics were invited from the United States to minister to the captives during the holiday season. They arrived with news of the hostages' families, since the prisoners had been unable to send or receive letters. We heard that 250,000 holiday cards were sent to them. A yuletide meal was planned with great fanfare, perhaps as a propaganda move, but I wanted to believe the captors had a soft spot for their charges.

The next day, I dashed off a letter to mail with a few photos that Pari had taken of the kids and me, knowing my family would receive them sometime in January. Feeling lonely that night, I crept into bed after the boys were asleep, only to hear the familiar gnawing deep in our bedroom wall. The rats were certainly tenacious. I tried not to think about their destructive potential.

Christmas Day came at last. Jason awakened Matt just after 6 A.M. and dragged him to the living room, where they admired the gifts that lay beneath our simply decorated tree. I had left those for Nas's family in the bedroom so the boys would not mistakenly open them. Nas was detained at his job site by worsening weather conditions, so I took some pictures with our faithful camera to show him later. I watched with amusement as Mathew clambered onto his tricycle, which Abdolah had assembled days before and Mina had hidden downstairs until the previous evening, when I brought it up after the boys were asleep. Jason sorted packages by nametags, handing some to Matt and keeping others for himself. Beside him sat the fire truck that he had unwrapped first. Soon he turned his attention to the favored toy and made engine sounds as he ran it over the carpeted floor.

Within minutes, toys, books, and sweaters surrounded the boys. Each had opened perhaps a half dozen gifts, and they were more than satisfied with Santa's delivery. Jason seemed to reflect a moment before asking,

"How did Santa get in? Our fireplace doesn't work."

"Santa is pretty clever. I'll bet he came through the balcony doors."

I showed him the half-eaten cookie and empty milk glass sitting on the mantel, as proof. Then I opened their gifts to me, beginning with the Bee Gees cassette that Jason had wrapped and placed under the tree. There also was a cute wall hanging that he must have gotten while shopping with Pari or Mina. Mathew handed me a colorful if unidentifiable picture that he had drawn on lined paper from my notebook. With great hugs, I thanked them profusely, and we enjoyed Christmas cookies and milk for breakfast.

Leaving them to their toys, I went into the kitchen to start dinner. Pari and Esmat would come with Mamanbozorg, and Mina and Abdolah also would dine with us. I had found a butcher shop and purchased a beef roast. Browning it on the stove with onion slices, I popped it into a roaster, surrounded by potatoes and carrots, and slid it into the oven. We also would have salad and warm bread, along with Coke, called "kuka." It was funny to see the exotic Persian script on the familiar Coca-Cola bottles.

The family arrived around noon, with excitement dancing in Mamanbozorg's eyes. She had never experienced anything like Christmas, and neither had the girls, although they had gotten ideas from television and magazines. Handing the ladies their gifts, I was pleased to see that each appreciated her scarf, perfume, or jewelry. Pari handed me a wrapped package, taking me by surprise. She also gave Jason and Matt small ones that turned out to be plastic cars and trucks.

"For me?"

She nodded.

"You don't celebrate Christmas!"

"You do."

Deeply moved, I opened the package to find a lovely printed chador of the kind I had admired on other women. I draped it around my shoulders to the guests' amusement, and then Pari showed me how to wrap myself gracefully in the delicate cloth folds. Though I had not yet taken to wearing the veil, I supposed the day would soon come. Pari knew, too, and had bought this gift to protect me since I did not have a clue where to buy or have one made. The chiffon fabric was soft and delicate, and made me feel feminine.

The roast was only a little tough. Everyone liked the Christmas cookies with their colorful, decorated tops, and I sent some home for Bababozorg and Esmat's fiancé, who would be calling later in the week. Esmat kept busy these days, finalizing arrangements for her transition from dutiful daughter to serviceable wife. Having packed her clothes, mostly jeans and tops, along with a dress or two, a few toiletries like cosmetics and perfume, and domestic items such as towels and blankets, in boxes that stood open in her room, she had become more thoughtful, and spoke less than usual. I could see the pending nuptials were weighing on her; I hoped her mind was filled with pleasant daydreams, not worried concerns.

As the kids fell asleep that night while chattering about their new toys, I tried on the chador in front of my bedroom mirror. I could not get it to fit right; the top kept sliding off my hair. Bunching it over the top of my head didn't look right, either. Peering at my image in the looking glass, I began to understand the value of veiling. Not only were female features indistinguishable for unwanted admiration, you could not even make out who was under the chador, thus protecting identification. Unwrapping myself, as though emerging from a cocoon, I folded the drapery and lay it in the bottom of the wardrobe. Putting on the veil represented an ideological surrender, and I was not ready for that. Some Iranian women still did not wear one. I would trust that a head covering would be adequate for now.

Turning on the television for hostage news, I couldn't get clear reception. I did manage to catch a few seconds of footage showing the prisoners eating Christmas dinner, flanked by captors and clergy. Perhaps there had been moments of comfort and hope for them. Years later, I read that Kathryn Koob and Ann Swift were able to meet with a priest, who offered them a private Christmas service. In addition, Kathryn's "sisters," the female students who guarded her, had brought a makeshift tree and helped to make decorations for it, along with providing sweets and a turkey dinner. She also received a King James Bible, leading to a lively discussion with her captors, who knew little of Christianity. Being a prisoner halfway around the world from family was tough, and Ms. Koob clung to her religious faith for strength:

> In the middle of noise and turmoil, Christ was born; and in the middle of all this noise and turmoil, I could celebrate anew. What a graphic example of His coming into the world to bring peace. I thought of the peace that had come when I needed it and how Christ had come when we needed Him. And my mind leaped forward to the scene at Pontius Pilate's palace. I could understand now much more clearly the scene of the crowd demanding the death of Christ. "Crucify Him! Crucify Him!" was echoed here each day with "Marg bar Cartare" and "Marg bar Ahm-ri-ka." Each day I listened to cries for death. I could see through Christmas to Lent and Good Friday.[1]

Alone in my flat, I switched on the radio and surfed stations to find Christmas music. Finally I heard ". . . O tidings of comfort and joy . . ." These would be needed for the days ahead.

A few days after Christmas, on my way home from class, I stopped at the newsstand. Blaring headlines filled me with dismay.

"Soviets Invade Afghanistan!"

"More Turmoil in the Middle East!"

"U.S.-Soviet Showdown?"

Varied accounts described the Soviet invasion of Afghanistan, one of Iran's neighbors. The Soviets had sent forty thousand troops to establish a Middle Eastern presence and protect regional interests, one account stated. Another news story reported that the Soviets planned to stake claims to oil supplies because of the U.S. embargo. Most accounts emphasized regional instability, especially since latent Afghan rulers had seized control and executed previous leaders. Hafizullah Amin replaced Mohammad Taraki, who was executed and replaced by

KGB-backed Babrak Karmal, brought in by Soviet paratroops. The long, difficult conflict would later be termed the Soviet Vietnam. Over the ensuing months, about five million Afghan refugees would seek asylum in Pakistan and Iran. Anxiety began to mount that the hostage situation was only the first in what was fast becoming a series of regional crises.

That evening, Nas came home unexpectedly due to required business in the village of Dasht Arzhan. Though Bababozorg no longer ruled, some residents still respected his leadership. Many longtime families looked to his sons, Abdolah and Nasrolah, for guidance or assistance. Village visitors to Bababozorg reported escalating conflicts between contentious factions. Nas and Abdolah were needed to settle a dispute there, and the kids and I asked to ride along. Nas agreed only when I promised to keep out of harm's way.

The day was cold and overcast. Following a forty-five-minute drive, Nas and Abdolah dropped the kids and me at his sister's house, a simple adobe dwelling adorned with lush carpets, wooden wall shelves, and traditional silk hangings, with a separate cooking kitchen that lay across the patio. The arrangement was uncluttered and charming. Jason dashed a few doors down to buy pop from the grocer's.

"Come right back," I called.

Tooran and I chopped greens and talked of Esmat's wedding and Aktar's engagement. Mithra, twelve, could run the household as efficiently as her mother; she helped mind the younger children and assisted with the cooking. Eight-year-old Mehran played a marble game with Jason. Moyzhda, the three-year-old, brought her doll to Mathew, who stared at it. Tooran's husband was a farmer. The larder was stocked with harvested produce and canned goods.

After finishing the greens, Tooran placed them in a roasting pot, and then made us tea. Taking a cupful in my hands, I stood in her doorway and looked out at the stirring view before me. A light snow covered the tips of dead grass blades poking through cold earth. Jason stepped outside and tried to make a snowball, delighting in the frosty flakes that turned to water droplets in his hand.

Staring across the road to the fields beyond, I noted that the moisture-soaked plain had turned brown, devoid of sheep and goat flocks that grazed here in warmer days. Their nomadic owners, proba-

Tooran with her sons

bly members of the Qashqa'i tribe, had moved south toward the Persian Gulf for the winter, leaving the fields looking cold and empty.

I recalled one of our visits for a picnic last summer on a hot day. Carloads of relatives had parked off the main road, waiting for everyone to arrive. Joking, laughter, and playful banter called from one car to another tumbled through the dry air. Mina's younger sisters and brothers with their mother came from town, along with Nas's older sister and some of her teenage children. Village cousins I did not know joined the growing cluster of family hovering near the cars. Though unfamiliar, the new relatives shared my son Matt's green eyes and blond hair, a throwback to their Aryan ancestors. Finally, we piled into the cars to form a caravan that angled across the dazzling green pastureland toward a distant point.

As our vehicle bounced over dried mud roads, some hardly more than cattle trails, I grew increasingly thirsty and asked a nephew in the back seat to pass me a Coke. I shared the frosty bottle of cola with Mathew, but it was no sooner gone than I wanted another. I had never been so thirsty and attributed it to the dusty road that crisscrossed large fields feeding herds of sheep, cattle, and even a camel with her baby. Urging Nas to stop, I told him and the boys to approach the camels so I could take a picture. When they got within twenty feet, the mother stood up and took a menacing step toward them. The boys were back in the car instantly—but I got my picture.

Thirty minutes later, we arrived at a garden oasis, with thick grass and mosses shaded by leafy foliage on slender trees. The women busily laid out blankets that soon held flasks of tea, sandwiches of kebab with greens on fresh bread, goat cheese, grapes, and apples. Thirty of us shared the repast while bottles of Bubble-Up, Coke, and Pepsi cooled in the nearby stream.

After eating, the children played quietly on the blankets or under the trees, with the youngest rocked to sleep on their mothers' knees. Men stretched out a little apart from the food, as women packed away leftovers and shook out unoccupied blankets. Leaning against a burgeoning shrub, I watched Nas doze off, Matt and Jason alongside, and listened to the drone of lazy flies. Midday heat pressed my eyelids to close. A little while later, we were roused for fresh tea. Revived by our rest, several girls and women followed the winding stream a hundred feet or so around huge, curving boulders to a silvery waterfall. Cool splashes of droplets against hot faces and arms were refreshing, and we rolled up jeans or lifted skirts to wade in the shallow pool below the tumbling stream. Large boulders partially secluded the area so the men could not watch, and a few of the more daring young women pulled off tops and jeans to bathe in their underwear, as giggling sisters and cousins kept guard for approaching males. I preferred swimming with just the women, where I felt less self-conscious.

Guzzling chilled soda pop while waiting for our hair to dry, we watched the sun dip in the afternoon sky before packing the vehicles. On our return drive across the plain, we stopped by a large tent of migrant shepherds that Nas knew from seasonal grazing. They invited us inside their tent, which was made of goat's hair or wool, and was propped by wooden poles. Spacious and airy, the tent, with its padded carpets, was welcoming, especially since it admitted the fresh evening breeze. I sat down on the carpet at a place indicated by our host. His wife, in Turkish dress, placed hot tea in small cups and saucers before us. Most wives sat apart from their husbands while in the company of non-family members. But not me! I sat beside Nas, and no one seemed to mind. At first, it didn't occur to me to sit anywhere else than with my spouse when we went visiting. Uneasily, the other women would re-main standing a moment or two, probably wondering whether to hint I should move or seat themselves elsewhere, hoping I would join. They gave up, however, and plunked down beside me, and soon everyone chat-ted comfortably. Later, after visiting more widely, it finally became apparent that men and women were segregated by sex, sometimes in adjoining rooms. By the time I realized this, however, my pattern had become established, and other wives and female relatives were seated among the men with no complaint from the patriarchs. In more con-servative environments, though, I sat with the women.

Mina and Abdolah arrived at the tent in their vehicle, along with a few more guests, although most of the others had returned to Dasht Arzhan. Mina joined me on the Oriental carpet. The tent's interior was comfortable, with cooking pots hanging on the walls, and it was fur-nished with a simple wooden table and folded bedrolls. It reminded me of an Old Testament tableau. I could imagine Abraham entertaining the three strangers.

I asked who owned the chestnut mare tethered outside, having ad-mired horses all my life. The tent master offered its use for a ride around camp. Delighted, I sprang up from my seat on the ground, asking Nas to help me mount. With a quick lift, I was aboard and enjoying the cool air that fanned my face while the agile Arabian darted this way and that around the cook fire, skirting the barking dogs and loping around the far side of the herds. Pulling Matt into the saddle before me, I took a slow turn around the woodpile, letting one of the younger cousins lead us so I could firmly hold on to my son. Returning, we dismounted and Nas sprang into the saddle. Lashing the mount into a gallop, he disappeared on the far end of the camp, beyond grazing flocks. He returned as the sky was turning gold and pink above the set-ting sun, looking like a hero of old as he trotted up confidently and sprang off his mount. We left our hosts with many thanks for their hospitality.

Matt and me on horseback at the nomads' camp

A minor incident reminded me of the class distinctions that could flame into walls of obstruction.

Returning to the village, we got out of the car. Milling near the store, I waited for Nas to finish a conversation with Tooran's husband so we could return to Shiraz. A village woman in heavy skirts, with a long braid and headdress, approached me in a reverential manner. Since the woman spoke in dialect, I did not catch the meaning of her first mumbled words. Then she grabbed my hand and kissed it five or six times. Listening intently, I finally understood the gist of her hyperbolic exclamations:

"The khan's wife is wonderful! Nasrolah khan is a strong man. His father and brothers are good. We are honored to have you in the village."

She paused to touch my hand to her forehead before adding more kisses, as I tried to pull away. Horrified by her gesture of submission, I stumbled between English and Farsi.

"No, khanum, you don't have to do that. I'm American—we don't do that. Here, let me shake your hand."

The woman, who appeared to be in her thirties, continued to murmur in Farsi, to which I responded as well as possible:

Nas inside a nomad's tent

"Your children are beautiful; mine are ugly. Yours look so healthy, like you, madam. See, I tend the water buffalo." She pointed to a distant herd that I could only guess at in the gathering dusk. "I will set aside one for each of your sons, and they will have their own herds one day."

"Thank you, ma'am, but your children are really cute."

Nas came up and said something to her. She bowed and quickly left. I did not know if she actually believed in the khan's superiority, since the feudal system had been legally abolished, or whether she was hoping for a foreign woman's favor.

"What did she mean?" I asked Nas, tucking a staring Jason and sleepy Matt into the vehicle's back seat.

"Ignore it," he said.

Later, I told Mina about the woman and her promise of water buffalo. She laughed. "That woman can't give the boys any water buffalo."

"Why not?" I queried.

"Our family owns the herd."

The incident was disturbing for someone like me, raised in a democracy. It felt awkward to be addressed as a superior, and I could not understand why leaders allowed others to prostrate themselves in a demeaning way.

Putting the long-gone summer memory back into storage, my thoughts returned to the present wintertime scene, where strife now divided neighbors and friends. Uncertainty lingered about the nature of relations between former chiefs and the farmers who had given them a percentage of their crops for their ongoing security. Occasionally, as now, those uncertainties would blaze into skirmishes that could quickly lead to violence if not competently managed. Perhaps Nas and Abdolah had addressed inequities among the warring factions today. Despite his apolitical stance, Nas shared my democratic sentiments, and he would feel toward the woman and other villagers as I had. I felt new stirrings of interest in issues I had not faced in the States. Here, I could witness the evolution of democracy as these people struggled to exercise and defend their hard-won rights.

On that late December day, Nas and Abdolah did not return until dinnertime, having reached a solution to the present dilemma following hours of negotiations with the feuding partisans. Preoccupied with supervising Jason and Matt, I caught bits and pieces of conversation after the men had returned and discussed it with Tooran and her husband, Jehan, and learned that insults had been traded, but serious tensions had been deflected.

It was nearly 9 P.M. when we climbed into Abdolah's Pekan to head back to town. With the boys leaning sleepily against me on either side in the back seat, Nas and Abdolah debated the hostile situation in front. Turning to look back at the quiet little village nestled against a snowcapped mountain range, I felt tranquil.

Then an astonishing image caught my attention. Hanging over the village in the sharp night air was the brightest star I had ever seen, making me think of the Bethlehem star on the night of Jesus's birth. Mentally calculating our position, I saw that facing west, toward Israel, was the best view of the star. Could this heavenly body be an echo of the biblical scene the world had celebrated a few days before? Perhaps God had placed it there as a symbol of hope in the strife-torn night. Drowsy from our drive and the droning of men's voices, I nodded off, hopeful of peace in days to come.

January 1, New Year's Day, is virtually uncelebrated in Iran, so we did not observe it in any particular way. Back in the States, I seldom did much to celebrate New Year's anyway, except that Nas and I had gone out to dinner once or twice. I spent the day sweeping rugs and sorting the boys' clothes, setting aside things they had outgrown, in a premature spring-cleaning session. During the semester break over the next two weeks, the boys and I spent hours by the propane heater. I sometimes played games with Jason, read to Matt, or wrote letters home.

On those chill, dark days, my spirits sagged. I longed to hear from Mom and Becky, but Abdolah had been unable to get a call through. Letters were slow, and some that arrived were taped, as though read by censors. Nas did not come home for the next few weekends, and the boys grew restless, sometimes running around the living room to expend their energy and try my nerves. We did not go out in public much, waiting to be sure it was safe, especially since I had not yet taken up the chador.

A letter from Becky, dated January 3, 1980, unnerved me.

> Bet you're wondering why nobody has written to you lately? Because in the newspaper they said no more mail to Iran. I called the post office today and they said mail was still going but they were discouraging some mail because of some of the prank stuff being sent. . . . Plus, I thought you might come home soon, too. . . . We really missed you on Christmas. There seems to be an outbreak of fighting all over there and I really think you ought to come home very soon. You say you want to stay as long as possible. Do you think they're going to announce a war and pass out invitations or let whoever wants to leave, go? I don't think that's how they do it. Remember Pearl Harbor? Sometimes I think it might be Revelations and I really get scared, but whatever will be, will be. If anything should happen I'd rather you guys be here altogether. What a morbid, depressing letter! It's just that I don't want anything to happen to you.

I tried to put worrisome thoughts out of mind. But in the flat were hungry rats, at campus were restless students, in Tehran were the militant captors, and in Afghanistan were the Soviets. Even the village had its share of tensions. Hope was becoming elusive. To avoid discouragement,

I read the New Testament at night, as my faith began to blossom in the rich soil of solitary reflection. By day, I played with Jason and Matt. I wondered how long the stalemates would last before chaos exploded or peace was brokered.

One morning early in January, on a day when the sun had actually broken through dense clouds, Pari arrived at nine o'clock. I was having a cup of tea while seated on a living room cushion, window blinds open, watching snowcaps form on distant mountains. I wished a few flakes would come our way. The boys had finished their breakfast and were playing trucks, with Jason's fire engine taking the lead in face-offs that sent the little matchbox cars spinning, to Matt's delight.

"Ready?" Pari asked cheerfully, neither pushy nor disappointed that I had forgotten some engagement.

"For what?" Where could we possibly go with the boys in the cold?

"Esmat's wedding is today," she said gleefully.

"Oh no, I forgot! I thought it was next week."

"Let's go," she urged. "Mina and Abdolah are waiting downstairs."

"You go without me," I suggested. "I feel sad for home. I won't be good company." My Farsi included the phrase—"my heart is tight—" in this case meaning I was homesick.

Pulling my arm playfully, Pari would not take "no" for an answer. Seeing her grab me, Jason tugged at my other arm to play. Then Matt joined the fray, pulling one of my legs.

"Okay, okay," I laughed. "You win."

I put on an Italian silk dress I had purchased from a trendy boutique several months before. I had splurged on the dress, which was pricier than my usual casual wear, so I would have something nice for special occasions. It had a calf-length skirt, and was suitable for Esmat's wedding. Blotting lipstick and eyeliner, I ran a brush through my hair and then dressed Matt, meanwhile instructing Jason to pull on dark pants and a sport shirt.

"You look nice!" Pari's tone was sincere.

"Thanks—so do you." Her dark auburn hair lay in heavy curls on her shoulders, and she was wearing faint lipstick—a rarity for her. Pulling on headscarf and coat, she smiled when I appeared in the bedroom doorway with her chador over my arm.

"Just in case," I assured her, knowing that family in the village did not expect me to wear Islamic dress. Still, with tensions building everywhere, it would not hurt to go prepared, and I could drape myself with it easily if necessary.

I slipped on a headscarf. While I disliked pretending to be something I was not, there was no point in taking chances. I grabbed the wrapped gift I had bought for Esmat's marriage weeks earlier, a matching gold necklace and earrings. Most women I met, even those who were poor, wore gold jewelry. It seemed to be universal and quite different from the gaudy costume jewelry that westerners often wear. The family had sent gold rings and a bracelet to me in the States after learning of our marriage. My favorite was Mina's gift of a slender gold ring carved in an filigree pattern, delicate and tasteful.

Mina and Abdolah stood by the car and got in their respective doors as we exited the house. Mina's shoulder-length dark hair curled slightly, with warm accents of color surrounding her expressive face. Her abdomen showed a slight bulge that evidenced a healthy pregnancy. Abdolah wore a sport coat over a dress shirt and dark slacks. Nas was at his job site. I was disappointed he was not coming. After all, weddings were supposed to be romantic. But at least Pari was with me, so I would not feel alone. My spirits lifted as Jason and Matt sang the tune Nas had taught them, "99 Bottles of Pop on the Wall," substituting "pop" for "beer" in the traditional version.

Reaching Dasht Arzhan in late morning, we got out of the car at Tooran's, and Jason scampered off to join the kids while Matt clung to my skirt. Evidently, village tensions had been put on hold to celebrate this happy occasion. Everyone knew Nas's family, of course, and all would be welcome at the day's events. Abdolah left to find some of his local cronies, while Mina, Pari, and I entered Tooran and Jehan's home. Tooran and Mithra were cooking in the kitchen, connected by a short walkway to the main house. Inside, it was small but toasty, and the smells were wonderful: simmering stew, steamed rice, baked lamb.

"What can I do?" I asked brightly.

Tooran shook her head with a grin. "Go visit. You're a guest."

"Not me!" I exclaimed, "I'm family."

Tooran motioned for Pari to lead me away, and the short girl laughingly grabbed my hand to take me outside, as Mithra seated Matt with pots and pans to bang together. Mina told her cousin she would return soon, and followed us. The temperature seemed to be at least fifty, though the sky looked like rain. I doubted it would snow. Due to the nearby mountains, Dasht Arzhan experienced more moderate weather than Shiraz did, another reason I liked coming here.

On this chill January day, the plain, once so fertile and green, now lay brown and desolate, the colorful tents gone south in search of winter pastures. Musing on their nomadic lifestyle, I wondered if mine were similar. Our life in Iran had seemed so promising just a few months ago, and now, like the brown terrain before us, it had withered somewhat. But spring always comes, I reminded myself. Touching my abdomen, I wondered what kind of world my baby would be born into. With this thought, I turned to Pari, who was gazing at the houses that lay behind us, some of them multilevel villas, and others little more than adobe huts.

As we started off, Tooran appeared in the kitchen doorway.

"Wait—you'll get muddy. Take these, and save your dress for tonight!" she called in Farsi.

I took the jeans and T-shirts she held out, passing a set to Pari. Mina already had disappeared into another house to visit someone with whom she had grown up.

"But Tooran," I protested, "these are your new jeans."

"Wear them—they will keep you dry and warm."

"But you haven't worn them yet!"

"I will later."

She disappeared into the kitchen as Pari and I headed into the other part of her house to change in a secluded room. My pregnancy was still early, and I could wear normal clothes. Soon we reemerged outdoors, just as the sun made another brief appearance. After checking on Matt, Pari and I made our way down the mud-crusted path to the road that wound past a handful of cottages before turning upward past similar dwellings. We held onto each other as we skidded through slippery areas, with Pari mindful of my pregnancy. Though I had experienced few symptoms, my previous miscarriage reminded me of the need to be careful.

"That's where our cousin lives, the girl who got engaged."

She meant Ashvar. With fair hair and light eyes, the girl looked more Nordic than Middle Eastern. I reminded myself that Persians are Aryan descendents, not Semites like the Arabs or Jews. Over the centuries intermarriage had produced mixed features and dark countenances. Still, in isolated areas like this village, you could find many who reflected Aryan bloodlines.

"Over there is our villa," Pari pointed to a three-story structure partially obscured by a mud wall. "That is where I was born."

I recalled strolling past it last summer. "Can we go inside?"

Pari nodded. I would get to see more of how Nas and Pari's life had been while they were children. Stepping carefully around a branch that lay across the path, we came to an arched opening and entered the courtyard.

The place resembled a European villa, with pools filled with dust instead of water, and decayed vines that must have been graceful when tended. An overturned pot reminded me of the former life that had been abandoned in the move to the city.

Crossing the patio, I noticed a portico surrounding the open square, topped by two floors of enclosed rooms. We ascended a steep stone staircase to the next level. I felt as though I were in a medieval castle. The structure was built around a square courtyard. On the second level, we moved from one large room to the next. Many were connected, and some faced east to greet the rising sun. Others boasted large fireplaces with hearths for cooking and heat. Such areas would be sought in winter. A few rooms opened to imposing mountain faces that dispelled summer heat. Large, open windows invited cooling cross-currents.

"There's Bababozorg's room. The next one is Nas and Abdolah's room. Beyond that is the one I shared with my sisters."

There was plenty of space for a large family. In some corners stood wooden storage bins or benches. I could imagine the place full of young children at play or the older ones sweeping and cooking. Nas and his brothers would return after a day of hunting the mountain quail, called "capk," which the men so much enjoyed. Sometimes the birds' heads would be fried and eaten as a delicacy, something Pari liked. A wintertime favorite in the village and elsewhere was "osh," a thick porridge made of vegetables and grain, eaten with warm bread. People occasionally cooked a sheep head. I hurriedly ate and left the dining area on those mornings when two dull eyes framed a boiled head.

Pari led me to another worn staircase at the corner of the second story, this one ascending to a narrow tower. Looking out from the top, I saw housetops below. I thought of King David, who had watched Bathsheba bathing in her garden. Then I remembered Nas's confession of spying on the neighbor girls' harmless conversation. From here the mountains looked purple, offering a magnificent view.

"Why did your family leave the village?" I asked Pari.

She turned from the window, and I followed her down the steps.

"Life in the village is a lot of hard work. We carried water every day—in summer and winter. The animals had to be fed and watered. Sometimes the crops had to be watered, too. If the weather got bad, we could lose the harvest and have no food."

"Don't you miss living here?"

I could imagine myself in a hammock as the evening breeze lifted my hair while I leafed through a book. Obviously, my vision differed from Pari's experience.

"Shiraz is easier. But I like to come here for a visit."

I fantasized about returning in the summer with potted plants and muslin curtains. It would be delicious to curl up on a divan or find a comfortable bench for warm summer days, like going on vacation, I mused. We descended the last flight of steps. In the courtyard, I looked around once more, filling my memory with images for the future.

CHAPTER TEN

A Wedding and a Warning

T TOORAN'S, IT WAS TIME TO HELP. MINA RETURNED A few minutes after we did, and all of us worked together cleaning leeks, spinach, and dill for khoresht sabsi ("sabsi" means "greens") that we simmered on top of the stove. Next, we peeled, sliced, and fried strips of eggplant for khoresht badan joon, which Iranian women especially love. The eggplant was nestled among sautéed chicken parts, bathed in tomato sauce, and baked in the oven. Other village households were preparing additional savory dishes, as could be seen in the spirals of smoke climbing from neighboring dwellings and the tantalizing odors that teased our nostrils. I fed Jason and Matt bread and butter to hold them for the wedding dinner that would be served in the early evening at an aunt's house.

When we had done all we could to complete Tooran's contribution, we changed into our wedding clothes with time to spare. Jehan and Abdolah returned from wherever they had gone and discussed how to transport the large pots of stew to the feasting place. They decided to pack everything into the truck, with Tooran and Mehran holding it all in place.

The rain had passed. Mithra took Jason and Matt to the aunt's house with their cousins, while Pari and I leisurely strolled through the village as the late afternoon day grew dim. As though to match the celestial brightness of the earliest stars, lanterns and electric lights blinked on, one by one, throughout the two hundred or so dwellings as we made our way along the crooked path past several small and medium-size houses to the brightly lit villa halfway across the village. Chilly now, we paused only briefly to enjoy the lingering rosy tint on the horizon.

Glancing at the rugged precipice behind us, I asked Pari if there had ever been an earthquake here. Iran has endured major quakes that had claimed thousands of lives. In fact, during our recent visit to the dentist on the sixth floor of a downtown office building, a dental assistant had come running from the back to the waiting area to ask if I had felt the tremor. I had not, but when Pari emerged a few minutes later, she urged us to get to the ground floor quickly, taking the steps instead of the elevator.

"Yes," Pari replied, following my glance to the mountain's steep crags. "Once at night when we were sleeping, the ground began to rumble. It sounded like thunder."

"What did you do?" I asked breathlessly.

"Bababozorg yelled for everyone to get outside so the house wouldn't fall on us. No one was hurt."

We quickened our step on the narrow road before the silky darkness enveloped everything. I visualized a lion jumping into our path and repressed a shudder.

The sound of an Oriental melody played by flute drew our attention as we found the villa's opening arch. Crossing the courtyard where clusters of guests stood talking and laughing, we moved quickly along the first floor walkway leading to the steps that would take us to the upstairs nuptials. Passing two village women who appeared to be about the same age in traditional village dress, seated on stools beside a huge pot over an open fire in the courtyard, Pari greeted both by name while the heavier one stirred the pot's contents with a long-handled spoon.

As we continued on our way, Pari said, "They are my uncle's wives."

Surprised, I looked back. The two women seemed much alike, almost like sisters. And they appeared to get along, though maybe there were hidden rivalries. The new regime had reinstated polygamy as a permissible Islamic practice. A man could have up to four wives as long as he provided for their needs equally, including housing, food, marital rights, and children. Women were not permitted to have more than one husband, however, probably to ensure the legitimacy of their offspring.

"Do they argue about their husband?" I asked cautiously, thinking of the biblical Rachel and Leah.

Pari shook her head. "They are one family."

"I couldn't do that," I muttered.

Pari shrugged. "What can a wife do if her husband brings home another woman?"

"Divorce him!" I said defiantly.

"Women don't divorce very often. Their lives would be hard, and people would criticize them."

I was incredulous. I thought it best for couples to stay together if possible, especially with children involved. But I viewed divorce as a necessary back door for intolerable situations. Pari said she knew a woman who had divorced and remarried, but she was from an upper-class family, so little had been said about it. There was that class thing again.

Reaching the villa's second floor, I followed Pari along the external corridor that connected the upstairs rooms. The balustrades were strung with tiny white lights and Chinese lanterns. We passed rooms filled with people seated on rugs, drinking tea, and chatting. In one room, a dozen or more men were seated in a semicircle. Village hats and jackets distinguished the locals from their city cousins. In the next room, several women, many in village skirts and veils, were whispering and laughing as they exchanged family news. A little farther down the outside corridor were women organizing the dinner that would be served in a large, open chamber where a fireplace blazed with heat and light. Children darted from one area to the next, grabbing grapes from fruit-filled platters or tugging a mother's skirt. Over all, the rhythmic music vibrated against the walls like a heart within its cavernous confines.

"Let's go see Esmat," Pari suggested.

We moved along the balustrade to a room on the other side of the open square where a soft light shone behind curtains that covered the entryway. Pushing back the curtains and entering, Pari called, "It's us," and we stepped into the room, pulling the curtains closed. Throned on

a high-back chair sat Esmat as I had never seen her. Stiff and unmov-
ing, she appeared drugged, but probably was only frightened. Or maybe
the women had given her something to calm her nerves. Unused to
much attention at home, here she was the reason for the occasion, the
jewel of the party. Female attendants including cousins and nieces had
dressed her in a beautiful robe of gauze and silk. Gold coins hemmed
her veil. Esmat's face, painted white with cosmetics, was the perfect foil
for ruby lipstick and dark-lined eyes. Pearl earrings glistened in her
ears, and her rather thin brown hair was pulled into a topknot from
which curls escaped to frame her cheeks. The bride seemed exotic compared to those I had known in the United States.

The room had become a makeshift harem, with female visitors paying court to Esmat in her wedding finery. Household gifts for the couple's new life were stacked nearby. Young girls dashed in and out, giggling and staring, whispering questions about Esmat's bridegroom and
the impending honeymoon.

Esmat tried to smile as I kissed both cheeks, but her lips quickly returned to their frozen expression. I felt sympathetic, wondering what she
had been told to expect on her wedding night. Moreover, she had left
her parents' house for good; there would be no turning back. After
tonight, the next time she saw her family would be as guest, not as resident. I hoped Esmat's husband would treat her well. He had always
been polite to me, the American half of my identity a passport for slipping between the worlds of women and men, where, unlike Esmat, I
could speak freely to her fiancé. However, I had learned not to abuse
the privilege, and with time, I often preferred staying with the women,
although mixed company was a relief after hours of feminine chatter.

Pari's nudge drew me out of Esmat's chamber, and we returned to
the large dining room to help lay out the feast. Pari introduced me to
the aunt who was hosting the party, and the slender woman in her sixties, dressed in tribal skirts, kissed my cheeks, murmuring something in
dialect I could not understand. These were those of the Turkic tribe
from which Mamanbozorg had descended. Although the language was
similar, I did not comprehend it as clearly as Farsi. Motioning for us to
be seated, the aunt swept on to resume her hostess duties. I saw that the
dining area was a combination of two adjoining rooms that were loosely
segregated, as the women found places around the sofreh on one side,

and the men, on the other. Jason and Matt flanked Abdolah. The bride-groom was surrounded by youthful friends and assorted relatives at one end of the men's sofreh. He appeared happy and relaxed. Occasionally, laughter or amusing comments emerged from his section, though no one was raucous or rude. The bride remained segregated in her private chamber, served by attendants.

Without ceremony, the fifty or sixty guests began to fill their plates with steamed rice and juicy stews, passing warm sheets of bread from one person to another and spooning servings of "maust," yogurt with dill and cucumbers, onto the rice. Cold water was our beverage, a welcome change from sugary soft drinks. Some villagers ate with their hands, deftly scooping balls of rice and stew with slender fingers, dropping nary a grain. Jason had mastered this technique, but Matt, eyeing his brother and uncle, was trying, somewhat unsuccessfully, to follow suit. I opted for silverware.

Bababozorg had come for this special occasion, driven by a nephew and arriving with Mamanbozorg. I waved to them, and Mamanbozorg joined Pari and me. Nasrin and Mina sat down near us. It was a cozy gathering in a room that was decorated only with wall tapestries and a fireplace assortment of decorative wooden and metal bowls.

Mithra brought me a squirming Mathew. Catching Abdolah's glance, I motioned that Matt had been safely returned so he wouldn't go looking for him. Settling beside me, Matt was sleepy. He would rest well tonight—a good thing, since we would be camping in Tooran's living room near the hearth to escape the freezing night air that would chafe at the doors.

Each entrée was tasty and filling. Guests ate for several minutes, with few words. The aunt and her daughters, assisted by servant girls in baggy trousers, long tops, and headscarves, began to clear plates and utensils, along with a very small amount of leftovers. Sitting back, replete, we waited for tea and the wedding sweets that would be passed around. I asked Pari if we should help serve, but she shook her head "no."

The music began again while we drank tea and nibbled soft cookies or chewy taffy. Young and middle-aged women got up to dance, laughingly pulling one another to their feet. In the dim firelight, I was entranced to watch them link arms and snake their way around the women's side of the room, followed by laughter and throaty gurgles of exultation resembling Indian war whoops. The chain of villagers and city dwellers in traditional and modern dress threw long shadows. It was not long before the dancers edged into the men's side of the room to circle the entire area, spurred by the seated women and a few husbands and brothers. The scene was primal, with pulsing music, weaving feminine forms, and romantic firelight. I felt as though I had stepped back in time to join a nomadic campfire.

Someone whispered, "Nas has come."

Looking around, I did not see him and assumed the whisperer had been mistaken. With many relatives who resembled each other in the crowded room, it would be easy for a casual glance to guess wrongly at someone's identity.

But I heard it again as he sat down cross-legged beside me on the floor. I was pleased because he could have sat on the men's side, yet he had chosen to sit by his wife. Mathew climbed into his lap and soon fell asleep, as Nas stroked his back. Sitting beside him before the fire where the air was heavy with smells of cooking, I became drowsy. I wondered if the bride could hear our festivities from her quarters, and if she longed to be part of them. Perhaps she wished this part would never end.

Soon the dance wound to a conclusion. The groom stood, promptly joined by male attendants, or "groomsmen." Two young men dashed down the steps to bring his car for the bride and her belongings. Everyone got up and moved toward Esmat's room, blocking my view. I heard whispers and laughter, and followed the crowd as they took the last of Esmat's boxes downstairs and loaded them into the waiting car's trunk and back seat. Larger household things had been moved already; these were smaller wedding gifts.

Then Esmat was carried downstairs by her relatives and placed in the passenger side of her husband's car. There would be no religious service. The marriage agreement had been signed long ago during the couple's engagement party, which had occurred before my arrival last year. Now all that remained was for the groom to take possession.

Friends and families got into their cars and followed the newlyweds to a neighboring town where Khosrow had arranged the loan of a friend's private quarters for the night. There, trusted members of both families would wait to receive the couple's wedding sheets with proof of the bride's purity, ensuring the bargain had been properly fulfilled. The groom lived in Kazerun, to the south, in a house shared with parents and two unmarried sisters, but half of the dwelling was reserved for his marriage. There he and Esmat would begin their family while Khosrow taught at the local school.

We did not go with the bridal party. Nas carried Matt, and I led Jason by the hand to Tooran's house. Pari was staying with Mina and Abdolah at the aunt's villa. Tooran and Jehan had put their children to bed already, and the bedrolls they laid out for us looked well padded and inviting. Snuggling close to Nas's back as the boys slept, I felt content, tucked away from the cares of the outside world. Somehow, next to the mountains in this small house, I felt protected and safe, with no thoughts of rats, militants, or hostages. I savored the clean mountain air laced with a hint of chimney smoke that reflected peaceful coexistence with nature.

The next morning after a quick breakfast of fresh bread with jam and tea, we left early for Shiraz, as Nas had to return to his job. He had been able to get away just for the wedding, but was needed on the site as soon as possible. After he packed a clean change of clothes and left, boredom returned to our Shiraz flat. Being on semester break, there was little to do, especially since the weather was cloudy and cold. In a few weeks, we would return to a busier, more predictable schedule. But now I struggled to overcome the burden of ennui and loneliness when I felt cut off from my family at home and Nas at work.

During the second week of January, Pari brought the latest newsmagazines she had purchased during a short afternoon outing. When I pulled one from the stack, a headline grabbed my attention. The Ayatollah Khomeini's face filled the cover of *Time Magazine*'s January 7, 1980, issue. He had been named *Time*'s Man of the Year! In shock, I devoured the story, explaining to Pari what the article said when I finished. The Ayatollah expressed his sentiments toward the United States:

> Iranian feelings are not against the American people, but against the American public. When they refer to America in their slogans and denunciations, they mean the U.S. Government, not the U.S. people. I have received reports about large-scale, Administration-orchestrated anti-Iranian propaganda in

the U.S. The Zionists especially are doing all they can to poison U.S. public opinion against Iran. As a result, there may be ill feelings toward Iran in the U.S. as reported. But if the facts penetrate the Zionist-imperialist propaganda screen, if we succeed in explaining the truth to the American citizenry through the mass media, then the Americans will most probably have a change of heart about us and reciprocate our amicable attitude.[2]

The annual designation was given to a person who had made a significant impact on world events, and the magazine's editors felt the Ayatollah Khomeini filled the bill for 1979. Thinking it over, I wondered if he had been given that distinction with a view to fostering the hostages' release. If that were true, we would soon find it did not work.

Ironically, the same issue reported the results of a *Time* poll that indicated 66 percent of Americans felt that Carter was handling the situation "just right."

That evening after dinner, Mina told us that Iran's presidential election would be held at the end of January.

"President? What about Khomeini?" I asked.

She explained the Islamic Republic's new political structure allowed the Supreme Ruler, Ayatollah Khomeini, to supervise the president who would be elected. I asked another question.

"Can I vote?"

"You're an Iranian citizen, so of course you can vote," she affirmed.

Abdolah explained I need not register beforehand, but would "sign up" on election day at the poll. I had been reading about the promising candidate Abolhasan Bani-Sadr, who favored a moderate stance toward the hostage situation and modernization, as well. Building his campaign on a platform of nationalization, he seemed to be the kind of leader who might be able to unite the various factions whose inability to agree had led to the shah's exile and maybe even the embassy takeover. I was excited about casting my first vote as a citizen, since I had not exercised this privilege in the States. How odd that in a fundamentalist Islamic country I would learn more about the meaning of democracy and personal freedom than I had in my homeland.

Two days later, I ran into Zahra on campus when I stopped to pick up some books for the next university term. I wanted to get a jump on lesson plans and course syllabi for the classes I would teach, as well as those I would be taking.

"Salaam, khanum Kamalie, chetoreh?"

"Fine," I said politely, "and you?"

She would have her baby soon, I could see.

"I'm wonderful. How's your pregnancy coming along?" she asked in English with a meaningful glance at my abdomen.

"How did you find out?" I had not even told my family back home yet.

"We go to the same doctor."

"He's American-trained; isn't that a turnoff for you?" I tried to keep surprise from my voice.

"He's the best, they say. How far along are you?"

"Almost two months," I replied reluctantly. Hearing my curt tone, she changed the subject.

"Remember the hostages' Christmas on television? They were allowed to receive thousands of cards and eat a holiday dinner." She made it sound like a special holiday program.

"Nothing beats sitting around the Christmas table blindfolded and handcuffed."

"What?" Zahra asked, missing my irony.

Adopting a soothing tone with a brittle edge that would not be repressed, I responded, "I'm sure it was lovely; sorry I missed it. See you later," I added before heading for the stairs.

Occasionally, other campus colleagues would meet over tea to discuss the hostages' plight. Some of us worried the situation would turn worse, while others thought the prisoners would be released in the near future.

"Wait until Ronald Reagan gets elected," one of the male professors said. "The hostages will be released like *that!*" He snapped his fingers for emphasis.

"*If* Reagan gets elected, you mean," I spoke up. My recently awakened interest in politics prompted me to take a more active role in these discussions.

"Reagan's a hawk," another instructor, bespectacled Amir, chipped in. "The militants are waiting for Carter's term to be over. When Reagan is sworn in, they'll release the hostages. They don't want to surrender to Carter."

I valued Iranians' opinions, since after all, the crisis would affect them most.

On January 25, Nas was in Shiraz. With Abdolah and Mina, we drove to the poll for our area and voted for Bani-Sadr. Nas showed me how to indicate my vote on the ballot, and I could read enough Persian to understand the man's name and candidacy. Late that night, we heard that Bani-Sadr had won a four-year term as Iran's first president. Hopeful that he would move along hostage negotiations, we did not know that his term would be shortened. Government rivalries would lead the Majlis to initiate impeachment proceedings against him in June 1981.

The phone rang as I was heating soup for the boys' dinner. Mina was staying with her sister for a few days while Abdolah was in Tehran on business, so I had the house to myself. Though phones in both flats were connected to the same line, I always let someone downstairs answer, since I received few calls. But this evening, with no one else at home, I picked up.

"'Alo?" I used the Iranian greeting, expecting a local caller.

"Debbie—is that you?" My sister Becky's voice held excitement.

"Becky! How *are* you?"

Pent-up worries melted as her familiar voice caught my ear. I almost told her about the baby but decided to wait. I had miscarried at three months before and did not want to add to her worries.

Becky asked about cholera, as she had been reading about it in pharmacy class studies. I told her we had heard of no cases, but I would check with our doctor to see if there were precautions to take. I told her Matt and Jason were speaking Farsi. I recounted a recent incident when Matt was introduced to a little girl about six months older than he, a cousin from Tehran. Somewhat snooty, her parents praised the child's beauty and charm. I replied that she would make a helpful role model for Matt as far as helping him learn the language and develop social skills. At two and a half, he did not come into regular contact with other children his age. Just then we heard a ruckus in the hallway where we had left the little ones. Fearing someone was hurt, the girl's parents and I jumped up to see what had happened. We found Matt and Irsia face to face, spitting mad, as the girl yanked at his tricycle while using street Farsi to insult him.

"Tokh-me-sag! Pedar-sag!"

(You don't want to know what these mean, but they resemble English profanity having to do with "dog.") Horrified at her darling's vulgarity, the mother scooped up the preschooler and stuttered an explanation about where she might have learned such words. Hiding my smile, I told Matt to share his tricycle.

Becky laughed at the story before turning serious.

"Carter's administration is taking a more aggressive approach to settling the hostage crisis," she said. "At first, they wanted to try economic sanctions and pressure from Europe. Now that 1980 is here with the hostages still in Iran, Brzezinski is pushing for military action, though Cyrus Vance still thinks negotiations are the best way."

"You mean Carter might send troops to Iran?"

"The news said something about a naval blockade in the Persian Gulf with maybe twelve ships there already. But I don't know if they will do anything."

This was a stunning blow. So U.S. policy was shifting. I hoped there would be no civilian casualties, but this was my first war—I did not know what to expect.

"Debbie, is your passport ready?" Becky knew it had to be processed and notarized before I could leave Iran.

"No, but I'll ask Abdolah to get it ready—just in case."

"Look, if you don't want to leave, I'll come there."

"No!" My sharp tone caused the boys to look away from the cartoons they were watching. Lowering my voice, I continued. "You would stick out as a foreigner. It would be dangerous. Besides, we're safe."

Becky snorted. "Oh, you're safe, but I wouldn't be? That makes sense!"

"I can pass for Iranian, but you can't, especially since you don't speak the language. If things calm down by summer, you can come for a visit."

In answer to my questions, my sister said that Mom was doing fine, except for worrying about us. My next letter would arrive in a couple of weeks, I told her, and asked Becky to let me know if it appeared to be tampered with. The boys talked with her briefly but were disappointed to be told their cousin John was visiting his dad. They could write him a letter, I assured them·as Jason handed me the receiver.

"Stay out of trouble," Becky finished. "I'll try to call in a couple of weeks, unless something happens before then."

"Nothing's gonna happen. Tell Mom and Dad I love them. And keep studying—you don't want to stab a patient with a hypodermic in the wrong spot!"

With the spring term soon to commence, I went one day to the downtown administration building to register for classes. Nas had not been home for several days, and I hid my underlying uncertainties about everything—the hostages, village violence, and the critical community—under a semblance of contentment. I missed the academic bustle and eagerly sought to enroll so that I could renew friendships on campus. Beneath a sunny sky with birdsong in nearby trees, the day was lovely. But getting off the bus in front of the administration building, I was taken aback by the line of nearly a hundred slow-moving students.

I found a place behind the last person, a man who appeared to be in his mid- to late twenties, probably a graduate student. Reaching the desk several minutes later, the man ahead spoke in Farsi to the registrar, who directed him to another building a block or so away. As he stood to the side and replaced the identification card in his wallet, the registrar, a middle-aged matron in headscarf, gave me the same directions after checking my registration form. I didn't quite understand her explanation, so I asked again, this time in English. She looked a bit helpless. As she began to try out a few phrases in English, the man to the side said in Farsi for us both, "I'm going there; I'll take her." I felt fearful; what if this were a ploy to abduct the hapless foreigner? Revolutionaries were everywhere and could be anybody. Still, he had registered for classes—or had seemed to.

Seeing no recourse that would not make me look ungrateful, I thanked the woman and meekly followed the confident young man out the door and along the sidewalk to the next building, where we joined another lengthy line. At least we had made it safely, and this person had a courteous manner. There was a sure look in his eyes that made me feel he could be trusted when he nodded acknowledgement to my thanks of accompaniment. I knew that, apart from the scoundrels found in any society, Iranian men typically treat women respectfully, or at least the ones I met did. Relaxing my guard, I hummed a 1960s pop tune as my guide in front of me leafed through the course catalog he was carrying. I often hum or sing to pass the time, and thought my voice was too low for anyone to hear.

> There she was, just a-walkin' down the street,
> Singin' do wah diddy diddy dum, diddy do.

He turned abruptly, and I stopped midword, fearful he had heard and would disapprove. What if he reported me? Worse, could he have a chain or gun hidden in his jacket? I had worn a headscarf, still resisting the chador, hoping the university campus would be more tolerant of self-expression. Feeling for the scarf, I pulled it forward over my forehead and averted my gaze.

"What were you singing?" he asked in clipped English that revealed a British accent. Piercing blue eyes stared into mine from a face neatly trimmed with a beard. He looked Iranian—and he didn't. Perhaps one of his parents was European.

"It was popular years ago in England and the States. You probably don't know who sang it."

"Manfred Mann," he suggested with a gleam in his eye, "mid-sixties."

"How do you know?" Curiosity overcame my fear.

"I grew up in England," he said with a smile. "I should have introduced myself. Hassan Mehrnaz—pleased to meet you."

I mechanically took the hand he offered and shook it in a daze. I was not in the habit of talking with strangers, and I questioned this man's motives. Was he a spy? Was this conversation a trap? Didn't he know women were not allowed to talk to strange men or touch hands? Studying his features, I saw that he was attractive in a rugged way. He seemed to be somewhat reserved, as Nas was. Noting my frank stare, he grinned.

"Sorry, I didn't mean to throw you off. I've recently come back to Iran—two years ago, in fact. I'm an engineer for a Swiss company, and I travel a lot. So please excuse my manners." His candor disarmed me.

"That's okay," I assured him.

"So what other sixties music do you hum when no one is listening?" There was an amused glint in his eyes.

"Let's see if you can name the artist who sang 'Kicks,'" I challenged him, caught up in the game.

"Paul Revere and the Raiders. C'mon, you can do better than that."

"Little Red Riding Hood?"

"Sam the Sham—and the Pharaohs!" he replied promptly.

"You're pretty good."

"I've got a decent collection, not to mention being a former *Teen Beat* subscriber."

We discussed the Beatles's *Rubber Soul* album and confessed to enjoying Herman's Hermits and the Beach Boys, along with Cher and Marianne Faithful. Those stage names sounded oddly humorous as we talked about them in this faraway place. Yet, it felt good to reminisce on an innocent youth that seemed even more distant than our location.

Hassan explained his preference for the Hollies and Petula Clark. Nearly an hour passed as we exchanged views on music and events from our growing-up years, mine from the American side, and his from Britain. My hungry soul appreciated the cultural exchange, something I sorely missed from life in the States. While Pari and Mina were delightful companions, I enjoyed the social camaraderie that comes from a shared past. My new acquaintance seemed to be fun-loving and informed; I had forgotten how much I enjoyed thinking about light-hearted music and social movements of my youth, and laughing freely about things we both understood. We did not notice the line inching forward until it was Hassan's turn to register just inside the building's door. At the desk sat a secretary in a headscarf that hugged her shoulders. She crisply asked my acquaintance's name.

After Hassan had given his information, it was my turn. I moved past the registration table to the exit once more, preparing for my next stop, the bookstore. Hassan was waiting outside and turned to me with a grin.

"Thanks for chatting," he offered, stuffing his identification card into his pocket.

"And for tolerating my humming," I giggled.

"Maybe I'll see you on campus," he said brightly.

"I don't think so," I replied. "The engineering college is a long way from the humanities building." The gulf between us was fixed and could never be bridged.

With a quizzical look, his smile disappeared. He regarded me soberly for an instant before turning with a brief salute and the words, "Take care."

"Bye," I called in a low voice. He waved once while making his way across the lawn to the main street.

That evening, I wrote a long letter home, describing the wedding and the village feast. I told Mom and Becky how well Pari's English was coming along. I mentioned that Mina was nearly ready to deliver her baby but said nothing about mine. Nor did I mention the loneliness that often engulfed me on those long, dreary evenings. Folding the letter around Christmas photos and those of the camels, I wish I had gotten Esmat's wedding pictures developed. I wanted my family to know that we were in no immediate danger. With a new president and a fresh university term, our future should be brighter in the months ahead.

CHAPTER ELEVEN

Dark Days

THE NEXT DAY, I DECIDED TO GIVE THE FLAT A THOROUGH cleaning before returning to my studies in a matter of days. I vigorously swept the carpets with a hand broom, the long-handled kind that requires some bending, favored by Asians as more gentle to delicate carpets than electric vacuum cleaners. I enjoyed the forty-minute workout as one of the few exercises that helped expend calories and keep me fit.

Scraping debris into a dustpan, I felt a familiar twinge of pain in my lower abdomen, the type I was used to feeling a few days each month. Suddenly fearful, I dropped the broom and went to lie down. Jason was in school, and Matt was playing with his tricycle, pretending to fix a wheel that was not really broken. Over the next hour, I recognized symptoms of my monthly cycle.

Telephoning Mina at her sister's house, I explained what was happening. She listened with concern and said to call the doctor. Hanging up, I dialed his office. The nurse said the doctor was with a patient, and told me to call back if the flow or cramps became worse. Putting Mathew to bed for a nap, I lay down again. Tears flowed as I realized the baby I carried would never be born. My glance settled momentarily on Mamanbozorg's amulet lying on my jewelry box.

When Matt got up after a two-hour nap, I sliced an apple for him, resting again until Jason got off the bus at four. I waited for the waves of pain I was sure would follow. But they never materialized. Instead, I felt my usual menstrual cramps and a normal monthly flow. Had I really been pregnant?

The next day after breakfast, I called the doctor's office and this time spoke with him directly, explaining what had happened.

"It could be a missed abortion," he said kindly in his accented English.

"Abortion? But I wanted the baby."

"Missed abortion is a technical term meaning you miscarried early in the pregnancy and the embryo has been absorbed inside your body."

"You mean I won't miscarry?"

"Not in the usual way. The period you're having means your body is getting back on track. The pregnancy is gone. Call me if the cramps or bleeding become worse."

With a sense of anticlimax and disappointment, I went about my usual activities. Mina returned home later that day and sympathized with my loss. In the evening, we went over to Nas's parents' house where I told Mamanbozorg and Pari about losing the pregnancy. My mother-in-law shook her head as I handed her the amulet. All I wanted now was to forget and move on. I was glad I had not mentioned the baby to my American family. Nas said little about the miscarriage when he returned that weekend, but I could tell he felt down, too. New life is precious, planned or not. We spent a quiet weekend at home, watching television and visiting family. All too soon, Nas had to leave Saturday morning early to return to the construction site. Still depressed over the miscarriage, I watched him go, with sadness, wondering what the future held for us.

Responding to Becky's concerns about possible military action, I tuned more regularly into Iranian television and the BBC. Though there had been numerous meetings involving the United States and international entities like the United Nations and NATO, a joint approach could not be agreed upon. While many countries in theory supported the U.S. demand for the hostages' release, few were willing to join forces for decisive action. Better no action than bad action, I believed. Yet, I worried that an assault was being planned behind the scenes. I needed to know what was happening so I could take steps to protect the boys.

As if to parallel the growing external threat, the bedroom gnawing intensified. Temporary mild weather must have distracted the little beasts, since I had not heard them for some time, but now they were back with a vengeance. Night after night, I tried not to listen, hoping the sound would disappear. Maybe they would burrow out the other side of the building without getting into our apartment. Mina told me about a similar noise in her cupboards, and Abdolah promised to set traps.

When the temperature warmed a day or two later, I bundled up and covered my head firmly with the knit cap before venturing out to buy more newsmagazines. Having been in the house days without reprieve, I needed fresh air. Leaving Matt with Mina while Jason was in school, I made a quick bus trip downtown, got my reading material, and returned home. That evening after dinner, I read belatedly of the assassination of the shah's nephew in Paris. More recently, the United States had expelled fifty-six Iranian students who had entered the country illegally. Several reports highlighted the United States' growing frustration with nations that refused to pressure Iran. Some were sending aid or expressing sympathy to the Islamic Republic.

The United Nations Security Council got a 15–0 vote for the hostages' release, though nothing came of it. Even a judgment from the World Court was virtually meaningless, though prominent cities like Rome and Paris allegedly supported U.S. claims against Khomeini's government. The Carter administration questioned Tokyo's support, while the Soviets expressed sympathy for Iran. We heard scattered rumors of a proposed Soviet takeover that would rival Hitler's abuses. Danger was approaching from every direction. On Iranian television each night, a military instructor explained how to operate an automatic rifle or a submachine gun, referencing the mobilization of twenty million Iranian youths.

Tossing the magazines on the kitchen counter, I wondered why I bothered to read them. Would hostilities never end?

Nas came home that weekend. When I told him my fears that President Carter would take military action, he was skeptical.

"Carter doesn't have a backbone. His advisers pull him in a dozen directions. Nothing's gonna happen."

If Carter wasn't ready to act, the rats were. That night they made their move.

We went to bed about ten-thirty. I turned off the lamp on my bedside stand, pulled up the blanket, and closed my eyes.

A moment later I heard a scratchy movement behind the large wardrobe that stood against the far wall of the bedroom. On the adjoining wall was our dresser. Atop it lay a hairbrush, perfume bottles, and a paper bag of sponge hair rollers that I had gathered to throw away.

Holding my breath, I listened for the sound of more movement. Then I heard the bag rustle. It rustled again. The rats were attracted to the human smell on the rollers.

"Nas!" I whispered stridently, "Wake up."

"Huh? What?" he snorted.

"There's something in the room."

At the sound of my voice, the rustling stopped. Carefully reaching to my bedside stand, I wrapped my fingers around a paperback book and tossed it with all my might. It hit, and I heard a muffled scampering noise.

"Nas—get up! They're in the room!"

My voice was loud with panic, and he sprang to a sitting position. "Who?"

"Rats—over there!" I switched on the lamp beside me, fearing to find the dresser swarming with them. But nothing was there. Nas stared all around.

"Where?" he demanded.

"On the dresser, I heard them in that bag of rollers."

Jumping out of bed, he went to the dresser, pulled it out from the wall about a foot, and checked behind it.

"There's nothing here."

"The sound started behind the wardrobe—look there."

Tugging on one side, he moved half of the large piece of furniture away from the wall as I crept up behind him. There were no visible openings in the wall or on the floor.

"Maybe they're under the wardrobe," I suggested.

"I'm not moving it tonight," he groaned.

"Then push it back firmly against the wall. Maybe that'll cover the hole or wherever they came from."

Long after he turned on his side to sleep, I lay awake with the lamp on, waiting for the familiar sounds. Finally, I fell into a dreamless slumber.

Nas returned to his road crew on Saturday, as usual. I told him I would take the boys and stay downstairs with Mina and Abdolah if the rats came back. So far, Abdolah's traps remained empty. After Nas left, I went downstairs and tapped on Mina's door. She answered a moment later.

"Come in. I'll make tea."

"Is Abdolah here?"

"He went to town."

"Too bad," I said in English.

"Chee?" she asked curiously.

"I was hoping he could drop me off at the college bookstore. I need to buy another book before the semester begins."

"I can drive you," she offered.

"But you're tired." I gestured toward her belly, big with child.

She insisted, "I'll take you, and then go to the supermarket with Mathew. Afterward, we'll come back and get you."

I dressed Matt warmly and took him downstairs, where my sister-in-law was waiting. We got into the Pekan, and she dropped me at the curb of the campus compound. In the bookstore, I found my needed reading in short order and was waiting at the curb a few minutes before Mina and Matt were due to return. Time drifted by. Soon I had been waiting almost an hour. It was after noon. Had she stopped to see her sisters or visit her mother? Perhaps I had misunderstood the plan.

After another ten minutes, I decided to take the bus, since I felt uneasy riding in a cab by myself. The last time I had done so, the driver asked if I were American, and kept saying something that sounded flirtatious. When I told Pari and Mina, they laughed and then cautioned me, saying the man had been recklessly forward, using an expression that I loosely translate as "I like you." At least, I think he was flirting and not planning to murder me! After that, I avoided taking taxis alone. Pari advised me to say firmly "shut up" if anyone asked personal questions.

While midday temperatures had risen, it was still cool. I buttoned my jacket and pulled the knit cap tightly over my ears. Not having planned to walk outdoors, I knew that if extremists targeted me, the cap might not satisfy their demands for Islamic dress.

Nervously, I walked down the sidewalk toward the direction I expected my sister-in-law to come from. Traffic began to thin as commuters went home for lunch and the siesta. Increasing my pace, I turned on the road that should lead toward a public square where I could catch a bus. But the sidewalk climbed steadily, and soon I had left the business district. Now I was in a secluded suburb where the houses stood silent and watchful. Looking down the road I had just ascended, I realized there was no uphill road that I traveled to come to campus. I was lost! I turned around and began walking briskly downhill. Surely, I could find the right turn and get to the bus stop.

A man on a bike came into view, pedaling toward me. Whizzing past, he called, "Emrakaee?" ("You're American?")

Ignoring him, I continued my quick steps, resisting the urge to run. The man turned and zoomed past, grabbing my rear.

"Nakon!" I called sharply. ("Stop!")

But he turned again and again. Each time, he circled more tightly, like a vulture circling its prey. As his hand grabbed at me, I tried to dart out of reach. Truly frightened, I wondered if he would pull me into someone's shrubs and cut my throat, or worse. On his fifth pass, when I felt he was ready to spring for me, I caught a glimpse of a truck on the cross street just below.

"Nas—help!" I broke into a trot as the truck backed up and turned up the road in my direction. In a flash, my husband pulled to the curb as the cyclist sped away.

"What was he doing?" Nas's eyes shot lightning after the predator.

Climbing into the passenger side, I broke into sobs.

"He kept grabbing me. I was afraid he would—"

I couldn't bring myself to say it. Nas looked me over to see if I was all right. Realizing he should be at his work site, I asked, "What are you doing in Shiraz?" His rescue was nothing short of a miracle.

My husband's mouth tightened as he steered the car down the hill, making a left-hand turn leading toward the highway that began to look familiar. Now I could see where I had taken the wrong turn.

"I forgot to pick up the supplies we ordered. When I came back, I stopped at home, but no one was there. Abdolah called as I was leaving. Mina had a car accident, but she and Matt are okay."

"Accident? Where are they?" New panic gripped my heart.

"They were checked at the hospital. The doctor gave medicine to relax them both. They're at Reza's house now. It's closer to the hospital in case Mina goes into labor."

Pangs of guilt washed over me. Why had I let my pregnant friend drive?

"Did they get hurt?"

Pulling up to a stoplight in the downtown area, Nas explained what had happened.

"Mina's leg has a four-inch cut. Matt was thrown against the gearshift when the car went off the road. The doctor thinks he's okay, but he hasn't peed yet. We're supposed to call the hospital if he doesn't urinate in twenty-four hours."

Overwhelmed, I leaned my head against the dusty back of my seat. On top of everything else, now Mina and my precious child were injured. I could not handle it. As tears trickled down my face, I said, "If anything happens to Mathew, I can't bear it."

"Nothing's gonna happen. You worry too much."

I wanted to shout that he did not worry enough, but I knew an argument would not help. We had to stay calm.

At Reza's house, Mina was resting in a downstairs bedroom. The sisters offered consoling words as they led me to Mathew, lying on the sofa. I scooped him into my arms.

"Are you okay?"

He nodded and then rested his head on my shoulder. Matt did not complain when he got hurt; he just clung to me. Today that made me cry even more.

Then I went into Mina's room as the sisters explained her leg had been dressed and bandaged by hospital staff and should heal in a week or so.

"Is the baby okay?" I asked anxiously.

With a smile, she assured me it was fine, though he or she might come early. Abdolah would be here any minute. Nas said we ought to take Matt home, as Jason would arrive on the school bus soon.

As Mathew lay dozing in the truck's back seat, I spoke in a vicious whisper.

"I'm sick of everything here. I want to go home."

Throwing me a look of surprise, Nas shot back, "Go home, then. No one's holding you."

"Then get my passport fixed."

"You can go," he added sternly, "but the boys stay with me."

My tone changed.

"Nas, is this what you want for them? Political crisis, rats, car accidents, demonstrations? We have to give them something better."

"There's nothing wrong with life over here. If you can't handle it, go."

After a few moments of irritation, I wondered if maybe I was overreacting. Car accidents in the United States were plentiful. It could be that I was still hysterical from the encounter with the cyclist, or perhaps emotional from the miscarriage. I tried to remind myself of all the things I loved about Iran. It certainly had been fortuitous that Nas was able to find me when I got lost. But fear and guilt kept creeping back, like the rats in our walls.

By the next morning, Matt still had not urinated. Settling him gently on the red plastic chair we had been using for potty training, I coached,

"Come on, sweetie, make pee-pee."

He smiled at my funny words and grunted, but nothing came out. Urging him to stay seated, I got Dr. Seuss' *Hop on Pop,* a favorite of Matt's, and began reading. Several minutes later, he began to strain, and I heard a few drops hit the hard plastic bucket.

"Good boy," I exclaimed, "make some more."

Nas peeked in the bathroom doorway to watch as Matt, proud of himself, pointed below and said "Pee-pee," one of the few English expressions I had heard him use. He sat down and released a stream of fluid. Jumping up, he said, "I make pee-pee."

"Good boy!" I exclaimed, checking to see. Horrified, I saw it was bloody.

"Nas," I said in a firm but calm voice, "look at this." Glancing into the pot, he replied nonchalantly, "The doctor said that might happen."

Why had he not told me?

"Are you sure?"

"Yeah." He made a face from the doorway.

"Do we need to get Matt checked to be sure?"

"No. The doctor said it should clear in a day or two."

Relieved, I showed Matt how to wipe with tissue and saw that the urine was blood-tinged rather than pure blood, a comfort. Nas returned to work the next day—Sunday—but came home again Wednesday evening. I think he wanted to make sure we were all right. Plus, Mina was not downstairs; her mother wanted to look after her until the baby came. Abdolah often was gone, though he made a point of calling to see if we needed anything. I was glad to see Nas again, and hoped he would not have to leave soon.

The next day, Mina's mother invited us to dinner. Mina looked well, though she was resting most of the time. When she held open her arms to Mathew, he ran to her for a hug, and I saw tears form in her eyes. Reaching over, I squeezed her arm affectionately.

"He's fine. I'm grateful you're both doing so well. We have to keep you strong and healthy."

Smiling through her tears, she reached to hug me, too. I helped her to the sofreh, and all of us were seated for the meal of braised lamb with seasoned rice and salad, along with Pepsi and grapes for dessert.

After dinner, we sat back to have our tea when the phone rang. Fifteen-year-old Reza answered. His voice took on a sharp note. He handed the receiver to Abdolah. After a staccato exchange with the caller, Abdolah hung up and announced that he and Nas had to get to the village—tensions were flaring again, and someone had been shot.

"Can I go?" Jason asked eagerly.

"No—stay here!" Nas commanded.

"Wait, let us go. We can stay with Tooran."

I do not know why I wanted to go, but somehow I felt our family needed to stay together after all we had experienced. I did not want any-thing to happen to Nas.

"Matt stays here with Mina's mother. Get in the truck with Jason," he ordered.

The sisters wished us well, anxious thoughts written on their faces, and from the sofa Mina called "Khoda hafez." Abdolah and Nas jumped into the front seat, and we were on our way. They drove fast, and I grabbed Jason as we rounded curves. After forty-five minutes on the highway, Nas pulled the truck to an abrupt halt at the road leading from the highway to the village, where Jason and I spilled out and made for Tooran's door. She was chattering with another village woman about the breaking news, while children stood by silently, with open ears and wide eyes. Nas and Abdolah spoke briefly with Jehan, who joined them as they strode rapidly down the path toward the other end of the village. I wondered if I would see them again.

"Sit down," Tooran said gently, putting the kettle on for tea.

"What a beautiful tea set" I exclaimed, admiring the delicate, gold-rimmed glasses and saucers trimmed with mauve roses that she set before us. "Is it new?".

"Yes," she blushed, pleased by my compliment. "I bought it at the bazaar last week."

"Let me know which shop you visited, so I can see what else they have. I might get one, too."

"Then you must have mine," she said generously.

"Oh no! I will get one of my own."

"I want you to have it."

Taken aback, I remembered the quaint custom of bestowing a gift on its admirer. Sorry I had spoken without thinking, and horrified at taking this precious gift, I tried to reject the beautiful present, but Tooran would not let me. Settling the cups in their carton, she handed me the boxed set as I waited for Nas and Abdolah to return. Embarrassed by my careless praise, I regretfully accepted her tender offering. I could see the delicate dishes were expensive. Perhaps she had saved a long time for them.

"Thank you," I told Tooran, who always wore a smile, planting multiple kisses on each cheek while she blushed. "I will get you one like it at the bazaar."

I did not know if this was acceptable protocol, but she did not argue.

Then I stared down the rocky path to see if the men were returning yet. But it was nearly dark before I heard them arguing with another man as they approached the house. Abdolah's voice was raised, and I heard him yell something at a shorter man while making three jerky mock bows in a contemptuous manner.

As they reached the door, Tooran started to ask if they wanted dinner, which would soon be ready. She and Mithra were frying koo-koo, potato pancakes made with flour and egg, served with greens and yogurt. Brushing her comment away with quick thanks, Abdolah continued toward the truck, the other man beside him in animated argument. Nas's occasional statements sounded more moderate. At the truck, he motioned to Jason and me where we stood in the doorway. "Bereem." ("Let's go.")

We dashed to the truck, eager to be gone before the arguing men could break into a fight. My agitation caused me to forget Tooran's gorgeous tea set, though later I was glad I did. Perhaps now she would keep it for herself. Abdolah and Nas climbed into the vehicle as Jason and I huddled in the back seat. The other man, middle-aged and gruff-looking, pounded the driver's door as Abdolah started the engine, and we roared away.

"What was that about?" I asked. "Who got shot?"

"A boy. It was an accident. Someone was making threatening gestures with a rifle, and the gun went off."

Abdolah interjected at this point. "The men were arguing about a piece of land."

Seeing Jason's alarmed face, I let the matter drop. No sense in giving him more to worry about. Nas told us the boy had been taken to the hospital for treatment but should be all right.

By then, night had fallen, and it was very dark, with no sign of the star that had impressed me at Christmas. After we reached the highway and had traveled about fifteen minutes, we saw a roadblock ahead, with two Jeeps parked lengthwise across the road. In front of the vehicles stood six Revolutionary Guards in army jackets, holding rifles.

"Now what?" I asked with trepidation.

We braked to a stop. Two guards approached the driver's window, which Abdolah unrolled. They asked a few questions about our names, where we lived, where we had been, and where we were going. I stealthily pulled a blanket from the floor and wrapped it around me as a mock chador.

"Get out," I heard one say in Farsi.

Nas and Abdolah exchanged a quick look before complying. This was not a good sign. As we stood in the freezing night air, the guards searched our vehicle from front to back, peering into compartments and under seats. I had never seen a roadblock or been involved in a vehicle search. What were they looking for? Drugs? Weapons? Contraband?

Standing close to Nas with Jason at my side, I saw a faint bead of sweat at my husband's temple, odd given the cold temperature that showed our breath. After a couple of minutes, the guards finished and told us to move on. Another guard got into one of the Jeeps and moved it to let us pass.

"Whew," I whispered.

Putting them well behind us, after ten minutes or so Nas pulled out a handgun from a hidden pocket under the passenger's seat.

"It's a good thing they didn't find this," he said. "We might have gone to jail."

Shaken, I distracted Jason with a rhyming game. It was late when we stopped to get Mathew before returning home. I remember thinking, "This would make a great movie" before falling asleep with Matt tucked into bed between Nas and me, and Jason on the floor beside us. Almost certainly, things would settle down after all that had happened in such a short time. Though I had always dreamed of adventure, this was too real and too close.

Letters from Mom, Annie, and Becky arrived the next day. Even my father, who had never written before, included a few sentences of brusque greeting and concern at the bottom of my sister's missive. Mom and Annie wrote additional letters to Jason. Matt, of course, was too young to read, but they asked Jason to tell Matt they loved him. Mom's included a comic strip from the newspaper, while Annie had drawn a few stick figures, including one of Mom's cocker spaniel, Jodie, that made Matt smile.

I saved my sister's for last. "You need to get your passport ready," Becky wrote. "Some of Carter's advisers are pushing military action in response to the captors' latest announcement." She referred to Communiqué Number Seventy-Four that stated the hostages would be tried as spies, and if found guilty, could face execution. Noting that Mom's, Dad's, and Annie's letters did not mention these concerns, I hoped they were unaware of the escalating tensions.

I had just put the last letter down when the phone rang. It was Abdolah.

"Mina had the baby." His voice sounded ecstatic. "It's a boy!"

"We'll be right over," I replied happily.

When Nas got out of the shower, I told him the news. After he dressed, we drove to the hospital, leaving the kids with Mamanbozorg and Pari. Mamanbozorg looked at me sympathetically when we told her about the new arrival. But I knew she would rejoice, especially since it was the couple's first child, and they had waited a long time for him.

At the hospital where I had formerly taught, Mina looked tired.

"Did you see him?" her voice was weak.

"He's beautiful! He looks like you."

She shook her head "no." "He looks like Abdolah."

Staying just a few minutes, we left so she could rest. It had been a natural delivery, with little pain medication. Given her recent injury, she needed to sleep. As we moved down the hall, I heard the loud groan of a woman in labor.

"Khoda—Allah, oh Khoda!" she cried.

The accented voice was familiar.

Pausing by the door of the next room, I watched as Zahra writhed in pain, shaking back and forth as though to hurl the infant from her

Mina, Abdolah, and Ali

body. Wavy hair lay tangled around her shoulders as a nurse tried to calm her. In labor, Zahra clung to her Islamic identity by calling on the name of her adopted god, Allah.

"Are you all right?" I asked.

Her eyes widened. "What are you doing here? It's not your time, is it?"

A blush washed over my face. "I lost my baby. I'm here to visit my sister-in-law."

Collapsing onto the bed, she closed her eyes, murmuring a request for ice.

"Can I get it for you?"

"The nurse will do it," she snapped.

"Take care," I offered, catching up to Nas, who had sauntered down the hall to wait. Behind me floated Zahra's anguished cries. I swallowed tears, reminding myself of the two wonderful sons waiting for us at home.

CHAPTER TWELVE

The Beginning of the End

O utside, the sun shone feebly. We drove back to my in-laws' house, where Pari was making omelets for dinner. It still seemed odd without Esmat's bustling around, cooking dinner or tidying up. We had heard the young couple was doing well, but we had not seen her since the wedding.

Nas's parents insisted we stay and eat with them, so I laid out dishes while Nas talked with his dad, flanked by Jason and Matt. Since the accident, Matt had shown no further medical problems. His urine had returned to normal the day after the accident, and he seemed no worse for his ordeal. In fact, he did not seem to remember it, looking blank when I asked about the car and the hospital.

Over our meal, we talked about the spring term that would begin the coming week, and how cute newborn Ali was. Pari practiced her English.

"Do you want water?"

"May I help you?"

"This is a fine day."

Amused by her earnestness, I appreciated Pari very much. There was nothing hidden or deceptive about her. Open and natural, she was passionately devoted to family, her chief purpose in life. She was a peacemaker, seldom moved to anger. Once, when Mina's youngest sister's personal questions grew irritating, Pari urged me to overlook it. I wished more Muslims and Christians were like her. Chuckling to myself as I studied her intent expression in rehearsing the stock phrases, I remembered the one astonishing time she had flown into a rage at nephew Cyrus, twice her size, who had insulted her faith. Pummeling him with blows, she missed him with her foot and kicked out the glass window in the door instead, getting a bad cut as a result. Spirited and intelligent, Pari was unique.

Mamanbozorg made sure everyone got enough to eat.

"Bishtar," she urged, telling us to eat more. This dear woman had seen her share of trials. She flowed with the currents, wherever they might take her, with little thought for the outside world beyond her immediate haven of home and family.

Everyone was tired from the excitement. Nas promised to take his parents to see Mina and the baby the next day. We went home earlier than usual to get a good night's rest.

"Did you get my passport fixed?" I asked Nas that night in bed.

"You planning to leave?"

"If Carter sends troops, we may have to get out quickly."

Turning on his side, Nas muttered, "He's not that dumb."

Nas remained home the rest of the week due to unexpected problems at the work site. I was grateful to have him with us. On Saturday morning, he left at six-thirty, as usual, after I fixed eggs and toast for breakfast, though he declined my offer of a packed lunch for the road trip. Next, Jason boarded his school bus. Then it was time for me to get ready for the spring term that was about to begin. I was looking forward to a fresh perspective with new graduate classes and students.

I took a shower and put on a sweater with dark slacks. Helping Matt get dressed, I led him downstairs. Having prearranged a ride to campus with Abdolah on his way to work, we first dropped off Matt to stay with Pari. Mina should be home from the hospital today or tomorrow, but she would need time to recover, and she had her own baby to care for now. Pari, aided by Mamanbozorg, agreed to keep Matt for me. We would look into preschool options for fall term.

On campus, I stopped by the secretary's office to get a copy of my class list. She was not in, and the list was not in my mail slot. Strange. I had learned the previous week that our first assignment as graduate assistants would be to administer the placement exam, which would determine the students' enrollment in appropriate-level English classes. Other instructors likewise would be giving the exam, and we would be spread around campus in various classrooms to test the several hundred students seeking admission to Shiraz University. My exam would be given in the building behind this one; this I knew from a letter received at home the previous week. Classes would officially begin two days from now, following exam placements. I made my way down the steps. The first-floor tea kiosk was closed. In fact, the building appeared to be empty.

It was almost nine. Stepping into warm sunlight that hinted at spring, I saw few students as I followed the sidewalk and entered the next-door building. I looked for my assigned classroom and found it a few doors to my left. Students should be arriving and getting seated by now. Had I mistaken the date?

I looked out the window but saw no one on the lawn or pavement. Standing near the door, I glanced up and down the empty hall. Then the glass doors opened, and the Asian girl who had shared my drama class scurried in. Seeing me, she asked about her room number.

"Down there," I pointed.

As her heels clicked on the tiled floor, I had an eerie feeling. Another instructor's head popped out of a classroom farther down the hall.

"Lily—how are you?" I had not seen her since before Christmas.

"Great—where are the students? Isn't the placement exam scheduled today?"

"I thought it was."

A tall figure entered the doors at the other end of the building and strode rapidly toward us. As he approached, I saw it was Dr. Vajdin, who spoke without stopping as he passed.

"Emergency meeting—second-floor conference room in the foreign languages department."

Lily and I exchanged alarmed looks before I grabbed my purse.

"C'mon," I called through adrenaline-clenched teeth as I bolted from my classroom, "Let's get out of here." Looking the opposite way, I saw our Asian colleague dart from her room.

"Hurry!" I called. The three of us followed the direction taken by Dr. Vajdin. Pushing through glass doors, we crossed the patio, at last catching a glimpse of the huge crowd of students milling near the front gates of the campus compound. Hundreds, perhaps thousands, of male and female students were listening to the man I had seen loitering outside my classroom. He appeared to be ranting about imperialist literature and Western pollution, cheered periodically by his listeners. Fifteen or twenty armed Revolutionary Guards lined the iron fence surrounding the campus. Were they there to prevent students from leaving? Or to keep others from getting in? My heart pumped wildly as we slowed our gait so as not to appear hurried. I felt like we were foxes slipping past the hounds.

Reaching the front building, we dashed inside through the back door and up the steps to the languages department. Breathless, we paused by the secretary's desk to ask what was happening, but she still was not in. We rushed to the conference room at the end of the wing. Inside, a dozen Iranian and foreign instructors appeared agitated. A couple stood by the window. Others sat in metal folding chairs, chatting nervously or looking around with anxious expressions.

"What's going on?" a Mexican woman of about thirty asked from the door.

George turned from the window where he was watching events below. He generally helped advise students and new instructors. Today, he looked grim.

"The Revolutionary Guards have ordered students not to take the placement exam. They say we're a nest of spies—like the embassy staff. They're demanding a new curriculum cleansed of imperialist philosophies." He coughed nervously.

Dr. Vajdin entered the room, closing the door behind him. To our surprise, he locked it. Lily and I looked at each other. The Chinese lady seemed preoccupied.

"Everyone, please sit down. There's been a change of plans."

"That's putting it mildly," I whispered to George, who took a seat on my left.

With a funny look, he asked loudly enough for everyone to hear, "Did you get a grade on your research paper?"

"The one for Modern American Drama?"

"Yeah."

I pulled it out of my satchel. "It was in my mail slot. The comments are all negative, and there's no grade on the paper." I already had received a grade of "A" for the course, but I could not figure out why the paper did not have a grade, since it was a major assignment.

"Read a few paragraphs," George said pointedly.

Shaking my head, I leafed through the eighteen-page paper. Then fear clutched me as the implications hit home. Slowly I read aloud to the others, who were staring, wide-eyed: "Arthur Miller's *The Crucible: A Play for All Seasons.*"

Someone groaned, and I looked up briefly. "The play is about the 1692 witch hunt in Salem, Massachusetts. A handful of teenage girls got carried away and began accusing innocent people of wrongdoing, some of whom were hanged because of it."

"Go on," George urged, as several colleagues stared at me.

"Here's an excerpt," I offered tentatively.

> Like Salem, Iran's youth first perpetrated the "witch-hunt" in Iran, in the manner of the revolution they fought last year, and more specifically in the establishment and continued sanction of the Islamic Republic of today. Like Salem's girls, they wished to rebel against economic influences, and to set up a new authority with themselves as the "voice" of that government. . . . The youth of Iran overran the American Embassy in Tehran and held the lives of approximately fifty hostages in their hands. Their egos, like those of the girls of Salem, are no doubt inflated with the same type of self-importance. . . . It was evident that the court officials were reluctant, if not positively against, admitting any contrary evidence to their proceedings. . . . A statement from an Iranian press report, which runs along the same lines concerning today's Iran: "Imam Ruhollah Khomeini . . . asked Revolutionary Courts Prosecutor General Hojatoleslam Qodussi to shut down all publications whose views are contrary to those

of the Islamic Republic, to arrest their writers and editors and
bring them before the Revolutionary Courts for prosecution."
(*Iran Week,* August 24, 1979)

"This doesn't look very promising," I joked in an effort to lighten
the mood. "But the instructor's comments are critical, and there's no
grade," I countered.

"What do the comments say?" someone asked.

Everyone listened as I read aloud once more:

> In a research paper you do not "hope" or sound patronizing,
> . . . a real artist, which we hope Miller to be, does not use art,
> here the play, as a means of propaganda or didacticism, and
> that openly too.

Glancing up, I added, "I don't think the professor liked it."

"Weren't you afraid to put critical ideas in writing?" Christina asked,
looking up from the stack of student registrations she was checking.

"It didn't occur to me not to," I said slowly. Some in the room were
shaking their heads.

"So you're the imperialist," a woman said in a low voice.

"What?"

Lily protested, "She didn't mean anything." Dr. Vajdin listened intently but did not offer comments of his own.

"What was your course grade?" George asked.

"I got an A."

He shook his head. "It doesn't make sense." After a pause, he
added, "Remember the guy you thought might be spying outside your
classroom?"

"Yes, but I can't prove it."

"Never mind," George sputtered, "he was. Your name was mentioned."

"To whom?"

A sharp tap on the door grabbed our attention.

"Who is it?" Dr. Vajdin asked tensely.

"It's Dr. Jehani." The department head unlocked the door to admit
the suave professor who even now remained calm before pushing the
dead bolt once more.

"The Revolutionary Guards are trying to whip the students into a frenzy!" he announced.

A stunned silence broke over the room, as though we all had been struck mute. Then it passed as many spoke at once.

"Will they—?"

"What should we do?"

"Is there a back way out of here?"

"They're headed this way!" George had stood and now pointed through the balcony door. Armed guards in khaki were moving toward our building, followed by dozens of students shouting something I could not understand. As they entered the building, we heard their yelling and scuffling downstairs. Cheers broke out, and a clamor was heard on the steps.

Something hit the door with a loud bang. Angry voices yelled for us to open it.

Lily and I stared at each other. She seemed so young and innocent, but in my mid-twenties, I felt older and experienced. I edged toward the balcony and grabbed Lily by the wrist, pulling her with me as George tensed. Dr. Vajdin conferred in rapid Farsi in a low tone with Dr. Jehani, who made a decisive statement.

"Stand back," he called to the mob, "and I'll come out."

We shrank back as another blow hit the door, followed by more loud voices. But a moderate tone was heard, as though convincing the assailants to calm down and move away. Hearing shuffling feet and then quiet, Dr. Vajdin quickly unbolted the door to let out the other man, then shot the bolt again. I stared at the ground below us through the balcony entrance, wondering how many bones would be broken if I jumped.

"Everything's going to be fine," I reassured Lily.

Silently I prayed, and then wondered what would happen to the kids if I were killed or taken prisoner.

A quick tap prompted our chairperson to open the door quickly as Dr. Jehani slid through and bolted the door again.

"They're willing to negotiate," he began, "but they demand we meet their terms."

"Great," I thought, "we could be here for days—or months, like the embassy hostages." The balcony looked even more inviting.

More yelling broke out. Dr. Jehani called something through the door in a calm tone as the rest of us waited in stunned silence, looking at him and each other in terror. I inched closer to the balcony. Another step or two, and I could jump when the mob broke through the door. I shot a knowing glance at Lily, who returned a slight nod. George intercepted our look and studied the balcony for himself. Even if the jump did not cause serious injury, the armed guards might prevent our escape, or they might send students after us.

Again the voice of reason implored the guards to move away. We heard shuffling feet. Without speaking, Dr. Jehani motioned for the other professor to secure the door as he exited. Loud arguing was heard, followed by lowered voices that revealed sharp dissension.

Silence followed for the next several minutes.

A rapid succession of soft taps made us jump. Dr. Vajdin hesitated before opening the door. Dr. Jehani entered, looking flushed. This time he did not bolt the door behind him.

"They've gone for now. Go home at once. They may return."

Grabbing our things, we darted down the steps, first checking the halls and peering outdoors through windows to be sure the mob had really left.

This time I knew where the bus stop was. Looking back to be sure I was not followed, I tried to make my way nonchalantly to the stop and blend in with the five or six waiting passengers. Stooping a little to hide my face, I climbed on board the first bus that stopped, willing to ride all over the city and change buses if necessary to avoid standing in an exposed public area. Settling near the front, I pretended to look for something in my purse so other passengers would not see my features. Thankfully, I was wearing the headscarf, but I actually longed for the chador. I could see how willful and selfish my refusal to wear it had been.

The ride seemed interminable, but finally the middle-aged male driver pulled to the curb in my neighborhood. Looking around as I stepped to the pavement, I saw that the way appeared to be clear, and I took quick steps to reach home. Abdolah was on his lunch break, awaiting my telephone call for a ride, as arranged.

"What happened?" he asked in dismay.

Explaining quickly, I ran upstairs to change clothes. Pulling on a jacket, I sprinted for the door and locked it behind me to go get Matt at Mamanbozorg's. I stopped on the first step, turned around, unlocked the door, and ran to my bedroom. Opening the wardrobe, I pulled the folded chador off a shelf and slipped it around me. Staring into the mirror, I saw someone I did not know, a frightened woman of uncertain identity. Pulling the veil awkwardly around my face, I clattered down the steps and bolted through the door, accompanied by Abdolah, for Nas's parents' house. He appraisingly glanced over the chador but said nothing.

Within a few days, we were notified that the students had gone on strike, and the university would close for an indefinite period. Ironically, Nas's road construction project was put on hold, as supplies became increasingly harder to get due to shipping constraints. He returned to Shiraz to find another job, but nothing was immediately available. It was a good thing we had saved a sizable portion of Nas's pay to support us between jobs, so we were not hurting for money, but uncertainty held us in its grip.

Jason's school remained open, and he reported ongoing friendships with playmates and teachers. Matt and I spent a lot of time with Mamanbozorg and Bababozorg while Nas negotiated building contracts in town. I enjoyed helping Mina with baby Ali. His huge, dark eyes stared at me as though wondering who I was. I did not know myself, anymore. Now I wore a chador whenever I went out in public. Nas did not mention it, though Pari commented that I looked nice as she adjusted some of the folds.

With each week, hostage news emerged with ominous overtones. An attempted suicide was discovered and prevented. Another hostage, caught trying to escape, was severely beaten by his captors. There were hints of psychological torture, that one captive was falsely told his mother had died. Other staff members were confined to small spaces, manacled to a dining room table, and taken to the next room only to eat or to use the bathroom. Some slept three to a bed. Outdoors, sunlight, and exercise were limited privileges.

Another letter from Becky said that U.S. troops were practicing maneuvers that might be preparation for a hostage rescue. Reportedly, the United States would not attend the summer Olympic games. Nightly, Iranian television broadcasts condemned the United States as "the great Satan."

"Did Abdolah fix my passport yet?" I asked Nas one night after we had gone upstairs.

"No."

I took a shower and washed my hair, emerging from the bathroom with a towel around my head.

"Do you have my passport?"

"No."

That night in bed, I faced Nas's back in the dark. A faint gnawing could be heard once more in the wall.

"Nas?"

No answer.

"I want to go home."

No movement.

"I know we thought it would work this time, and I love this country. Your family has been wonderful. But there is too much at stake."

He remained silent. Unsure of whether he was asleep or awake, I plunged on.

"The boys feel the tension, at least Jason does. Now Mathew's been hurt."

"The same things happen over there," he snapped.

"But here, lots of things are going wrong. There are rats in our bedroom—"

"The only rats are in your imagination!"

"I want what's best for the kids. The university is closed, so I can't teach or study. There's nothing to do. We can go home for a while and come back when things settle down."

His back stiffened. "People don't keep jumping from one continent to another. Settle down and wait it out. You Americans are impulsive."

I began to cry, and my voice quavered. "I'm scared. I can't handle this anymore. I don't even know who I am. I need time to sort things out."

"Then go," he bristled, "but I told you, the boys stay here. Come back when you're ready."

"I'm not going without them."

"Suit yourself."

"Just get my passport notarized, okay?"

He didn't answer. I let it drop, but I would return to the attack soon.

The days became warm and sunny, a welcome reprieve from the wintry cold. One day, we went to visit Nas's sister Fatemah in her small village at the edge of her husband's pomegranate orchard near Kazerun. We would stop and see the newlyweds, Esmat and Khosrow, who lived a few miles north of Fatemah. I hoped the trip would help me thrust off my gloomy mind-set. Jason and Matt were excited about a change of scenery. I tried to smile and remain upbeat for their sake.

Skirting the mountains on the four-lane highway, we admired the inspiring view as Nas told the boys tales of bears and lions that had once roamed the region south of Dasht Arzhan. The boys listened, enthralled, and even my attention was captured.

Halfway to our destination, we stopped at a roadside bazaar where nomads and villagers sold embroidered blouses, clusters of dried dates and figs, and local curiosities at prices so reasonable I hated to barter. I bought a white, long-sleeved blouse that tied at the neck. It was edged with colorful embroidered flowers along a connecting vine. Purchasing some figs, I ate one after another as we got back in the truck and resumed our journey.

"Better check them first," Nas warned.

"For what?"

"Worms."

Feeling sick, I tossed the rest of the fruit out the window. Immediately I regretted not checking for worms before discarding them, so at least I would know if I had eaten some. But, on second thought, I did not want to know.

The temperature climbed to a comfortable level as we made our way south. Just before noon, we left the highway for a single-lane dirt road leading across a pasture toward a cluster of small homes at the base of a mountain. Taking a steep, winding drive to the uppermost house, we arrived at the home of Fatemah and her husband. Three children between the ages of four and ten stood in the yard, staring as Fatemah came out in village dress, raising her arms to embrace us as we got out of the truck.

She was pretty. I could see why her husband had come back for her, even after marrying a wealthy woman. Mohammedi had sought Fatemah's hand as his first choice of bride, but Bababozorg had declined the offer for reasons that remained unclear. Growing a commer-

Fatemah and her son

cial pomegranate orchard, Mohammedi had married a well-off widow who had given him a son. Unable to forget Fatemah, however, Mohammedi returned with a second suit, to which Bababozorg finally agreed. Fatemah seemed perfectly content here. Her cheeks were rosy and her eyes bright. Her adorable children appeared happy and healthy.

   She led us indoors and said her spouse would return soon. Across the terrace, from a separate part of the house, came the older wife. Dignified and aloof, she smiled a greeting and waved, though she did not join us. Looking out on the surrounding terrain, I saw the view was beguiling. Groves of trees, pastures filled with livestock, and the first signs of green hinted that spring would soon arrive. Everything was fresh and natural, and I felt peaceful.

We handed Fatemah the confectionary chocolates from Shiraz. Profuse in her thanks, she insisted we sit down while she served tea. Mohammedi appeared shortly. His English was passable, and he thoughtfully spoke a good deal of it with Nas for my sake. Within an hour, Fatemah was serving roast chicken, salad, yogurt, and rice. Afterward, Mathew napped while Jason kept running to the bathroom with diarrhea, a consequence of eating fly-covered watermelon the day before, despite my warnings. Thankfully, I had stuffed a large amount of tissue in my carryall bag for this purpose.

I made sure Jason drank boiled water, and after another hour or so, his stomach settled down. Sitting on patio benches in the midafternoon, we drank more tea and admired the sun's journey toward the western mountain chain as shadows began to spread.

"We'd better go," I heard Nas tell Mohammedi. "We have to stop at Khosrow's house."

Fatemah and her three children kissed us good-bye. Soon we were back on the highway, with their promises to bring fresh eggs to Shiraz soon.

Thirty minutes later, we pulled into a small town. Off the main road was a large dwelling fronted by the usual privacy gate. A young man, possibly Khosrow's brother, opened to admit us, and there was Esmat, somewhat more sedate than she had been at home, but with a complacent look on her face. She kissed us, murmuring pleasant greetings. Leading us to their partitioned part of the house, she promptly brought the customary tea and fruit. We gave her the things Mamanbozorg had sent, which included a few cooking pans and towels, along with confections we had bought for them. Khosrow's mother and two sisters, as well as the young man who had admitted us, came in briefly to be introduced. Their extended family arrangement was practical here, but I did not think it would work for me. Khosrow came in a few minutes later, and we had a pleasant visit for nearly an hour, which is short by Iranian customs.

Then we were on our way home. The golden sun was just setting on distant peaks, leaving rosy streaks like afterthoughts in its wake. Climbing the mountain highway once more, I felt myself relaxing for a doze. It had been a long day, and the mountain air had done us good.

Our visits with the sisters had been fun, but I looked forward to getting home for the night. The familiar depression of recent days was beginning to settle on my thoughts like crows on a carcass.

The days crept by. I continued coaching Pari in English. With more practice time, she would pick it up well. Abdolah had mentioned that a hotel was to be built in the village the following summer, and maybe Pari could work there if her English improved.

I did not give up on the idea of going home. But there was the matter of the exit tax. Though we had the money to pay it, I was sure Nas would not want to. I could ask Becky to send my savings from the States, but there was no guarantee she could withdraw it from the bank or that Iran's Bank Melli could process a transfer. I wondered if I should give up and stay here.

The March days were exquisite. Families began to enjoy outdoor excursions once more, as the snows receded and new grass appeared. Now Rooz, the Persian New Year, came around March 20 or 21 each year. In the week that followed, families would dress in their finery, place springtime symbols of flowers and eggs on the table, and make frequent visits to each other in celebration of the renewal of life. We had commemorated Now Rooz in the past with Iranian friends. One year, we had shared a home-cooked lamb dinner in a combined celebration of Now Rooz and Easter with two other Iranian-American couples. This year, I would make Jason and Mathew aware of the Easter theme of Jesus's resurrection. Jason was learning about Islam at school. Would he get in trouble by mentioning Jesus? Since confirming my Christian faith in Iran, I felt it important to teach my children these beliefs, too. But I would keep it low-key to protect them from confrontations with militant Muslims.

We decided to take a day trip to Persepolis, also called Takte Jamshid. The citadel of Iran's past rulers, with remains of stone columns and artwork, draws thousands of tourists from all over the world to the site where Alexander the Great defeated Iran's king, meshing Western and Eastern cultures. I wondered how our lives would differ if the Persian king had defeated Alexander and claimed Greece. Would schools teach Iranian classics instead of those by Homer and Sophocles?

Pari came with us on our excursion. As we approached the historical ruins, the scene was breathtaking. Climbing a plateau to the ancient fortress, we wandered the stonework and mused on the teeming activity that must have enlivened the palace complex in a bygone era. Massive stonework reflected a monumental heritage, while ornate inscriptions and drawings of rulers, warriors, and beasts depicted a mythic legacy. No wonder Iran's modern rulers claim ancestral lineage.

Reminding the boys to watch for poisonous lizards and snakes, I found Nas sitting on a fallen block, and climbed onto it beside him.

We stared out onto the facing plain. I wondered what Xerxes felt as he watched Alexander's approaching army. Did he realize the dynasty was doomed? Or did pride inspire him to put up a fight he expected to win?

Glancing at Nas's profile, I wondered if his family descended from the noble line. No matter, it was here and now that concerned us. He pulled something like a cigarette out of his pocket and lit it, taking a drag.

"Have you thought any more about our leaving?"

He stared ahead, taking occasional puffs.

I touched his arm tentatively.

"You can come, too. Get your master's degree in urban studies like you wanted to before. We can come back in a year or two."

He gave me a funny look, then put out the cigarette.

"I don't want to hurt you," I said. "But I think it's time to let go. We can't do anything more in Iran right now."

After a pause of several seconds, he said, "Go."

"Thank you." I laid my head on his shoulder, but he would not respond.

The next day, Abdolah told us which police office would notarize my passport. Nas and I were there by nine-thirty; Pari kept the boys. After a twenty-minute wait, the uniformed man in charge stamped a place near Nas's signature. Then we went to the bank. After a short delay, a brief discussion with the teller directed us to the bank across the street. Another pause occurred while a teller found the bank manager. Finally, we signed a form, and Nas surprised me by paying the exit tax with cash rather than by check.

Edging the car along the curb downtown, he turned off the ignition.

"Now what?" I asked, expecting a lecture.

"Airplane ticket."

"But I don't have the money until Becky sends my savings."

"Come on," he said gruffly.

The travel agent booked us on a flight that would depart within the week. Part of me felt sad to leave the land that had nurtured us in so many ways. But the other part was relieved to escape the unrelenting tensions that had been mounting for months.

We told Nas's family that evening. Pari was aghast.

"Stay," she pleaded. "Your sister can visit this summer." Since Pari could not solve the hostage problem, she would tackle the more manageable concern of homesickness.

"It's better for me to go there so my mother and father can see Jason and Matt," I explained.

Mamanbozorg shook her head. "Don't go. We want you to stay with us."

My heart was torn. Later that night after we returned to the flat, Abdolah tried to persuade us to wait a little longer. But I felt the time had come for us to return to the States. So much had recently happened that I did not want to see what was next.

When the departure day came, Nas drove us to the airport, just as he had more than two years before. As we boarded the plane for Tehran, I saw tears in his eyes. The boys clung to him. I almost changed my mind.

Then I caught my reflection in the glass window. Covered from head to toe in dark cloth, I looked like a Muslim convert. My face wore a serious expression. It was not the smiling, confident face I remembered.

Waving from the plane's door, I saw Nas turn abruptly to leave the terminal, and I wondered if we would ever meet again.

Over the next twenty-four hours of our journey, I reflected on all that had happened. From culture and hospitality, to faith and politics, I was grateful for the diversity of experiences that had enlightened our two stays. When our jetliner touched down in Germany for a stopover, and we exited the carrier's doors, I pulled off my chador with a sigh. Stuffing it into my carry-on bag, I descended the ramp holding Jason and Matt's hands. Slowly, I began to feel like my old self, but I was different, too. After a five-hour rest, we boarded a longer flight to the New World. I wondered if my grandmother's thoughts were similar to mine when she had sailed from Europe.

In New York, my sister was waiting at the boarding gate. I did not see her face in the crowd, and she did not recognize me as I strode past with the boys' hands in mine.

"Deb! Is that you?" Her expression was incredulous.

Exhaustion washed over me.

"Yes," I answered tiredly. "I think so."

Epilogue

So ended my personal relationship with Iran. The hostages' ordeal lasted much longer. In April 1980, a U.S. rescue attempt failed, resulting in the deaths of eight servicemen. Afterward, the hostages were split into groups and stashed in various locations around the country. When Iraq invaded Iran several months later, the government was forced to deal with military issues. Finally, the fifty-three hostages were released on January 20, 1981, on the inauguration of President Ronald Reagan. Former President Jimmy Carter flew to Germany to meet with the newly released Americans. Billions of dollars in Iranian assets remain frozen in court entanglements, and the United States pledged not to interfere with Iran's internal affairs.

Shiraz University closed while anti-imperialist curriculum changes were made. Many Western colleagues returned to their nations of origin, and we have lost touch. A colleague's letter dated April 7, 1981, was my last communication with my former academic life:

> I resigned due to improper health from the committee.
> Dr.—left for England; Dr.—for U.S.A, and Dr.—? All your
> classmates have gone to their home town. . . . I don't know
> when we'll assume our teaching duties again. But we are
> impatiently looking forward to the end of the war [with
> Iraq], which has really caused a lot of problems. We hope
> this will be a new year of peace and quiet. . . . Keep well.

Nas came to the States six months after I did, but we did not return to Iran, and we were unable to reconcile. Sadly, divorce followed the next year. Bababozorg died in 1981, and Mamanbozorg passed away in 2001, while both of my parents passed between those dates. I keep in touch with Pari by telephone and letters. Mina and Abdolah's son Ali is married and now lives in Texas; they have visited several times. Some of the nephews and nieces, with parents or independently, emigrated to Europe and America for college. A few lost life or limb in the Iran-Iraq War. Others remain in traditional occupations that employed their ancestors. I hope to see these former family members again someday.

Jason grew up fast, it seemed, and served a stint in the U.S. Army. Afterward, he earned a bachelor's degree in English and has become a champion for social causes, processing grant requests from nonprofit organizations. Mathew learned English quickly. He earned a political science degree. My sister Becky is a critical care nurse.

Today I teach college English. When the thirst for adventure hits, I attend a conference or take a trip, including some that are overseas. The universe of ideas is infinitely more secure than the physical worlds shaped by religion and government. As my father used to say, you can lose everything but what you know.

My residence in Iran under two rulers taught me much about that country, and more about myself. From taking my spirituality for granted, I have since become a committed Christian. After not voting in the United States before moving to Iran, I now participate in every election. I have learned to question everything—my government, my faith, and my ideals—rather than take any of these precious things for granted. The chador helped me understand differences between two great nations and the need to acknowledge and respect their distinctions.

Should the embassy takeover be forgotten? Forgiveness is a better approach. In 1998, former hostage Barry Rosen met with one of the embassy takeover organizers, Abbas Abdi. Rosen described plans for attending the meeting arranged by the Center for World Dialogue as one of the toughest decisions he ever made. His comments there addressed the need for mutual understanding, although he did not support the idea that the militants had good reason to take over the embassy. But he sympathized with Iranian complaints about U.S. support of the shah's repressive regime.

In 1999, former hostage Kathryn Koob published a book about her experience. *Guest of the Revolution* balances the difficulties of captivity with the ironic amusement of domestic care provided by young, idealistic, if militant females. Ms. Koob displays remarkable feeling for the land and people while promoting her reliance on faith and forgiveness. Even her language reflects a hospitable relationship with Iran when she calls herself a "guest" rather than victim or prisoner. She refers to the girls as "sisters," and males as "brothers," though perhaps directed to do so, and likened the girls' nighttime chatter and giggles as reminiscent of a slumber party, with herself a mother hen. Koob believes Iran should take its place in the international arena: "However angry we might be about the hostage crisis, Iran is a country full of wonderful people, intellect and culture, and should be part of the world community."[1]

On March 17, 2000, Secretary of State Madeleine Albright made a speech that offered a formal acknowledgment of the United States' past interference in Iranian affairs:

> In 1953, the United States played a significant role in orchestrating the overthrow of Iran's popular Prime Minister, Mohammad Mosaddeq. The Eisenhower administration believed its actions were justified for strategic reasons; but the coup was clearly a setback for Iran's political development. And it is easy to see now why many Iranians continue to resent this intervention by America in their internal affairs. Moreover, during the next quarter century, the United States and the West gave sustained backing to the Shah's regime. Although it did much to develop the country economically, the Shah's government also brutally repressed political dissent. As President Clinton has said, the United States must bear its fair share of responsibility for the problems that have arisen in U.S.-Iranian relations.[2]

Although the speech was probably intended as something of an apology, Ayatollah Khamenei, Iran's chief leader, took a dim view of Mrs. Albright's words:

> What good does this admission—that you acted this way then—do us now? ... An admission years after the crime was committed, while they might be committing similar crimes now, will not do the Iranian nation any good.[3]

Iran's militants acted contrary to international law in taking hostages. Massoumeh Ebtekar, spokesperson for the students who staged the embassy assault, explained years after the event the group's motivation:

> The young men and women who participated in the embassy takeover did so based on their convictions that their action was in line with the Imam's policy. We believed then that action was essential; we were determined to take a stand against past and possible future humiliation by the United States.[4]

Clearly, broken relations between these two countries have grown out of misguided actions. Recently, new fears have surfaced over Iran's use of nuclear energy. How will an Iranian atomic bomb affect U.S.-Iran relations? Some scholars like Dr. Jerome Corsi, whose views appear in *Atomic Iran,* maintain a dire outlook: "Many do not yet realize how real the possibility of nuclear war will be the minute the Islamic Republic of Iran gets its first deliverable nuclear weapon. And that day is imminent."[5]

David Farber summarizes our nation's inadequate attempt to deal with Iran in a responsible way:

> The Iranian hostage crisis could have been an interesting lesson in international affairs. Most Americans, however, including Jimmy Carter, treated it instead as (to paraphrase) the mad act of evildoers. As a partial result, American policymakers did not respond directly to the underlying problems that produced the Iran hostage crisis. That failure led, indirectly, some two decades later, to an evil act by vicious killers morally blinded by fanaticism. Thinking past the act of terrorism to the strategy of prevention has not been an American strength.[6]

All of us wear veils of one kind or another. Most are invisible, like our deeply held values. Drapery concealing self-disclosure prohibits the development of mutual trust. Yet, covering oneself at times is expedient not only for self-protection, but also in respecting others' boundaries and in displaying fidelities. Azar Nafisi seethed at political coercion forcing her to wear the veil in maintaining a public persona. Militants who overran the embassy veiled their personal motives under the patriotic banner of Islamic idealism. Kathryn Koob describes an eighteen-year-old captor as nervous and agitated when conducting the initial search of Ms. Koob, becoming more so when told to repeat the search. How did the girl's patriotic duty mesh with her innocent upbringing and educational goals? What veils, tangible or imagined, was she forced to wear in manifesting her role as a militant captor? In adopting a persona, we slip under a mantle that projects a single facet, often an assumed one, of our character. Yet, veils reveal as much as they hide. They add another layer of meaning to our lives, representing ideologies and commitments that otherwise remain hidden. Though Iran remains under the chador of Islamic fundamentalism, there are deeper meanings of the country's heart and soul that lie beneath this surface cover.

If the United States and Iran can set aside past grievances and current distrust, we can create a reciprocal partnership of international trade and strategic support. Iran is rich in history. Its people are warmhearted and generous. We must never overlook these strengths in admiring its resources. Establishing a respectful relationship on equal footing can provide advantages to both nations, healing the twenty-seven-year-old breach. The new century offers fresh opportunities for forgiveness and reconciliation, and for interdependence. Setting aside prejudice and power plays, we can collaborate to establish an enduring partnership.

Notes

Introduction

1. "Iran rejects U.S. effort to launch talks." *Akron Beacon Journal*, January 11, 2004, A6.

Chapter Two

1. "Darius the Great: Naqs-I Rustam Inscription," http://www.livius.org/da-dd/darius/darius_i_to1.html (accessed 4/25/2006).

2. "Traditional Zoroastrianism: Tenets of the Religion," http://tenets.Zoroastrianism.com/ (accessed 10/24/2003).

3. "Forgotten Delights," http://www.forgottendelights.com/essays/Iran.htm (accessed 10/24/03).

4. "Poet Seers," http://www.poetseers.org/the_poetseers/hafiz/would_you_think_it_odd (accessed 11/18/2003).

5. "Persia or Iran," http://www.art-arena.com/history.html (accessed 6/30/2006).

6. "Islam in Iran," http://www.revision-notes.co.uk/revision/37.html (accessed 11/18/2003).

Chapter Five

1. Abolhassan Mobin, "The Aryan Movement," http://www.iranchamber.com/history/mohammad_rezashah/mohammad_rezashah.php (accessed 11/18/2003).

2. Kenneth M. Pollack, *The Persian Puzzle: The Conflict between Iran and America* (New York: Random House, 2004), 42.

3. "Persia: Brief History," http://www.Sedona.net/pahlavi/gvt.html (accessed 10/24/2003).

4. James A. Bill, *The Eagle and the Lion: The Tragedy of American-Iranian Relations* (New Haven: Yale University Press, 1988), 81.

5. Barry Rubin, *Paved with Good Intentions* (New York: Oxford University Press, 1980), xi.

6. National Security Archive, "The Iran Documentation Project" http://www.gwu.edu/%7Ensarchiv/iran/index.htm (These materials are reproduced from www.nsarchive.org with the permission of the National Security Archive.) (accessed 6/30/2006).

7. "Biographies," http://www.Sedona.net/pahlavi/biograph.html (accessed 10/24/2003).

8. David R. Farber, *Taken Hostage: The Iran Hostage Crisis and America's First Encounter with Radical Islam* (Princeton: Princeton University Press, 2005), 98.

9. Farber, *Taken Hostage,* 75.

10. "Democracy in Iran," http://www.angelfire.com/home/iran/ (accessed 6/30/2006).

11. "Ayatollah Khomeini," http://www.iranchamber.com/history/rk-homeini/ayatollah_khomeini.php (accessed 10/28/2003).

12. Appendix F: Statistics, http://www.fas.org/man/dod-101/ops/war/docs/3203/appf.pdf (accessed 10/28/2003).

13. "Jimmy Carter Library," http://jimmycarterlibrary.org/documents/list_of_hostages.phtml. (accessed 10/28/2003).

14. Farber, *Taken Hostage,* 5–6.

Chapter Six

1. *Time,* December 3, 1979.

2. Azar Nafisi, *Reading Lolita in Tehran* (New York: Random House, 2003), 167.

3. *Time,* November 19, 1979.

Chapter Seven

1. *Time,* November 19, 1979.

Chapter Eight

1. Dr. Rashad Khalifa, *The Arabic Quran and Its Authorized English Translation,* http://www.submission.org/efarsi/arabic/sura21.html (accessed 2/7/2006).

2. Ibid. (accessed 2/7/2006).

Chapter Nine

1. Kathryn Koob, *Guest of the Revolution* (Nashville: Thomas Nelson, 1982), 85.

Chapter Ten

1. *Time,* January 7, 1980.

Epilogue

1. Kathryn Koob, "Hostages Recount Their Captivity," http://rescueattempt .tripod.com/id16.html (accessed 4/25/06).

2. Pollack, *Persian Puzzle,* ix.

3. Ibid., xxv–xxvi.

4. Ibid., 154.

5. Jerome R. Corsi, *Atomic Iran: How the Terrorist Regime Bought the Bomb and American Politicians* (Nashville: WND Books, 2005).

6. Farber, *Taken Hostage,* 8.

Bibliography

Beckwith, Colonel Charlie A., and Donald Knox. *Delta Force*. New York: Harcourt Brace Jovanovich, 1983.

Bill, James A. *The Eagle and the Lion: The Tragedy of American-Iranian Relations*. New Haven: Yale University Press, 1988.

Corsi, Jerome R. *Atomic Iran: How the Terrorist Regime Bought the Bomb and American Politicians*. Nashville: WND Books, 2005.

Farber, David R. *Taken Hostage: The Iran Hostage Crisis and America's First Encounter with Radical Islam*. Princeton: Princeton University Press, 2005.

Follett, Ken. *On Wings of Eagles*. New York: William Morrow, 1983.

Koob, Kathryn. *Guest of the Revolution*. Nashville: Thomas Nelson, 1982.

Milani, Mohsen M. *The Making of Iran's Islamic Revolution: From Monarchy to Islamic Republic*. 2d ed. Boulder: Westview Press, 1994.

Nafisi, Azar. *Reading Lolita in Tehran: A Memoir in Books*. New York: Random House, 2004.

Pollack, Kenneth M. *The Persian Puzzle: The Conflict between Iran and America*. New York: Random House, 2004.

Rubin, Barry. *Paved with Good Intentions*. New York: Oxford University Press, 1980.

Sick, Gary. *October Surprise: America's Hostages in Iran and the Election of Ronald Reagan*. New York: Times Books/Random House, 1991.

Index